145369

Maximum
Life Span

Maximum
Life Span

ROY L. WALFORD, M.D.

W·W·NORTON & COMPANY
New York • London

Figure 3.1. Adapted from R. J. Wylie, W. L. Beeson, and J. W. Kuzma, "Is There a Younger You Inside?" *Life and Health*, October 1978, p. 5.

Figure 3.2. Adapted from F. Bourlière, *The Assessment of Biological Age in Man*, Public Health Papers, no. 37 (Geneva: World Health Organization, 1970)

Figure 3.3. Adapted from A. Leaf, "Getting Old," *Scientific American*, 229:45, 1973.

Figure 4.2. Adapted from R. Hart and R. Setlow, "Correlation between Deoxyribonucleic Acid Excision . . ." *Proc. Nat. Acad. Sci., U.S.A.* 71:2169 (1974).

Figure 5.1 (A) Adapted from C.L. Goodrick in *Science News* 1 December 1979, p. 375; (B) R. Weindruch ct al, "Life Span . . .," *Science* 215: 1415–18 (1982); (C) M.A. Rudzinska, "Overfeeding and Life Span . . .," *J. Gerontology* 7:544 (1952).

Table 7.1. Adapted from *Nutrition Action*, July, 1980, Center for Science in the Public Interest.

Figure 7.3. Adapted from *Nutrition Action*, September, 1981, Center for Science in the Public Interest.

Figure 9.1. Adapted from M. Riley, M. Johnson, A. Forer, *Aging and Society: A Sociology of Age Stratification* (Russell Sage Foundation, 1972), p. 10.

The text of this book is composed in Baskerville.
Composition and manufacturing by The Haddon Craftsmen, Inc.
Book design by Jacques Chazaud
Illustrations by Ann Morris

Library of Congress Cataloging in Publication Data
Walford, Roy L.
    Maximum life span.
    Includes index.
    1. Longevity. 2. Aging. 3. Life span,
Productive. I. Title.
QP85.W315   1983   612'.67   82–12605

ISBN 0-393-01649-8

W. W. Norton & Company, Inc., 500 Fifth Avenue, New York, N. Y. 10110
W. W. Norton & Company Ltd., 37 Great Russell Street, London WC1B 3 NU
    3 4 5 6 7 8 9 0

This book is dedicated to my children,
Lisa, Morgan, and Peter,
and to Martha Walford and Susan Ritman
for their love and forbearance.

Contents

Acknowledgments

I am grateful to Jill Taylor for expert editorial, secretarial, and library research assistance; to Susan Ritman for her splendid help with nutritional data; to Helga Bradish for secretarial help; to John Thomas, Martha Walford, Jody Sibert, Alan Harrington, and Dr. Kathleen Hall for incisive comments on the manuscript; to Ann Morris for her highly innovate illustrations; to Wyn Chamberlain, Nick Douglas, and Dr. G. P. Yadav for instruction in Indian medical and yogic lore; to my agent, John Brockman, and to George Brockway and Mary Cunnane of W. W. Norton Company, for their encouragement and advice; and to my numerous colleagues, particularly Drs. William Hildemann, Jean Dausset, Edward Schneider, Richard Weindruch, and Kathleen Hall, and my students and technicians, in particular Edith Zeller, for the pleasure of sharing their knowledge, expertise, and enthusiasm. My own research has been supported by the National Institutes of Health, the American Cancer Society, the Gerontology Research Foundation, Gerontix, Inc., the Paul Glenn Foundation, and individual donors.

Preface

An article bearing the optimistic title "Conquest of the Future" appeared in the June 1941 issue of my high school magazine, "The Literary Parade." In that article at the age of seventeen I wrote, "Elders have received positively no gain from science concerning expectant life span . . . (but) death is not a necessary adjunct of living matter." These words recall vividly to my mind an early intense fascination with aging, a somewhat surprising interest for a high school student to be expressing in the midst of the social orientation of forty years ago because the modern era of gerontology, the science of aging, in which life-span extension is no longer considered a mere Faustian dream, had not yet dawned.

But I had my reasons even then.

It seemed to me (and still does) that a person's allotted span of life is simply too short to permit a satisfying exploration of the world's outer wonders and the realms of inner experience. We are cut off in the midst of our pleasures, separated too soon from our loved ones, shelved at the mere beginning of our understanding, and laughed at by the gods. Life-span extension became my primary task, an intellectual adventure and personal challenge in its own right and a key to the others.

PREFACE

Now, in 1982, I believe that gerontologists are not far from achieving substantial prolongation of human life span. Indeed it seems fairly certain that maximum life span could already be prolonged up to 130 to 140 years by the exercise of very stringent measures. While I do discuss these measures in considerable detail, this book is not primarily a "how-to" manual about retarding aging. My purpose here is to describe the various domains of the science of biological gerontology from the historical, theoretical, practical, and social aspects: not only "how-to" but "wherefrom" and "why."

The field of gerontology has a long, magical, turbulent history peopled with myth-makers, fools, quacks, and some of the greatest intellects mankind has produced. The book will touch upon their times, their lives, and their lies as well as detailing some of the struggles out of prejudice and superstition into the opening possibilities of modern aging research. I will outline the major current theories of aging, those which, in my view, may soon coalesce into a unified theory that can help us achieve extension of maximum life span by measures less demanding than those now available. Chapter 4 is devoted to these theories. But to comprehend the information and what it portends you must begin by understanding survival curves. Survival curves comprise the initial and most fundamental raw data of gerontology; so right at the beginning, in Chapter 1, I will deal with the meaning of these curves, and will also undertake to demystify the numerous stories about historical persons or populations who supposedly lived to extraordinary ages.

To understand the practical applications of aging research, you will need to be informed about the general phenomena of aging, how the body's vital functions slow or change with aging, how functional age may differ from chronological age, and how functional age can be measured. Are you biologically younger or older than your actual years? Chapter 3 provides this information.

You will want to know whether anything can be done right now to improve an individual's survival chances. What preventive health measures can be gleaned from present gerontologic knowledge to enhance our probability of still being alive and well when the maximum extension breakthroughs take place, as I predict they will, during the closing seventeen years of this century? This gerontologic knowledge is not well-known by the ordinary health professionals, or where known is apt to be regarded by them as more controversial than it actually is. Several chapters and the appendices are devoted to this important practical subject. I do want to stress, however, that the stringent dietary program of "undernutrition without malnutrition" which is outlined in this book and which I personally follow, plus some of the recommendations about vitamins and food additives, are based on experimental research in animals. Thus far they have not been thoroughly tested by scientific studies in humans. Should you decide to follow these or similar programs, I urge you to first consult your own physician and to be guided by his or her advice.

In the closing chapter I examine the probable effects on society and on the individual of maximum life-span extension. Will extension lead to overpopulation, an increasingly elderly, senile electorate and social stagnation, or will its results be opposite to these gloomy projections? What will you do with yourself if you have 150 years to dispose of? I believe that the effects of life-span extension will be outstandingly positive for mankind as both social and individual animals, will help solve many of our dilemmas, and revolutionize human potential.

"May you live in interesting times," runs an old Chinese saying. Whether we heartily approve of the twentieth century or not, we are at the very least living in interesting times. Let's hope they last and that we last too. Recent progress in gerontology gives abundant life to this hope.

While the present book is intended for the layperson, I am not writing a protracted essay that merely uses science as metaphor for homespun philosophy about life, destiny, or the mysterious wisdom of nature. My object has been to be clear and accessible and specific for the careful reader, trusting that the subject matter will touch the heart and pull at the mind. And I have been careful to include enough anecdotal and diversional material to relieve the tension of running into

PREFACE

word conglomerates like bis-hydroxytoluene or the major histocompatibility complex, and concepts like DNA-repair, cell fusion, and the notorious Hayflick limit. Through these complexities I am privileged to be your guide.

And may you live in *many* interesting times.

Roy L. Walford, M.D.
Suite 1215
1015 Gayley Ave
Los Angeles, CA 90024

Maximum
Life Span

1

How to Think about Life Span

I want to prove (says the Gilgamesh of the clay tablets)
. . . that the boundaries set up by the gods are not unbreakable.

Marvelously fitting to the life-and-death inquiry we're engaged in is the fact that mankind's first recorded epic,
the 5,000 year-old story of the adventurer king and hero, Gilgamesh, is a gerontological myth (Gerontology = the study of
aging) about a quest for the secret of immortality.[1] Told on
twelve broken tablets rescued from the dust of the capital city
of ancient Sumer, the epic also unwinds as a revolt against
Death, and therefore against authority, the authority of the
gods themselves; it presages why much of gerontology remains emotion-charged even today, indeed perhaps more so
now than ever before, because this time around in the cycle of
history—in our own time—the rebellion may succeed. The
philosophical side of the epic reflects at least two of the major
and still current opposing views about aging and dying: one,
that since death is inevitable, we should simply adjust to it and
be satisfied with developing a rich life; two, that death is a
crime against consciousness. Finally, the Gilgamesh legend
resembles the later story of our own Judeo-Christian ancestors, Adam and Eve. Gilgamesh bravely found, then foolishly
and tragically lost, one of the fruits from the Tree of Life.
Adam and Eve were expelled from the Garden lest they eat of
the Tree of Life, "and become as one of us." In both stories

one message rings outrageously clear: the gods gave Death to man and kept Life for themselves.

The task of the modern researcher into aging is to remake the myths, to avoid the tragic flaws of heroes like Gilgamesh, to slip past the flaming sword in the garden east of Eden and steal the fruit from the Tree of Life, indeed to make off with the tree itself, to smuggle it past the Customs Service (even past the Food and Drug Administration), and to plant it in our midst. The desire to be physically immortal, or at least to live much longer and in full health, has been humanity's oldest dream, and the day is no longer distant when we may enjoy the metaphorical fruit of that fabulous ancient tree—in the lives of our children or even, with luck, in our own. It's already possible to live to be well over 120 years if you start young and, as we shall see, take the necessary (albeit exceedingly stringent) measures. In my own laboratory at the UCLA Medical Center we have extended the maximum life span of fish by 300 percent.

It's high time. Not only for fish, but for us. Unless we aim for extending the outer limit of life span, which can only be done by slowing down our actual rate of biologic aging, we are as populations (although not as individuals) approaching the end of the possibility of medical progress. We may learn to prevent or find remedies for all known diseases and still not expect to live longer than the longest-lived of our ancestors. Let me explain what I mean by this surprising statement, and in the explanation slide into the primary subject of this opening chapter: how to begin to think about the biology of aging, what basic concepts to grasp so you can judge the validity of what is being talked about and can recognize whether someone else does too. Combatting death, the crime against consciousness, does not in these biologic terms involve transcendence of self like the Hindu and not-so-Hindu mystics try for, or reincarnation, or the collective immortality of a "people" such as the Jews. First of all and perhaps most importantly it involves understanding survival curves.

Look at Figure 1.1. The curves describe the patterns of

Survival curves in human populations.

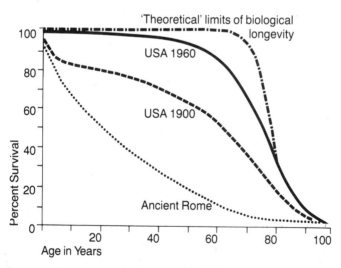

Survival curves in human populations: ancient Rome, USA 1900 and 1960, and the curve resulting if all diseases were cured but the basic aging process still continuing ("theoretical" limits...).

Figure 1.1

human survival in early and recent times. The vertical axis on the left indicates the percentage of survivors remaining in the population as the population ages across the horizontal axis. The horizontal axis denotes age in years. Each curve begins with 100 percent alive at birth and gradually decreases as people die off. All curves would cross the zero point at about 110 years. It's hard to visualize the 100- to 110-year region on such a figure because the numbers of survivors in that region are so small, increasingly less than one in ten or fifty thousand. Still, a few people do live to be that old, and always have, since recorded time.

We'll concern ourselves with two points on each of these and similar population curves: first the *50 percent survival,* the age at which half the original population of all those born has died; and second, the *maximum survival,* the age of the absolutely longest lived very few survivors.

The 50 percent survival has increased from about 22 years in ancient Rome to about 40 years in the middle of the last century, to 49 years in the United States in 1900 (Figure 1.1), to 67 years in 1946, 72 years in 1960, and about 74 years today. Now for a surprise: the maximum survival of about 110 years hasn't changed *at all* since even before ancient Rome. It has probably never changed since we became what we are, *homo sapiens,* some tens of thousands of years ago.

Here's why these two measurements behave differently; the 50 percent survival reflects mainly our genetic susceptibility to various diseases, plus interactions with the environment. These vary from person to person, race to race, and according to where you live. Maximum possible life span, on the other hand, is determined by some sort of innate, ongoing time clock that ticks out the rate of biologic aging. This rate is inherent in each of us not so much as an individual characteristic but as a species characteristic. A few persons in antiquity lived to be 100 to 110 years or slightly older. The same is true today. The outer limit of life span has not been budged at all by anything we have been able or at least willing to do so far, all our sciences notwithstanding, nor by anything which has happened in the way of social improvements. The Bible is correct in spirit if not quite in literal fact: the days of our years are not fixed at three score years and ten, but at one hundred and ten.

Certainly, on the average, our prospects for living to a healthy and productive old age are better today than in the past. The 50 percent survival has increased progressively as humanity staggered through two earlier eras of epidemiologic change. Before the Industrial Revolution the human setting was what A.R. Omran[2] rightly called the Age of Pestilence and Famine, extending from ancient times through most of the eighteenth century. Cholera, typhus, smallpox, and plague marched across the earth, rivaling one another to see which could slaughter the most people. In the fourteenth century the Black Death (bubonic plague) carried off one-third of the population of Europe. Its symptoms were extravagently described by the dramatist Antonin Artaud:

> Before any pronounced physical or psychological sickness appears, red spots appear all over the body, the sick person only suddenly noticing them when they turn black. He has no time to be alarmed by them before his head feels on fire, grows overwhelmingly heavy, and he collapses. Then he is seized by terrible fatigue, a focal, magnetic, exhausting tiredness; his molecules are split in two and drawn towards their annihilation. His fluids, wildly jumbled in disorder, seem to race through his body. His stomach heaves, his insides seem to want to burst between his teeth. Buboes appear around the anus, under the armpits, at those precious places where the active glands steadily carry out their functions, and through these buboes the anatomy discharges either its inner putrefaction, or in other cases, life itself.[3]

Truly, death was everywhere before and during the Middle Ages, death public and ugly and brutal, and the world views of our ancestors were forged in visions of constant death and the stink of decaying flesh, as were their tombs and monuments, their songs, their arts and literature, their descents into Hell and invocations of the shades. Raymond of Aguilers wrote about the capture of Jerusalem by the Christians in 1099, "They rode in blood up to the knees and the bits of the horses by the just and wonderful judgement of God."

But the judgment began changing in the eighteenth century.

The onset of the Industrial Revolution ushered in the Age of Receding Pandemics, wherein at least the devastations from the major infectious diseases began to decline. Orthodox medicine can't take much credit for this improvement because it didn't actually begin its impressive disease-conquering advances until the twentieth century. Those great, earlier pandemics receded because of the social changes of the early Industrial Revolution: better family hygiene, greater personal cleanliness, improved nutrition. At last, during the span of lives still being lived, orthodox medicine and the Industrial Revolution interacted to bring us to where we are now; the Age of Degenerative and Man-made Diseases.

Our age has been made possible because the 50 percent survival has increased so rapidly in modern times. Smallpox, which had been with us since at least the time of the Egyptian pharaohs, has been wholly and everlastingly eradicated, really a splendid triumph of international cooperation and preventive medicine. And tuberculosis, the "White Death" of the nineteenth century, responsible for about 20 percent of all deaths in Western countries during that period, is now only a small-time killer. Measles, which once affected nearly everyone, has become almost extinct. Cases of whooping cough have come down from 250,000 patients in 1939, to 2,000 cases last year; diphtheria, from 200,000 in the 1920s to fewer than 100 today; mumps, from 152,000 as late as 1968, had dropped to 16,000 just ten years later.

We've largely conquered the last century's killer diseases.

If we conquer our own century's epidemics, heart disease, cancer, diabetes, arthritis, and the other degenerative maladies, can we keep on increasing the 50 percent survival indefinitely? No, not by these conquests alone. We come up against an ancient barrier, the finality of the biologic process of aging, which is not a "disease" to be cured like the others. Figure 1.1 taught us that while the 50 percent survival has been increasing through the centuries, maximum survival hasn't. A very few people lived to approach 110 years of age in ancient times. No matter how many additional diseases we cure, if we don't decelerate the basic aging rate, we merely rotate the survival curve a bit more to the right, clockwise about that stubbornly fixed 110-year point. We can call these rotational efforts "rectangularizing technologies." Rectangularization is still going on. The death rate for heart disease fell more than 24 percent in the last ten years; for stroke, 33 percent; for influenza and pneumonia, 37 percent. The majority of health efforts at present are aimed one way or another at decreasing the tolls from these late-life diseases even further, i.e., at rectangularizing the human survival curve.

From what, then, will people die if the major killer diseases become completely controlled but the 110-year maximum survival is not extended? The answer is, accidents. Even today with the late-life diseases still plaguing us, the causes of death for persons over 65 years of age are, in order of frequency, heart disease, cancer, stroke, influenza and pneumonia, arteriosclerosis, and accidents. Accidents are the sixth main cause of death. They come before diabetes, emphysema and asthma, liver cirrhosis, and kidney infection.

Table 1.1 shows the ten leading causes of death in the year 1860, 1900, and 1970 for all age groups and not just the over-65-year-olds. In 1860 accidents didn't even make the top ten; in 1900 they caused 4.5 percent of deaths, and in 1970, 5.9 percent. The increase in accidental deaths partly reflects changes in environment, like the flight of population from country to big-city living. It also reflects the increased average

The ten leading causes of death.

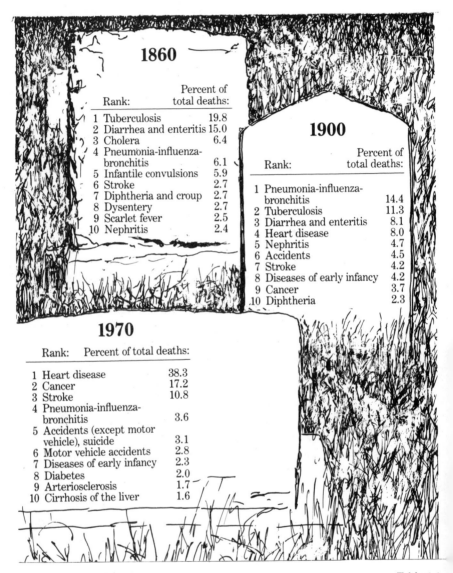

1860

Rank:		Percent of total deaths:
1	Tuberculosis	19.8
2	Diarrhea and enteritis	15.0
3	Cholera	6.4
4	Pneumonia-influenza-bronchitis	6.1
5	Infantile convulsions	5.9
6	Stroke	2.7
7	Diphtheria and croup	2.7
8	Dysentery	2.7
9	Scarlet fever	2.5
10	Nephritis	2.4

1900

Rank:		Percent of total deaths:
1	Pneumonia-influenza-bronchitis	14.4
2	Tuberculosis	11.3
3	Diarrhea and enteritis	8.1
4	Heart disease	8.0
5	Nephritis	4.7
6	Accidents	4.5
7	Stroke	4.2
8	Diseases of early infancy	4.2
9	Cancer	3.7
10	Diphtheria	2.3

1970

Rank:		Percent of total deaths:
1	Heart disease	38.3
2	Cancer	17.2
3	Stroke	10.8
4	Pneumonia-influenza-bronchitis	3.6
5	Accidents (except motor vehicle), suicide	3.1
6	Motor vehicle accidents	2.8
7	Diseases of early infancy	2.3
8	Diabetes	2.0
9	Arteriosclerosis	1.7
10	Cirrhosis of the liver	1.6

Table 1.1

age of today's citizenry. People over 85 experience four times as many death-causing accidents as those between 65 and 74. The declining general vigor of the aging process leads to increasing susceptibility to accidents, and to complications and deaths from smaller and smaller accidents. Grandpa totters into the bathroom at three A.M., slips on the bath mat, falls, breaks his hip, and develops pneumonia and dies.

Often the elderly are the victims of changing trends. The oceanfront suburb of Venice, California, where I live, has witnessed a recent upsurge in the popularity of outdoor roller skating. The many older people who live in Venice do not, quite naturally, participate in the fast, freewheeling sport. One aspect of the new vogue is that many of the skaters wear headphone radios in order to hear a continual disco beat for their skate dance. They often skate backward down Venice's boardwalk and although they look great, the disco-dancing skaters cannot see very well over their oscillating shoulders, and with the headphones on they certainly can't hear the shrieks of warning given by the victims with whom they are about to collide. If they run down a young person, it's just a fun fall, but several oldsters have been killed by being ricocheted off skaters. In retaliation the oldsters occasionally throw a barricade across the boardwalk and the unwary skaters splotch into that.

Being neither old nor an avid skater, I am able to remain an observer of these phenomena, and in Venice by the ageless sea I observe one instance of the truth of the generalization that the primary cause of death among people of very advanced age is accidents, a vulnerability to otherwise minor trauma.

Maximum survival is defined as that age reached by the few, longest lived individuals in a large population. Genetically determined and characteristic for each species, maximum survival has the remarkable property, as I've already said, of being virtually independent of the environment. The great eighteenth-century naturalist Georges Buffon displayed precocious insight into survival characteristics when he wrote:

If we consider the European, the Negro, the Chinese, the American, the man highly civilized, the savage, the rich, the poor, the inhabitant of the city, the dweller in the country, so different from one another in every respect, agree on this one point, and have the same duration, the same interval of time to run through 'twixt the cradle and the grave, that the difference of race, of climate, of food, of comforts, makes no difference in the duration of life, it will be seen at once that the duration of life depends neither upon habits, nor custom, nor the quality of food, that nothing can change the fixed laws which regulate the number of our years.

Buffon was talking about maximum survival and he put it well, especially that part about "the fixed laws which regulate the number of our years." Despite all the progress in social and health sciences since antiquity, nobody today reaches an age greater than the longest-lived old Romans, Greeks, or even the Sumerians over whom King Gilgamesh ruled.

How do we know the maximum life spans of different animals and of our own species? For experimental laboratory animals, like the mice and fish used in my own research, the method is simply to set aside fifty to one hundred animals and maintain them unmolested and under optimal conditions until the last one dies. This generates a survival curve showing the percent still alive at each age until the end. For non-laboratory animals like lions and walruses, sheep, turtles, and bulls, maximum survival data are derived from two chief sources: zoo data, and the records of thoroughbreds. Because zoo records are exact and many zoo animals are captured while still very young, the oldest recorded age for a particular animal from the combined zoos of the world gives a rough idea of the maximum life span for that species.[4] Life spans for some common species are shown in Table 1.2.

Precise records are also available for prizewinning thoroughbred animals who've been allowed to live out their natural life spans under the best conditions, well fed, well exercised, and cared for. Examining the British General Stud Book

The maximum verifiable life spans for a number of animals.

Animal:	Years:
Tortoise	150
Man	113
Asian elephant	60
Orangutan	58
Gorilla	55
Chimpanzee	50
Golden eagle	50
Whale	50
Horse	40
Grizzly bear	35
Domestic cat	30
American buffalo	26
Lion	25
Rhesus monkey	24
Dolphin	23
Dog	20
Domestic goat	20
Moose	17
Kangaroo	16
Rabbit	15
Vampire bat	13
Skunk	8
Rat	4
Mouse	3½
Shrew	2

Table 1.2

for thoroughbred racing horses, gerontologist and sexologist Alex Comfort[5] found the highest ages reached to be a little over 30 years. Poignantly, the last entry on a number of the old stallions was "fell dead while servicing a mare." Some years earlier, in 1873, William Thoms,[6] deputy librarian of the House of Lords, had examined similar "thoroughbred" data from peerage and baronetage books, one of the few sources of accurate human life-span information available before birth registration was begun in the nineteenth century. Thoms could find only a single instance of a peer or baron living to be over 100 years. The books do not cite how the lords met their deaths.

Because birth registration is relatively recent, it is virtually impossible to authenticate historical or even current claims of great age in humans. The oldest person with fully acceptable credentials was Fanny Thomas who lived to be 113 years and 215 days and died in April, 1980, in San Gabriel, California. Attributing her longevity to the fact that she ate applesauce three times a day and never married, so "never had a man to bother me," Miss Thomas was survived by four nieces, one nephew, fifteen grandnieces and nephews, forty-five great nieces and nephews, and sixteen great-great nieces and nephews. In 1979, United States social security records, which are generally based on birth certificates, listed a total of 11,891 persons who were 100 years of age or over. At 111 years, George Washington White, formerly a fireman on the Southern Railways famous 97 Crescent Limited, was the oldest individual on the list.

Claims for ages substantially in excess of 110 never seem to pan out, although they often make interesting reading. Three of the most famous supposed super-centenarians were the Englishmen Thomas Parr (who allegedly died at age 152), Henry Jenkins (169) and the Countess of Desmond (140). "Old Parr" was even honored for having reached such a great age by being buried in Westminster Abbey where his gravestone declares that he had "lived in the reigns of ten kings," namely from 1483 to 1635. But these and other reputed superlong lives are all hokum, as shown by painstaking investigations of the aforementioned William Thoms, who incidentally remarked, "Let no one who has the slightest desire to live in peace and quietness be tempted, under any circumstances, to enter upon the chivalrous task of trying to correct a popular error."

Popular errors there were indeed. In 1799 James Easton[7] collected information on everyone who, between A.D. 66 and 1799, supposedly lived more than 100 years. Unlike Thoms, Eastman was completely uncritical in his assessments. Two of his 427 synopses will illustrate how legend and anecdote creep into history.

Attila: died 500 A.D., 121 years of age.

King of the Huns. Hearty and strong at such great age, he led to the altar of Hymen, as a second wife, one of the most beautiful princesses of the age, and the next day he was dead of excess.

Jonathan Hartop: died 1791, 138 years of age.

Of the village of Aldborough, near Boroughbridge, Yorkshire. His father and mother died of the plague in 1666; and he perfectly well remembered the great fire of London. He had been married five times; and left seven children, twenty-six grandchildren, seventy-four great grandchildren, and one hundred and forty great great grandchildren. The third wife of this very extraordinary man was an illegitimate daughter of Oliver Cromwell, who gave her a portion, amounting to five hundred pounds. Mr. Hartop lent the great Milton fifty pounds, soon after the restoration, which the bard returned him with honor, though not without some difficulty, as his circumstances were very low. Mr. Hartop would have declined receiving it, but the pride of the poet was equal to his genius, and he sent the money with an angry letter, which was found among the curious possessions of that venerable old man, Mr. Jonathan Hartop, who died at 138 years of age.

Besides the above examples of inadequately supported and preposterous accounts of individual longevity, claims for super-longevity surround certain modern isolated population groups: natives from Vilcabamba in Ecuador, the Hunza tribe in India, and a group from the rugged Caucasus mountains in Russia. These population stories are modern counterparts of one of the old gerontological myths, namely, that in some far-off land and due to special circumstances (which we might hope to discover if we're smart) people live to extraordinary ages. No birth records exist to substantiate these longevity claims. In the Caucasus it's a great honor to be old, and the older the venerable ones get the more they are honored, so the more they exaggerate their ages. There's a tendency when you're middle-aged to say you're younger than you are; but when you're quite old, to say that you're even older. An 85-year-old man is just another codger in the public eye, but let him reach 105 and suddenly the local newspaper glorifies him in two chatty column-inches. Strangers congratulate him on his birthday. It's not an honor to be just old, but it is to be very, very old.

In the Russian Caucasus, a villager supposed to be 130 had his picture appear in the government paper, *Izvestiya*. Later, *Izvestiya* received a letter from this man's fellow villagers who identified him as a World War I deserter from the Russian Army who had used his father's documents to escape remobilization. In reality he was not 130 but 78 years old. According to Russian gerontologist Zhores Medvedev,[8] there are hundreds, perhaps thousands of similar cases. Because the social scene is biased toward great age and the state propaganda machine delights in Russia's having the oldest people in the world (it looks like Communism is really good for you!), the crafty oldsters maintain the masquerade and maybe even grow to believe it themselves. But Mikha Jobua of the village of Chlou is certainly not the 125 years he claims to be, nor Khfaf Lasuric of Kutal the 128 he claims, nor is Muslim Shirali 167. There's no hard evidence whatsoever for any of these claims, or for similar ones elsewhere.

A recent example of a seemingly authentic longevity claim

which nevertheless turned out to be false concerned Charlie Smith,[9] who died in October, 1979. Charlie said he was an ex-slave, and at one time was accepted as being 137 years of age, the oldest person in the United States. His assertion that he'd been brought to the U. S. from West Africa as a youth had been endorsed by Social Security officials who believed they had found documents proving Smith's sale into slavery in New Orleans in 1854 at the age of 12, when Franklin Pierce was president of the United States. For a time, Charlie Smith was listed in the *Guinness Book of World Records*, but he was dropped from the 1980 edition because a marriage certificate turned up which required a revised computation of his age. In reality Charlie Smith was only 104 years old. All these super longevity stories finally explode just like Charlie Smith's.

The truth is that since mankind began, in all generations, the maximum attained life span probably stands between 110 and 120 years. To extend that maximum has been the classical goal of gerontology since its venerable origin in ancient China in the time of Lao-tzu. Let us therefore begin to inquire what will happen when the goal is attained, when life span is extended not only in myth but in fact, because at last that time is not far off. Figure 1.2 shows again the survival curve for the United States in 1960, but now I've added a new curve reflecting a survival pattern with maximum life span assumed to be 140 years. The two small bell-shaped curves under the larger ones represent the frequencies in advanced age of the so-called "diseases of aging": cancer, heart disease, diabetes, stroke, arthritis, and the others. These diseases do not actually underlie aging. On the contrary, they are largely secondary to the decline in resistance and adaptability which accompanies the aging process. As secondary manifestations of aging, they begin appearing about the time the survival curve starts swinging steeply downward. If the successes of science result in a curve with maximum survival at 140 years, the "diseases of aging," although not cured, will have their times of onset postponed commensurate with the delay in the downswing. So instead of slumping over with a heart attack at age 62 on the subway as at present, you'll suffer the same fate at age 115 on the space shuttle. You'll have gained fifty-three years and taken a trip to the moon.

The 90-year-old man of the future will have the physical vigor of a 50-year-old man of today. By substantially prolonging life span, at one swoop we will have greatly postponed the onset of the major diseases of our society. In this age of Degenerative and Man-made diseases, substantial postponement is a kind of "cure"—perhaps a better and cheaper way to cure the killer diseases than trying to pick them off one by one, as medicine is trying to do at present. Maximum life-span-extending technologies will give as a bonus the postponement of heart disease, arthritis, cancer, diabetes, all of them. This is the first message of Figure 1.2.

The second message concerns the percentage of senile or debilitated people in today's population compared to the percentage expected in a longer-living, 140-year-maximum population. Let's assume for the sake of illustration that everyone in the terminal hatched portions of the two survival curves in

The effect of extension of maximum life span.

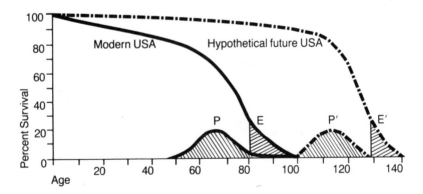

Effect of extension of maximum life span in modern USA and in a hypothetical future USA on the frequency at different ages of the major diseases of aging (P and P') and on the occurrence of feeble or senile oldsters (E and E') in the population.

Figure 1.2

Figure 1.2 is senile. We see (and it is easier to see than to say) that the hatched portion of the longer curve is a smaller fraction of that entire curve than the hatched portion of the shorter curve is of its curve. With prolongation of maximum life span the percentage of persons in the total population who are senile or debilitated actually decreases. Another pleasing and surprising result!

This second message has important implications for public policy. The social support system for the aged in the U. S. costs a staggering amount of tax money. The way things are, it will always be increasing. Federal programs for the elderly cost about 112 billion dollars in 1978. *Even without inflation* they are expected to rise to 350 billion by the early twenty-first century[10] and will total something like a quarter of the nation's entire payroll. The over-65-year-old age group will increase from twenty-three million in 1976 to thirty-two million in the year 2000 and to forty-five million by 2020.[11] By the year 2000 there will be seventeen million persons over 75 and five million over 85 years of age in the U. S. alone. These population increases are predicted even without the added prospect of significant life-span extension. Under our present system they add up to more old-age homes, more nursing care, more subsidies, and more money to take care of more sick, senile, and debilitated old people. As an earlier revolutionary, V. I. Lenin, once asked in another desperate context, "What is to be done?"

Our long-term efforts should be for prevention ahead of treatment. The National Foundation for Infantile Paralysis faced a similar kind of policy decision in the 1940s and 50s. It could have invested all its resources in perfecting better iron lungs. If that had been the choice, we would now have the best designed, most comfortable iron lungs imaginable, inhabited by thousands of polio victims. Instead of iron lungs, the Foundation invested heavily in basic research on the conquest of polio. It was certainly the wiser decision. My point is that old-age homes and all the vast social support structures continuously accumulating to care for the helpless aged are the iron lungs of gerontology. Improvements in the social, economic, and medical support system for the elderly will merely provide symptomatic relief for an expanding problem. Extending maximum life span will diminish the size of the problem.

Having understood the significance of 50 percent and maximum survival, we can use the principles learned from studying the curves to ask questions which will teach us how to use the principles more widely. This is a prototype of scientific method called building understanding upon itself (which is why the whole edifice needs occasionally to be demolished and reconstructed, as by a Lavoisier or a Darwin . . . but that's another story).

Is the commonly held opinion true that women age more slowly than men? They do indeed enjoy a longer 50 percent survival. Eighty percent of female children live to be 65 years or older compared to only 67 percent of male children. Women over 65 are the fastest growing segment of the population. The ratio is expected to increase still further by the year 2010. In the over-100-year category, there are today about 8,500 women but only 3,000 men in the U. S. Social Security register.

In fact, however, it's probably not true that women age more slowly than men, because there's no difference in maximum life span between the sexes. The observed differences in 50 percent survivals are secondary to environmental changes in the past half-century. In 1900 there was no sex difference in 50 percent survivals, and there were as many men as women over 75 years of age.[12] The relative upsurge in male mortality since 1900 can be traced to smoking (lung cancer, heart and respiratory disease), more accidents (automobiles), and more alcoholism among males. Where these factors are not operative, as among the Amish, men live as long as women even now. Furthermore, in today's population at large, as shown in Table 1.3, the difference in remaining life expectancy for men and women narrows as the population becomes older.[13]

Table 1.3

Remaining life expectancy* once you've reached a certain age.

Men*	Age	Women*
24.5	50	30.4
20.6	55	26.2
17.0	60	22.1
13.9	65	18.3
11.1	70	14.7
8.7	75	11.6
6.9	80	9.0
5.5	85	6.9

At age 50 men expect to live another 24.5 years; women, 30.4 years—a difference of 5.9 years. By age 85 the difference in life expectancies is only 1.4 years. Osborn Segerberg[14] recounts that at the 1971 White House Conference on Aging a number of women delegates campaigned for increased gerontological emphasis on older women because there were more of them, until a male delegate countered that there were more older women because so many men were having a problem living as long.

Insistence on the evidence of survival curves will also help us penetrate the claims of scientists like Ana Aslan (GH3 or Gerovital), the assertive nonsense of pseudoscientists like the cellular therapist Paul Niehans, testicular grafters like Serge Voronoff, and the U. S.'s own grand quack, John Romulus Brinkley.

Since 1951 Dr. Ana Aslan, a Rumanian physician, has been treating the elderly with her preparation of novocain known as Gerovital. In 1957 she reported that over 5,000 persons had received the treatment. Included among her patients have been such celebrities as Charles de Gaulle, William Somerset Maugham, and Konrad Adenauer. Every year thousands more people flock to Rumania to receive Gerovital therapy. No one from this large cohort treated for a long time has broken the maximum life-span barrier or even come close.

Gerovital may have some effect in relieving arthritic pain and is an antidepressant. One of the major problems of the aged is depression. In them, depression mimics the picture of organic dementia. Therefore, successfully treating old-age depression may look like central nervous system "rejuvenation," but there is no convincing evidence that Gerovital extends maximum life span. Of course, since humans live so long, it might just possibly be too soon to know. One study with the European brand of Gerovital did report that in a small series of the elderly, it augmented nerve conduction velocity and decreased secretion of an adrenal gland metabolite that normally increases with age.[15] On the other hand, a thorough review of the total Gerovital evidence, conducted at the Veterans Hospital in Los Angeles in 1975, yielded a negative report.[16]

Well-controlled appropriate animal studies with Gerovital should tell us whether it affects longevity. Aslan has conducted life-span experiments in rats.[17] In 1965 she reported a 21 percent increase in the life span of male rats treated with Gerovital, but no effect in females. The rat strain used (Wistar) was not optimal as it does not have a long natural life span. Although trumpeting the alleged age-retarding potency of Gerovital for almost thirty years, Aslan has not repeated (or at least not published) her work with any other rat strains, nor with genetically inbred long-lived mouse strains (which are readily available), nor with hamsters or other animals whose life spans are substantially shorter than man's, so that effects on maximum life span could be evaluated without having to wait for years and years. Why haven't other gerontologists run survival tests? It's because the supporting evidence for something that has been around now for thirty years and been so highly touted is so marginal that good scientists won't invest their time in a doubtful experiment requiring three years of work. They have better options. They could be wrong, because in fact, Gerovital has never been adequately tested for life-span extension in animals.

How to Think about Life Span

✳ Most of the evidence for Gerovital as an anti-aging therapy is based upon the least acceptable kind of scientific evidence, that of testimonials. Some people take it and swear they feel younger. Unfortunately, testimonials can be had for most anything you please: encounters with Bigfoot, cancer cures, UFO's, ghosts, and all by sincere people. Testimonial evidence is not necessarily wrong, but there is no scientific methodology capable of evaluating it. Maybe a ghost did in fact put its cold hand on Mrs. Comstock's warm thigh that night in the opera box, thus proving the survival of the spirit after death! I'll not be the first to deny it, because as evidence it cannot be adequately evaluated, but I'll be the first to doubt it, and for the same reason.

The Russian gerontologist, Zhores Medvedev, now in England, has pointed out that originally Dr. Aslan transferred old people from the dull atmosphere of Rumanian retirement homes into pleasant hospital surroundings, and gave them a lot of attention plus Gerovital. Of course they felt rejuvenated. When the Russians tried Gerovital on old people who were not leading dull retirement lives (Khrushchev, for example) the results were negative.

Dr. Paul Niehan's "cellular therapy" consisted of injecting patients with fresh cells from unborn lambs obtained by slaughtering their mothers. Konrad Adenauer, whose political acumen exceeded his medical discretion by a considerable margin, got this one too, as did Charlie Chaplin, Pope Pius XII, the Duke of Windsor, Bernard Baruch, Sir Winston Churchill, Christian Dior, and many others whose judgments were out to lunch. The trip to Niehan's elegant clinic in Switzerland might well be referred to as "Gullibles Travels."

After World War I, Serge Veronoff, a Russian physician living in France, accumulated a large fortune by transplanting ape testicles into old men as a form of rejuvenation therapy. I was informed by Professor Walter Starkie, formerly associated with the Abbey Theater in Dublin and later a lecturer on Welsh witchcraft at UCLA, that William Butler Yeats, perhaps driven to desperation by his fruitless courtship of the actress Maude Gonne, received a Voronoff testicular transplant. In the United States in the 1920s the complete quack in the form of John Romulus Brinkley transplanted lusty young goat testicles into old men, thereby amassing a sufficient fortune to buy a radio station and run for governor of Kansas. None of these several cellular and testicular gentlemen performed a single animal experiment to obtain actual lifespan data.

Are there animal or plant species which don't age at all? Let's answer that question and then let's see what their survival curves look like.

At a two-mile elevation near the California-Nevada border not far from Death Valley grow the gnarled, wind-twisted bristlecone pines. Narrow strips of bark sustain life in what outwardly look like nearly dead trees. The oldest bristle cone pine is merely thirty feet tall, but radiocarbon dating proves it to be 4,600 years old. However, despite the impressive antiquity of the pines, the record for survival is held by a bush! In Riverside, California, some of the desert creosote bushes have been age-dated with radiocarbon technics as going back 10,000 years. Bushes growing in round clusters or circles over twenty feet across are direct offshoots of clones of single individual plants which thrived millennia ago—but technically they are still the same plant.

Under good conditions, bacteria and yeasts, which are also clone-like, will go on multiplying indefinitely without signs of aging. The same is true for the more complex amoeba and for some other, but not all, one-celled organisms. *Paramecia* are single-celled organisms covered with fine hairlike filaments which beat rhythmically like oars to propel them forward or direct food into their mouths. Some strains age, others don't. In those which do, the time between divisions of the proliferating cells gradually lengthens until at last they fail to divide at all. "Rejuvenation" occurs only if sexual union takes place.

Aquatic flatworms possess a head that is formed in early development. Soon the cells of the head no longer divide but the body cells keep dividing. When a certain length is reached by the body, a new head is formed on one side and the worm divides in two, forming one new body with the new head, plus a second new body which carries the old head. The process continues. Finally the worm with the original head, passed on to successive bodies, dies, no doubt ripe with flatworm wisdom. But aging does not occur in the line of descent composed of successive rear-end animals. Among flatworms it pays to be last.

Sponges do not age. Nor do sea anemones. In the 1850s a number of sea anemones were collected from ocean waters near Arran, Scotland. Sixteen were kept in seawater-repleted jars and finally transferred to the aquarium of Edinburgh University. In 1940 they were all found dead on the same day. The sudden death of the whole colony could only have been accidental, not due to aging, so they clearly lived eighty-to-ninety years without signs of deterioration.

All right, then, why are we not up to our rears or even our ears in sponges, sea anemones, and flatworms? The answer takes us back to the subject of accidents as an important cause of death in populations. In the case of the lower animals, predation, or being eaten by someone else, can be considered an accident, and naturally an unlucky one. In the case of humans, it would also be considered an accident, although nowadays a rare one, we having devised more refined methods of predation. Figure 1.3A shows the kind of survival curve produced if aging and disease were halted and all deaths limited to accidents. The curve was actually generated by following the fate of a number of drinking glasses in a restaurant.[18] The glasses don't "age," but they are subject to accidental breakage at a constant rate. They don't "age," but neither are they immortal. The human survival curve beyond ninety-two years (Figure 1.3B) displays a similar shape, emphasizing that in very late life random accidents stand forth as the major fatality factor. For animals in the wild, whether they age or not, the main cause of death is accidents, and survival curves of wild animals are of this type.

If human aging were completely preventable but accidents continued at the same rate as today, the 50 percent survival can be calculated to be around 350 years and maximum survival 600 years. There would be a very long tail to the curve, a very small proportion of the population living to be a thousand or even five-to-ten thousand years old. If the accident rate were altered, the maximum life span would be different, but true physical immortality would remain unobtainable even if aging and disease were conquered.

Nature may abhor vacuums but she delights in paradoxes. A completely non-aging human population could be considered as one which had returned to its "natural state" insofar as the shape of its survival curve be concerned, because in the savage state as in the non-aging state, survival curves are governed by accidental deaths. The few physiologic decrements setting in with mid-adulthood are enough to tip the balance if you live in the savage forest and have to run from tigers. Rectangularized survival curves are therefore artifacts of progress, just as aging itself is an artifact of evolution.

The evolution of mankind has unique features in relation to maximum life span.[19] Within any general order of animals

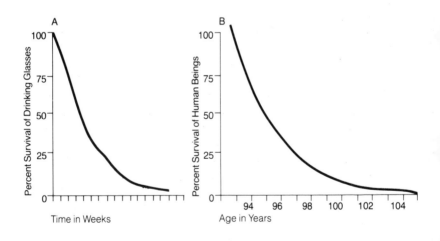

Comparisons of shapes of survival curves of drinking glasses in a restaurant (A), with the human survival curve beyond 92 years of age (B). Both typify death by accident rather than disease.

Figure 1.3

—primates for instance (monkeys, apes, and men)—a distinct mathematical relationship exists between brain weight, body weight, and life span. This relationship allows scientists to estimate the maximum life span of man's ancestors by examining the fragmented remains of their bones. Our earliest true ancestor, the still undiscovered "missing link," had a small brain, walked on its knuckles, and of course left no records; but it can be included in our calculations because of its evolutionary nearness to today's chimpanzee.[20] The cranial capacity and body weight of the "missing link" would have corresponded to a maximum life span of forty-three years. By three-to-four million years ago the fossil record reveals the presence at last of a genuine hominid or true man-like creature, *Australopithecus*, who walked upright, possessed a slightly bigger brain than the chimpanzee, and had a maximum life span of probably forty-seven years. A million and a half years ago we find *Homo erectus*, with a cranial capacity three-fourths that of modern man. A user of complex stone tools (and perhaps more importantly a user of tools to make tools), he enjoyed a maximum life span of seventy-two years. Between three million and one and one-half million years ago, as *Australopithecus* changed into *Homo erectus*, the brain doubled in size, enlarging from 500 milliliters to 1,000 milliliters. *Homo sapiens* (ourselves) only appeared 100 to 150 thousand years ago, with a brain size of about 1,500 milliliters. The human brain is not only bigger but has undergone extensive reorganization, and we can now live up to 100-to-110 years.

Now look at Figure 1.4. The degree of increase in maximum life span which has occurred quite recently in human evolution, namely the abrupt upswing in the curve since *Homo erectus*, has no parallel in evolutionary history. Since the increase does represent an evolutionary event, it must have resulted from natural Darwinian selection of mutated genes (genes are the fundamental units of heredity). But on the gene level even chimpanzees and men are nearly identical. And the arrangements of amino acids in their respective proteins (hemoglobin, for example) are 99 percent identical.[20] In the sense of structural gene similarities and differences, man and

Evolution of maximum life span.

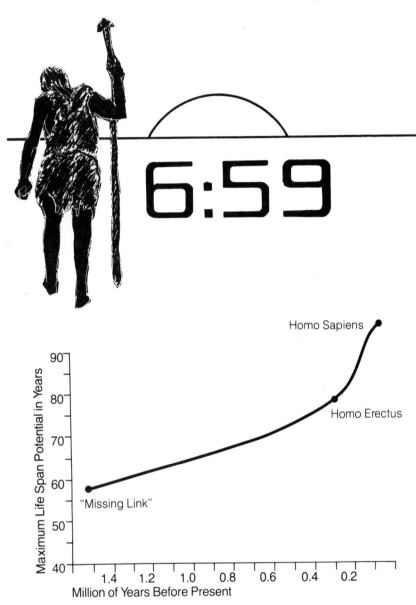

Recent evolution of maximum life span of hominid species leading to man. Note the big jump in life span in the last 200,000 years.

Figure 1.4

chimp are more alike than dog and fox. For this reason of near identity, and also because of the relatively short evolutionary time period during which hominid life span has doubled, the mutations responsible for the doubling could only have involved a few genes. Furthermore, we know the mutation rate for genes of ape and man, and during a 100,000 year period at most only half of 1 percent of the genes could have mutated. The genetic "program" for aging must therefore be written in only a few genes or gene systems, rather than involving the whole enormous hodepodge of heredity material. This is encouraging. It narrows the search. In my laboratory at UCLA, we have been able to identify at least one of these gene systems.

2

The Long March
of Gerontology

Almost twenty years ago in Budapest I visited the laboratory of Professor Joseph Balo, chairman of the Department of Pathology at the university. Most past chairmen of
Pathology in this oldest of the Hungarian universities had
been distinguished scientists. In line with this tradition, old
Professor Balo enjoyed renown as the discoverer of the enzyme "elastase." Formed in the pancreas, this enzyme is able
to dissolve elastin, the structural protein component of the
body's elastic tissue fibers whose deterioration with age causes
you to wrinkle up into a hag or a wizened wight.

After discussing the latest information about elastic tissue,
Professor Balo offered to show me around his department.
Walking through well-equipped laboratories, offices, animal
houses, several morgues, and an anatomy storehouse where
pickled dissection cadavers were hung up by ice tongs through
the ears, we arrived finally at the departmental library. Walls
paneled in old polished wood, easy chairs and ashtrays, rugs
thick enough to muffle the centuries, books both ancient and
modern: it was a charming, spiritually warm room. Splendid
oil portraits of all the past chairmen of the Department of
Pathology hung in chronological order on the ancient panel-
ing. The first portrait, by now some hundreds of years old, was

a bit cracked and faded; nevertheless, the first chairman gazed bravely and haughtily out at us from across the centuries.

There were eight past chairmen, as I recall, all giants of the autopsy table and many of them accomplished experimentalists as well. Professor Balo told me about each of his predecessors, lined up in order on the polished walls. He knew their private lives and peccadillos as well as their public careers. Ending our historical tour with the portrait of the immediate past chairman, we arrived at a vacant spot on the wall.

"And here," said Professor Balo with evident satisfaction, "is where I'll hang."

That was in the early 1960s. Today, as I write, it is 1982. He's hanging there now, I have no doubt—the discoverer of elastase, fully prepared to look out from across the centuries, perhaps from that vantage point seeing where *we* shall someday hang.

A fatalistic attitude about death, like Professor Balo's, is common, and extends to and embraces and nullifies the prospects of prolonging life. Death can also be denied by placing a taboo on mentioning it. Your friend is dying and you go to see him but you don't ask him what it feels like to be dying. You will probably never see him again, but the two of you don't engage in a serious discussion. You "cheer him up" by acquiescing in the taboo.

Since the very beginning, life-span extenders and immortalists have had to deal with various types of evasion and overall negative attitudes about their objectives. In recent times segments of the press and other media, when dealing with gerontology, have served up cloying mixtures of sensationalized longevity scientist and half-baked faddist. In addition, the past fifty years have seen the failures of at least three highly touted pseudoscientific remedies for aging: Bulgarian yogurt and fermented milk at the turn of the century, sex gland transplants in the 1920s, and Alexander Bogomolet's antireticular serum in the 1940s. Small wonder the *Encyclopaedia Britannica* didn't include a section on gerontology until 1957.

A historically older, subtler, more vexing category of negativism has been that of "apologism," which has always sought to provide acceptable reasons for the assumed inevitability of physical death. Immortality (or greatly protracted life span) is neither possible nor desirable (went the argument). Indeed, it is unnecessary (since death is not the end of things after all!). Immortality is not possible because it's against the Divine Order or the Natural Order, or because the "destiny" of animals, including humans, is death. Science shouldn't meddle because life (and hence death) has aspects which are epiphenomenal, mystical, and not to be defined in purely physical or chemical terms. Immortality is not desirable because you would end up disastrously wrinkled, decrepit, and senile, and who wants that? Or you'd grow overwhelmingly bored, ". . . living through a great blank eternity with [your] eyes open."[1] Society would stagnate under these conditions. Extending life span might interfere with evolution and, though harmful for the individual, aging and individual death are necessary for the evolutionary advancement of any species, including ours.

A puzzling aspect of apologism is the strong emotion often attached to many of the forms it takes. Apologists often portray extended life as a nightmare. When Tithonus, the brother of King Priam of Troy, married Eos, Goddess of the Dawn, Eos beseeched Zeus to grant her new husband eternal life, but she foolishly forgot to ask for eternal youth to go along with it. The deathless Tithonus grew older forever, reduced to a condition of pathetic, babbling senility. In the voyage to Laputa in *Gulliver's Travels*, Swift tells of the "Struldbrugs," mutant humans who don't die but keep aging and "find themselves cut off from all possibility of pleasure; and whenever they see a funeral they lament that others have gone to a harbour of rest to which they themselves can never hope to arrive." A modern version of the Struldbrugs are the "old ones" in the film *Zardoz*, which depicts an immortal society in which everyone is totally bored. They've seen all that life has to offer but still can't find the answer to the one and only overriding philosophical question, "What's it all about?" They agree to play endless roles, to pretend to be happy. Anyone who gets fed up with the hypocrisy and breaks the spell is parapsychologically zapped by the others and allowed to age . . . but these aging people still can't

die. The horror of decrepitude is added to that of boredom.
To punish man for accepting fire from Prometheus, Zeus
created Pandora and her box, which contained, among other
disastrous ills, old age, grief, and death. This particular variety
of apologism considers aging as punishment for an offense
against the gods. Adam and Eve were meted out the same
heavy judgment. By contrast, moderately long life may be the
reward for humble submission to the gods, as witness the
biblical Job.

The philosopher apologists, such as Epicurus, Lucretius,
Cicero, Marcus Aurelius, and the contemporary physician and
writer on death, Elisabeth Kübler-Ross, have laid many snares
to entice the immortalists—people like Roger Bacon, Francis
Bacon, Paracelsus, Descartes, and those of us in the modern
contingent—away from our goals. Or at least to divert everyone's attention elsewhere, or to argue that "whatever is, is
right!" Epicurus and Lucretius taught that overlong life would
become a dreary round of the same basic experiences, that it's
best to live fully, that accepting life's inevitable end even enhances its enjoyment. Hans Zinsser, the great bacteriologist
who died of leukemia in 1940, wrote that his last year of life
was the best of all. Knowing the end was coming, he savored
the beauty of every remaining day. All basically unimportant
matters were at last deeply comprehended to be unimportant,
and no trivial concerns interfered with his wonderful, final
leukemic year. Death is not bad, say the Stoics, only the fear
of it. And in recent years, Elisabeth Kübler-Ross has been
making death sound like the most appealing adventure life has
to offer.

> . . . dying can be one of the most beautiful incredible
> experiences of life. . . . Dying is a growth experience . . .
> the last big growth experience a human being has in this
> lifetime . . . a genuine positive submission."[2]

Christianity and Islam are particularly fine examples of
apologism. Both promise resurrection, salvation, and effortless bliss. If there's life after death there really is no death.

Rome herself, the mightiest temporal power in history, could not stand against the promise of post-death immortality. Socrates and Plato, religious rationalists, denied that death was the termination of identity. According to them, the soul lives a kind of afterlife either in Hades or Elysium. Most religions love death. They have a vested interest in it. They exist to sanctify it and give it meaning. Because of their teachings, we accept "natural" death (or try to) and seek to do nothing to counteract it.

The scientific apologists arrive next upon the stage of our historical inquiry, dancing in from the wings like a whole high-stepping chorus stretching across the centuries—see, there's Aristotle, Galen, Malthus, Cardan the Renaissance mathematician, and numerous moderns. Most of these gentlemen have taught that since aging is unavoidable, you may as well lie down and enjoy it, or since old age is a horrible and inevitable stage of life, let's be thankful death is around to put an end to its last, sad chapter. In his *Rhetoric* Aristotle painted old age as a strictly no-good time. According to him, the old are never positive about anything, are uncharitable, suspicious, without strong loves or hates, are generally cowards and perpetual alarmists, want most what they don't have, and are never so fond of life as on their last day. Death becomes a necessary release from foolishness! Cardan summed up his own attitude toward the late years of life, "Old age, when it comes, must make every man regret that he did not die in infancy."

These negative and self-reinforcing species of apologism are as common today as in former times and greatly impede the advance of gerontology. An enthusiastic acceptance of the idea of living very long has seldom been an attribute of thoughtful minds, due in large part to the numbing effects of apologism in all its forms. But the great Chinese alchemist and life extension advocate, Kung-Ho, had this to say of his apologist contemporaries: "As to Wen-Tzu, Chuang-tzu and Kuan-ling Yin Itsi, sometimes they equalize death and life, saying there is no difference. They consider life as hard labor and death as rest. They are not v orth bothering with."

Just as apologism benumbs, certain past and present

gerontological myths lead us into vain searches and useless preoccupations.[3] These myths are the more treacherous because of their aesthetic appeal. The antedeluvian type of longevity myth maintains that in primordial antiquity life was far longer than today. Genesis 5:9:29 asserts, as we see from Figure 2.1, that Noah and everyone before him lived substantially longer than the post-flood patriarchs, who in turn lived longer than degenerate, modern man. The Greek poet Hesiod tells of a golden age in the past when people lived a long, long time, never actually growing old but slipping quietly into sleep and gentle death at their appointed times.

Longevity myths display two negative aspects: first, the idea that aging and a shortened life are somehow a punishment for sins and represent a fall from grace; second, the myths state or imply that men were purer and wiser in the Golden Age of a distant past, and our current task is not so much to discover for ourselves as to *re*discover what they once knew. Even today many nonscientific longevity seekers waste time looking for lost keys and interpretations to allegorical texts.

Hyperborean myths do for space what the antediluvian myths do for time. In some far off but very real land (the Island of the Blest, according to the Greeks Strabo and Pindar and the Roman Pliny) dwell fortunate humans with remarkably long and healthy lives. "Hyperborean" means "beyond the north wind," so it's difficult to get there. "There" is where the Golden Age still persists, and Hindu, Persian, Celtic, and Chinese cultures all have legends telling us where "there" is. The "Shangri-La" of the novel *Lost Horizon* is a contemporary hyperborean myth. Non-fictional modern hyperboreans include the supposedly long-lived population isolates: the Hunza in the mountains of Kashmir in India, the inhabitants of Vilcabamba in Ecuador, and our friends the Soviet senior citizens of the province of Abkhazia in the Caucasus. As I've shown in the first chapter, none of these modern hyperborean isolates can be properly documented to support the claims of extreme longevity. Indeed, a painstaking investigation of civil and church records by scientists from the Universities of Wis-

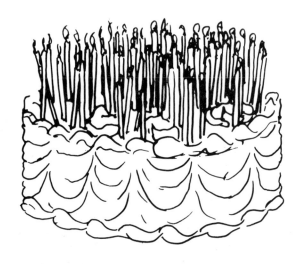

Age of the patriarchs at the time of their death.

Before the flood:		After the flood:	
Adam	930	Shem	600
Seth	912	Arphaxad	436
Enos	905	Salah	433
Cainan	910	Eber	464
Mahalaleel	895	Peleg	239
Jared	962	Reu	239
Methuselah	969	Serug	230
Lamech	777	Nahor	148
Noah	950	Terah	205
		Abram	175
		Isaac	180
		Jacob	147

Figure 2.1

consin and California, in company with Ecuadorian scientists, revealed that the oldest living villager in Vilcabamba was merely 96.

We continue to fantasize that we might achieve our breakthrough the easy way, evading the patient labor of understanding, by a nostalgic return to a time before now; by a journey to a distant, almost inaccessible and usually mountainous place; or simply by jumping into the jacuzzi with a fistful of sprouts and granola.

The jacuzzi is the modern equivalent of yet another captivating myth, the legend of the Fountain of Youth. Once there was a Hindu Pool of Youth. Once there was a Hebraic River of Immortality, flowing out of Eden. And deep in the faraway jungles Jupiter transformed the nymph Juventas into a Fountain of Youth. She gave forth sweet odors and whoever bathed in her became young and healthy. In a later age, a similar fountain attracted Ponce de León, a page in the royal court of Aragon who accompanied Christopher Columbus on his second expedition to the New World, to organize in 1512 an expedition specifically to discover "the springs of youth," supposed to bubble on an island called Bimini. Ponce de León merely discovered Florida where he was killed by an Indian arrow at the age of 61.

We note in later ages the touching European faith in mineral waters, those of Bath, Bad Godesberg, and Vichy, to name several. These spas began as holy wells, pools, and springs where one prayed first and was healed afterwards. The 120°F hot springs of Bath, in England, were used first by the Celts, then the Romans. Sul, the British goddess of springs, protected the bathers. But in 1745 the Abbé Le Blanc, in his *Lettres d'un francais,* described the transformation effected in a later generation of English ladies by the waters of Bath: they "for one glorious and by no means virtuous month enjoyed a nature cure that was as primitive in fact as in appearance it was made to look civilized."

The Holy Grail, sought so vigorously and so vainly by the knights of King Arthur, represented an allegorical image of the Fountain myth, whereas to the alchemists of the Middle

Ages the Fountain need not be an external bath but could be taken internally as an elixir, the "elixir of life." It's a mistake to regard these alchemists as merely forerunners of modern chemists, bent on preparing impossible concoctions. Alchemy was equally a system of mind and inner being employing concrete imagery: the stone, the forge, fire, the transformation, the bursting flower of gold. Nature was not merely quantitative, as science from Newton on has restricted itself to assume, but qualitative. The concept of a nature in perpetual qualitative change has been omitted from modern science, which deals rather with perpetual quantitative movement—the motion of atomic particles, for example. In the alchemical tradition a primal substance exists and evolves into the rest of matter by a sort of inorganic evolution or mutation. The primal substance can change other elements without itself being used up, and can thus be likened to a universal catalyst or enzyme. "Transformation" involves not only lead into gold, but mortality into immortality, or (as in Chinese alchemy and Taoism) man into hero and demigod (the *hsien*, in Taoism, as we shall see). Why not? Behold, the tadpole is transformed into the frog, the caterpillar into the butterfly. Why not man into *hsien*?

A great pioneer in an age not yet ready for his kind of insight, a product of monasticism, the medieval university system, and personal genius, the Franciscan friar and alchemist, Roger Bacon, in his life and work call to mind Faustus's admonition to Mephistopheles in Marlowe's version of the Legend:

Go and return an old Franciscan friar,
That holy shape becomes the devil best.

Proposing, like the erudite Aristotelian he was, that aging results from loss of "innate heat," Bacon placed his chief hope for combating it in pharmacology and alchemy, asserting that man ought to be able to extend his life span by at least a hundred years. He tried in his writings to keep just short of heresy but did not always succeed, and passed some years in prison. For example, in his *Opus Magnus*, he compares the philosopher's stone and "the elixir" to the fruit of the Tree of Life in the Garden of Eden. Clearly heretical! Shall the alchemist create in his retort what God forbade to Adam and Eve?

> . . . The body of Adam did not possess elements in full equality . . . but since the elements in him approached equality, there was very little waste in him; and hence he was fit for immortality, which he could have secured if he had eaten always of the fruit of the Tree of Life. For this fruit is thought to have elements approaching equality . . . Scientists, therefore, have striven to reduce the elements in some form of food or drink to an equality or nearly so, and have taught the means to this end.

Shining in isolated splendor on the last night of the Middle Ages and leading into the Renaissance, university lecturer, great physician, outcast and vagabond, a man whose life probably gave rise to the Faust legend, Paracelsus (born 1493, died 1541 in a brawl at the White Horse Inn in Salzburg) brought alchemy to its highest point, where it became a western equivalent of the spiritual disciplines of the East, an internal discipline held together by an external system of ritualized chemistry. Today we finally recognize as a probing legitimate question, whether modern science with its strictly quantitative orientation has not avoided inquiring into the true nature of reality, and the most advanced thinkers are considering again a unified view of the mind/matter duality. Alchemy can be seen as the forerunner of this ultra-modern movement, a movement which in the centuries ahead might well supersede what we now view as the most productive approach to the sensorial world—namely, our present scientific system of thought. Alchemists sought what Paracelsus wrote of as "the ultimate matter of anything, that state in which the substance has reached its highest grade of exaltation and perfection," in short, what Aristotle had labeled the fifth essence (the other four being earth, air, fire, water) and what others copied from Aristotle as *quinta essentia.* (So today we say "quintessence.") To understand the cosmos, to make gold, and to live forever, one needs a lot of quintessence, even today.

Something of the enticing flavor and frustration of alchemical writings can be sensed in a brief quotation from alchemist Basil Valentine's book, *The Triumphal Chariot of Antimony,* in which he describes how to concoct the elixir of life.

Take equal parts of this precipitate and of our sweet oil of Antimony; put into a well-closed phial; if exposed to gentle heat, the precipitate will gradually be dissolved and fixed in the oil: for the fire consumes its viscidity, and it becomes a red, dry, fixed, and fluid powder, which does not give out the slightest smoke.

Keep reverent silence: for now the King enters his bridal chamber, where he will delight himself many months with his spouse; and they will only leave the chamber when they have grown together, and produced a son who, if not the King of Kings, is at least a King, and delivers his subjects from disease and want. When you have reached this point, my friend, you have the Medicine of men and of metals; it is pleasant, sweet, and penetrating, and may be used without any risk. Without being a purgative, it expels all impure and morbid matter from the body. It will restore to you health, and relieve you of want in this life; nor can you ever discharge to God your obligation of gratitude for it. I fear that as a monk and religious man I have transcended the proper bounds of reticence and secrecy, and spoken out too freely. At any rate, I have told you enough; and if after all that has been said you do not discover the secret, it will not be my fault.

Attempts to prolong life by mental gymnastics mixed with pharmacology go back to well before the medieval alchemists, to ancient China and the system of the *Tao.* The attainment of great longevity, even immortality, was the chief original goal of Taoism. Tao means "the way," and immortality was what it was the way to. It was believed that through mastery of Taoist techniques, one could become a *hsien,* a self-actualized immortal human or demigod. We have no close western equivalent for the *hsien,* although the occasional association of great magicians who, some claim, control the real world are in the *hsien* tradition. If you had mastered the secrets of primal substances and quintessences and become a *hsien,* you could control external reality and be like a great magician, fly through the air, change the weather, assume different animal forms, be invisible, immortal, and ageless.

The three components of Taoism were naturalism, empiricism, and the development of special skills. The *hsien* or immortals were those who had won eternal life by mastering a number of techniques. Everyone begins life with a fixed amount of some vital substance, which he must conserve as one of the first steps toward longevity. Conservation involves progressing toward a state of "effortless action" whereby optimal results in the business of life are obtained with the smallest expenditure of energy. A modern version of this Taoist doctrine is the concept of specific metabolic rate, by which is meant that each animal is endowed at birth with a fixed amount of energy to use up in its lifetime. Most species have received about twenty-to-forty million calories per pound weight per lifetime. Man is an exception, he has eighty million. The maximum life spans of species differ in part because they use up their total energy endowments at different rates: thus, shrews in 1½ years, mice in 3½, and hummingbirds in 8.

The Taoist techniques were respiratory, dietary, gymnastic, sexual, and meditative, the latter running through all the others. To progress toward becoming a *hsien* you must reduce your rate of breathing, on exhalation swallow the breath for nourishment, and while the breath is inside, direct it on a prescribed route through the body and up into the brain, the chief organ to be rejuvenated because it controls the others. For diet: abjure grains, meat, wine, and many vegetables; subsist mostly on roots and fruit; finally, as the higher state be approximated, subsist on breath for meat and saliva for drink. Dietary and breathing techniques will prolong life sufficiently to allow time for preparing the elixir of immortality, which contains the bright red mineral cinnabar (mercuric chloride) and gold. It is, as they used to say, "potable gold."

Kung fu was invented to be the gymnastic of the Taoists,

its purpose, to remove "obstruction" within the body to the internal circulation of the breath and of the sexual essences. Like the Indian practitioners of Kundalini Yoga, the Taoists set great store in preserving the sexual forces, perhaps an earlier version of the modern scientific idea that the hereditary material, the DNA in the sperm and the egg, which passes on the traits of the species through large stretches of time, is immortal or probably still better, continually and wholly self-repairing, whereas the DNA of the body's other cells does not survive the death of the individual.

In Taoist practice, as in Kundalini Yoga, during sex you must raise your generative force. But don't ejaculate, meditate! And, mixing the internal breath with the generative force, send the latter upward to vitalize your brain. Ritual meditative sex, wherein the body was the seeker's alchemical crucible, was an appealing aspect of the *Tao*—certainly more so (or at least to us) than the diet of roots and gold and fruits. By following and mastering these techniques, the student gradually changes his physical body into a purer, more subtle material. The bones become as gold, the skin as jade, and further transformation supervenes toward the state of the transparent diamond body of a *hsien*. The Taoist master Chao Pi Ch'en ends his book, *The Secrets of Cultivating Essential Nature and Eternal Life*, as follows:

> The training should continue no matter how long it takes until the four elements scatter, and space pulverizes, leaving no traces behind; this is the golden immortal stage of the indestructible diamond body. This is the ultimate achievement of the training which now comes to an end.[4]

That was long ago, but their end was a new beginning. From the Taoists' and alchemists' view that all is one to the premodern and modern version of the mind/matter, mind/body duality is a leap from the marvelous into the practical and the piecemeal accretion of data. Leaping, we land first among the hygienists, nutritionists, emerging modern scientists, and philosophical pundits: men like the abstemious Renaissance nobleman, Luigi Cornaro, who followed a restricted diet and lived to be 103, or astronomer Edmund Halley, whose famous comet comes round every fifty-three years, perhaps to remind us that Halley constructed the first human survival curve, using data from the Polish city of Breslau. We encounter the illustrious German physician, Christopher Hufeland, whose book *Makrobiotik* (its initial title was *Art of Prolonging Human Life*), published in 1796, recommended a thoroughgoing lifestyle regimen which distinguished between the goals of simple hygiene, to maintain health (i.e., to optimize 50 percent survival), and of "makrobiotik," to attain great longevity (i.e., to extend maximum life span). We come to philosophers such as Descartes, Francis Bacon, Benjamin Franklin, William Godwin (father of Mary Shelley, who wrote *Frankenstein*, a sort of gerontologic treatise in its own right—the monster does not age) and the French encyclopedist Condorcet. Though we call them "philosophers," all sought practical methodology. Among his other accomplishments Ben Franklin, for example, invented the lightning rod, a stove which gives more warmth than open fireplaces and is still in use (the Franklin stove), bifocal eyeglasses (at age 74), and the public library.

These eager intellectuals were influenced by mankind's new orientation, the Idea of Progress, the idea that patient work will carry us forward to greater knowledge and fuller lives. They wanted to live longer to see how much better the future would become. A letter written in 1780 by Benjamin Franklin to the chemist Joseph Priestley illustrates this enthusiastic position.

The rapid progress "true" science now makes, occasions my regretting sometimes that I was born so soon. It is impossible to imagine the height to which may be carried, in a thousand years, the power of man over matter. We may perhaps learn to deprive large masses of their gravity, and give them absolute levity, for the sake of easy transport. Agriculture may diminish its labor and double its produce; all diseases may by sure means be prevented or cured, not excepting even that of old age, and our lives lengthened at pleasure even beyond the antediluvian standard.

Franklin's prophecies may come to pass much sooner than he thought. During the nineteenth and first half of the twentieth centuries, scientists made continued progress in "true" science and in practical medicine, with emphasis in aging studies on the simple collection of data: mortality tables, actuarial information, the life spans of animals, and descriptions of senescent changes in organs, tissues, and cells. Preoccupation with the actual diseases of aging led the French physician Jean Martin Charcot to begin the development of what we now classify as geriatric medicine.

Charcot was head of the Salpetrière Hospital in Paris, a huge seventeenth-century saltpeter factory that had been converted into an enormous hospital for the aged and indigent, and which represented a veritable museum of living pathology. One of the great clinicians and teachers of his century, an accomplished stylist, an urbane, handsome professor during one of the heydays of Parisian intellectual life, and married to a rich and socially prominent woman, he exercised enormous influence on the medicine of his time. His treatise, *Clinical Lectures on Senile and Chronic Diseases,* published in 1867, represented a turning point in the history of aging studies. Wary of grand designs for preventing aging, of "the nonsense of innate heat," imbalanced humors, and such leftovers from authoritarian antiquity, Charcot pointed the study of aging clearly in two directions which are still fairly well maintained today:

(1) to search for central themes or causes of aging;
(2) to describe the facts of aging, the organ changes, the physiology . . . in short, to define the aging process as it appears, and with emphasis upon the diseases of aging.

This emphasis found its next major proponent in Dr. I. G. Nascher (1862–1944) who in 1914 coined the term "geriatrics" in a textbook by that title which he could not get published for two years because the medical publishing firms of the time thought the demand for it would be nil. (Their position is partially understandable in that the percentage of old people in the total population was far smaller in the early part of the twentieth century than today.) Nascher was the first to propose that geriatrics be established as an independent discipline in medical schools. Although his ideas were largely unimplemented and ignored during his lifetime, he is now regarded (even more than Charcot) as the father of geriatrics. He linked his career to it for thirty-five years. His last paper, "The Aging Mind," was published one month before his death at the age of 81.

Eccentric half-geniuses, half-fools also populated the domain of gerontology during the transition period from the Enlightenment to now. In 1889, 72-year-old Edouard Brown-Sequard, who had taught at Harvard and London and finally was occupying one of the most prestigious professorships in France, reported at an executive meeting of the College of France that for three weeks he had been injecting himself with a watery extract of the crushed testicles of dogs, had "regained at least all the strength I possessed a good many years ago," and had even satisfied the amorous inclinations of his new young wife. Within a year thousands of physicians were giving a similar extract to eager old Frenchmen. But alas! It didn't work, and Brown-Sequard promptly fell into disgrace. He had not discovered "the elixir" but only a new way to excite the nervous system. Either he had received surviving sex hormones from the crushed dog testicles or had autosuggested himself into a last-chance erection. His young wife soon left him. While undoubtedly a brilliant physiologist (first to study the effects of cutting the spinal cord), he is only remembered today for his brief performance at the College of France, a prefulfillment of Andy Warhol's proposal, "Everyone can be famous for 15 minutes."

The second genius-fool was Élie Metchnikoff, whose genius aspect had won him a Nobel prize in 1908 for demonstrating that the body defends itself against bacteria by mobilizing an army of cells (the phagocytes) which gobble up the invaders. Later, Metchnikoff hatched the idea that aging may be secondary to poisoning from toxic products liberated by putrefaction in the large bowel. He sought to ameliorate the putrefaction by drinking large amounts of sour milk, believing the lactic acid in the milk would alter the bacterial flora of the gut. Then he recommended sour milk's cousin, yogurt, an important staple in the diet of Bulgarian peasants. Visiting Bulgaria, Metchnikoff had been told that the nation numbered 1,000 centenarians for every million citizens, and that deaths at ages 110, 115, or even 120 were not uncommon. The supposedly long-lived peasants ate a special form of curdled milk called "yogurt," prepared with a living culture of lactic acid forming bacilli. As further support for this colonic theory of aging, it was believed at the time that animals which have no colons, such as parrots, eagles, and tortoises, may be extremely long-lived. So Metchnikoff built his house of intellectual cards, all jokers, beginning with the misinformation about Bulgarian longevity (a typical hyperborean myth). After eighteen years of sour milk and yogurt, Metchnikoff died at the respectable but unremarkable age of 71.

Other famous colonic theorists can also be cited. Jazzman Louis Armstrong swore by strong nightly laxatives, and actress Mae West, who lived to be over 80, attributed her constant good health to daily cleansing enemas. But there is no substantial evidence that intestinal putrefaction has anything to do with aging.

With the notoriety followed by the dramatic failures of expedients like those of Brown-Sequard, Metchnikoff, and later the Russian biologist, Alexander Bogomolet, who injected antibodies against the immune system as a sort of "tonic," plus claims of pseudoscientific fringe promoters such as Niehans and Voronoff (cell therapy, monkey testicle transplants), and the activities of outright charlatans like the American John Brinkley (goat testicle transplants), research on the biology of aging fell into partial disrepute, not only in the public eye but among the scientific community. This occurred despite quite worthy contributions by scientists such as Raymond Pearl (factors which reduce metabolism and/or retard growth may delay senescence); C.S. Minot (senescence may result from cellular maturation, in that the mature, differentiated cells of adult animals become increasingly less capable of growth and self-repair); Sir Peter Medawar (senescence is a by-product of evolution because simple postponement of expression of harmful genes until beyond the reproductive age removes them from the selective counterforce of evolution); and Sir Macfarlane Burnet (senescence is secondary to mutational events, especially among cells of the immune system), to name but a few. The portrait of gerontologists as not-quite-respectable biological visionaries, or frustrated Fausts, persisted until at least the mid 1960s—yet another form of apologism whereby the effort to extend life span is somehow regarded as an inferior, slightly ignoble, or slightly crazy activity compared to the rest of science. However, even while entangled in these psychological impediments, plus the very real slowdown in biological research engendered by World War II, our own modern era in gerontology was being ushered in.

The American Geriatrics Society was founded in 1942 in Atlantic City, shortly thereafter the Gerontological Society of America, and in 1949 the International Society of Gerontology. The first issue of the *Journal of Gerontology* was published in 1946, of *Experimental Gerontology* (child of Alex Comfort) in 1964, and of *Mechanisms of Ageing and Development* (child of Bernard Strehler) in 1972. In 1948 the Federal American Gerontology Center under the leadership of Dr. Nathan Shock became a full branch of the National Heart Institute. In 1958 Shock initiated the famous Baltimore Longitudinal Study on Aging, beginning with 660 persons ages 20 to 96. These volunteers receive a variety of physiologic, psychomotor, and chemical tests every eighteen months, to see what indicators turn out later to have been good health and survival predictors, (so-called "biomarkers" of aging) and to determine by following the same individuals over a long period (until death) how bodily and mental functions change with age.

The research and many of the researchers of our modern period—which I predict will historically be regarded as having extended to about 1990, by which time regimens for maximum life-span extension may well have been tailored into their first successes in humans—are described elsewhere in this book.

Geriatrics and gerontology are now rather suddenly being established as an independent discipline in many medical schools. In 1978 the first privately endowed professorship in geriatrics in the United States was set up, the Irving S. Wright Chair of Geriatric Medicine at Cornell University Medical Center, occupied by the gifted immunologist, Dr. Marc Weksler. But certainly the most promising recent event for gerontology, and perhaps the most historically significant event since the time of the Tao, was the establishment of the National Institute on Aging (the NIA) in 1976, marking a commitment by the government to give research in aging the general visibility and prestige it had not previously enjoyed. Public Law 93–296, dated 31 May 1974, reads in part as follows:

The Congress finds and declares that:
(1) the study of the aging process, the one biological condition common to all, has not received research support commensurate with its effects on the lives of every individual;
(2) in addition to the physical infirmities resulting from advanced age, the economic, social, and psychological factors associated with aging operate to exclude millions of older Americans from the full life and the place in our society to which their years of service and experience entitle them;
(3) recent research efforts point the way toward alleviation of the problems of old age by extending the healthy middle years of life;
(4) there is no American institution that has undertaken comprehensive systematic and intensive studies of the biomedical and behavioral aspects of aging and the related training of necessary personnel;
(5) the establishment of a National Institute on Aging within the National Institutes of Health will meet the need for such an institution.

Getting Public Law 93–296 formulated and passed was not easy, and owes much to the active support of a former track star at Stanford University, Senator Alan Cranston of California, the Democratic Whip of the Senate, who set an age-55 world record of 12.6 seconds in the 100 yard dash, and in 1975, at the age of 60, won the "King of Capitol Hill" bicycle race between members of Congress. The support of the lanky Capitol Hill King was needed because at first the idea of a National Institute on Aging met vigorous opposition from the other National Institutes of Health, the reasons being that it was to be developmentally, and not primarily disease, oriented, and because it would sponsor social and behavioral research—areas the others deemed inappropriate for a collection of Institutes devoted to biology. Nevertheless, the NIA was enacted into being, and, as events proved, chose well its first director, psychiatrist Robert N. Butler, who at the age of 49 on 3 May 1976 began his job as NIA director and on the same day won the Pulitzer Prize for his book, *Why Survive? Being Old in America.*

To the extent that the NIA receives adequate congressional funding, the enormously promising, rapidly developing techniques of modern biology will be brought to bear on the problem of deciphering the riddles of aging and extending maximum life span, with, as we have seen, at least the quasi-cure of cancer, senile dementia, stroke, heart disease, and other maladies of aging by postponing their times of onset, as well as by direct cures for some of them. The cost-effectiveness of research advances in gerontology and geriatrics can hardly be overstated. Nursing home care for senile dementia alone, which is preventable and not a necessary component of aging (see next chapter), stands at 12.5 billion dollars yearly. The figure for such a conceptually simple problem as urinary incontinence is even more, about 21 billion dollars. Moreover, the NIA is responsible for research, not only in the biology and medical aspects of aging, but in the social and behavioral sciences as well. While increasing yearly, its level of funding (currently about 80 million dollars per year) is hardly adequate to such a broad mandate, or such an obvious public health need, and in fact stands at less than one-tenth that of the National Cancer Institute and one-fifth the monies devoted solely to heart and lung research.

Private donations for research on aging, even though we all

47

age, reluctantly or otherwise, are minuscule compared to the amounts given for research in specific diseases. Diseases do not afflict everyone, are not universal, so they can be personalized. They are frequently more attractive to fund raisers because famous people can be identified with each of them, and have even (e.g., Lou Gehrig's disease) given their names to them. The relative paucity of private funding coming in for aging studies is also due to the various forms of apologism about death still very prevalent in our society, and to a curiously persistent fatalism about whether anything can really be done. People forget that of man's three classic dreams, the transmutation of metals, going to the moon or planets, and extending life span, the first two have already been realized (and in our own lifetimes). They have trouble accepting the idea that the postponement of death and the retention of functional vigor into great age may well be realities that many of us will live to experience, and whose arrival we can hasten. We shall see further evidence in coming chapters that the state of the art of gerontology is vigorous and challenging and well beyond its infant stage.

3

The Hieroglyphs
of Aging

M ost people want to live long enough to grow old but at the same time dread old age. Today we are entering an era of progress in the biological sciences as startling as that which occurred in physics earlier in this century when relativity, quantum mechanics, nuclear power, and the computer sciences enlarged the human domain. In this coming era we shall learn at least some of the great secrets of the life process, the nature of evolutionary change and the formation of species, how development proceeds from fertilized egg to complex organism, how we think, what consciousness is, and how we age. True, extensive further research will be required before aging can be wholly stopped or reversed, so that the wrinkled old become young, smooth, and flexible again, repossessing the splendid energy of youth. But at least in animals the relentless advance of aging can already be substantially slowed, and by methods, some of which seem clearly practicable for man. I believe that the retardation of human aging, with extension of maximum life span, is not a distant but a near prospect. Backed by a gathering body of scientific evidence, the various ideas about the fundamental nature of the aging process are beginning to connect, forming a base for the realization of an ageless dream.

Before we plunge into these fascinating ideas about what actually causes aging and how to prevent it or slow its advance, we need to ask what aging really is and what are its features. Some people do seem to age more slowly than others, and parts of a person may age at different rates. Do you have the mind of a 30-year-old in a 60-year-old body, or the reverse? How does the brain, that vital organ whose possible deterioration into senility is one of the medical scare topics of these times, age? Can senility be prevented? To what other diseases does aging make you susceptible? What are the major hallmarks of aging, if any, in organs which may not be overtly diseased: the kidneys, heart, lungs, bones, and the vast meshwork of connective tissue that holds the separate parts of the body together? Do certain diseases cause accelerated aging; if so, what can we learn by studying them? If some treatment becomes available which promises to decrease the rate of aging in humans, how can we ascertain whether it will work? In mice this is easy. A two-to-three year experiment will tell us if the treated mice live longer. A similar experiment in humans would take fifty to one hundred years, far longer than the entire career of an investigator. The only way out of this dilemma is to measure the rate of aging in humans over a short stretch of time, say three to five years, to determine if the treated humans are aging less rapidly. What then are the "biomarkers" of aging which might allow us to make this estimation of "functional" age? These are some of the questions we need to ask to bring the phenomena of aging into focus, and to begin a wide-ranging discussion of the kinds of relevant research being done in the various branches of gerontology.

Five approaches, which can best be framed as questions, lead to the scientific study of biologic aging:

(1) What hidden processes determine the marked differences in life span between species?

(2) What regulates the differences in life span between strains or races of animals of the same species, or between identical and nonidentical twins?

(3) What are the time-induced structural and functional changes in the vital organs and individual cells and parts of cells? Do tissues age independently or as a result of a central

controlling process, e.g., a hormone, or a "clock" somewhere in each cell or centrally in the brain?

(4) How or why do certain diseases lead to accelerated aging, and what experimental conditions lead to accelerated aging in animals?

(5) By what mechanisms do several procedures in animals lead to a *de*celeration of the aging process, to an actual and impressive extension of maximum life span?

Although subject to environment, life span is determined ultimately by heredity, with a large variance existing among species. A mouse lives three years, a chimpanzee forty-five, and man one hundred. The reasons for the differences, which must involve the evolutionary origin of aging and longevity, are still unclear. One clue is that the ability of different species to repair their own heredity material, their DNA, after some types of injury correlates with their maximum life spans: the higher the repair rate, the longer the life span. Of course, correlation is not necessarily causation (one might falsely conclude that fire engines cause fires because they are often seen together). Other matters that seem related to life-span differences between species include a few of the many known metabolic processes, like the ability of the bodily machinery to transform a pre-cancerous agent into a cancerous one (here the correlation is inverse: the greater the ability, the less the life span) and the amounts in the cells of some natural chemicals (SOD to name one) which serve to neutralize the damaging by-products of oxygen metabolism. These by-products are called free radicals. While oxygen is necessary for most life forms, it has undesirable side effects which damage the tissues. These correlations underlie several theories of aging which propose that different sets of genes (the basic units of heredity) insure a certain level of accuracy in cell division and metabolism, and that this level varies with each species and determines the life span characteristic of the species.

We've seen evidence from Chapter 1 that only a limited number of genes govern the rate of aging and also that man and chimpanzee are merely 1 percent different in protein structure. In aging and speciation, therefore, we must be dealing with a limited gene repertoire in which each gene has multiple influences—in short with so-called "regulatory" genes, those which do not themselves determine structure but simply orchestrate the actions of other genes. A wholly fresh and exciting biology of genetics is unfolding. A new type of genetic unit, for example, called the "transposon" has been discovered. It's a set of "jumping genes," which can skip from one part of the DNA molecule to particular locations elsewhere, and then jump back.

Some of the secrets about gene structure, cancer, speciation, and, therefore, aging will also come from the new "hybridoma" technology, whose potential as a key biologic tool is regarded by Nobelist Renato Dulbecco as "greater than anything we have ever had." When an animal is injected with a substance such as a protein, ragweed pollen, or the cells of another individual or species, his immune system manufactures antibodies which combine with various parts of the foreign material and eliminate it or neutralize it. These antibodies, which are tiny protein substances made by the white blood cells, attach themselves to only one type of the thousands of markers covering the cells of the injected material. A solution of antibodies all reactive with the *same* marker would provide a powerful probe for determining the ultrafine points of structure and function. However, an injected animal does not make merely one type of antibody. To afford optimum protection, his different white blood cells churn out a sort of shotgun blast spectrum against the many different portions or markers of the injected substance. Drs. Georges Kohler and Cesar Milstein discovered in 1975 that if you fuse a kind of tumor cell (a myeloma cell) with an antibody-producing white blood cell, you can produce a hybrid cell known as a "hybridoma," one that will grow freely in tissue culture like the tumor cell but produce the single type of antibody (called a monoclonal antibody) of the fused individual white blood cell. Monoclonal antibodies are already allowing new adventures into the dissection of similar but nonidentical molecules, and will help us quantify and typify the accumulation of damage in DNA as a function of age.

Rapid developments in genetic engineering have been made possible by gene cloning and the now famous recombinant DNA technology, whereby small parts of the genetic material of one species can be inserted into the developing cells of another. The white-footed deer mouse and the ordinary house mouse are related cousins, yet the deer mouse's maximum life span is seven years, compared to three years for the house mouse. Inserting selected genes from the deer mouse into developing embryos of the house mouse, and finding whether they increase life span in the latter, will allow us to identify those genes to which we gerontologists ought to be paying closest attention.

Besides their utility for ferreting out the reasons for life-span differences, various species of animals are worth studying gerontologically because they offer experimental advantages peculiar to the species. With the lowly bread-mold fungus Dr. Kenneth Munkres of the University of Wisconsin performed a brilliant analysis of genes relevant to one of the major theories of aging.[1] He found that the same gene family which regulates life span also regulates the level of the body's intrinsic chemicals for neutralizing the damaging by-products of oxygen metabolism, the free radicals. My colleagues and I have suggested that the early protective anti-free radical system may have given rise during the long course of evolution to the genes that regulate the immune system, which we know is at the very least a "pacemaker" for aging.[2]

Investigators have used the small roundworm, *C. elegans,* to show that certain enzymes, those necessary catalysts which drive biological processes forward, may be normal in amount but structurally abnormal with age: present but not entirely accounted for. Deactivated enzyme molecules accumulate because the machinery for degrading and eliminating altered proteins (all enzymes are proteins) becomes less effective with age.

The fruit fly, the one-celled microorganism called *Paramecium,* the annual fish, the sturgeon, octopus, guinea pig, pigeon, mouse, rat, and monkey all have peculiarities which make them suitable in particular ways for doing studies which bear upon specific aspects of aging. The short-lived annual fish teaches us that internal, core body temperature greatly affects the rate of aging in higher vertebrates. The guinea pig is the only known mammal besides man and other primates that does not manufacture its own vitamin C in its own body, so it can be used to analyze whether large doses of vitamin C might influence aging.

Mice are superbly suited for studying differences in aging rates between individuals of the same species. Because of their genetic uniformity, the most useful mouse colonies are the so-called "inbred strains." Brothers are mated to sisters down through the generations until finally all the mice of any one strain are exactly identical. However, each strain is different from the others, hence the individuals of different strains are as different as you please to breed them. We can, therefore, on an enormous scale and on a far more controllable subject, repeat Professor Kallmann's famous human twin study. In the 1940s he began comparing intellectual patterns with aging in 134 pairs of identical and nonidentical twins born prior to 1889. Repeated testing over the next ten-to-twenty years showed that heredity influences individual differences in mental abilities late in life. But even this extensive twin study was numerically too small to be conclusive. Inbred mouse strains, on the other hand, are like hundreds of sets of identical twins. It is even possible to breed strains which differ from one another at only one gene region among the several hundred thousand genes in the cell nucleus. Using such strains, Dr. George Smith and I at UCLA were able to pinpoint one of the gene regions which regulate maximum life span. It is called the major histocompatibility complex, or MHC. There are probably another eight or ten (maybe as many as seventy) genes or collections of genes involved in aging. A mouse strain described by Drs. Elizabeth Russell and R.L. Sprott of Jackson Memorial Laboratories is characterized by the deposition in the cells of the brain, heart, and elsewhere of yellow-brown granules of pigment called lipofuscin, which also accumulates in similar cells in human aging. The insoluble aging pigment may grow to occupy substantial space within the old cells. What it is and how it accumulates can best be studied in these genetically predisposed mice, which also show premature death. Another valuable mouse strain, whose designation, NZB/W, sounds like a radio station, displays a high incidence of autoimmunity, wherein the immune system turns destructively against the body itself. Auto-antibodies against the DNA genetic material do much of the anti-self damage. NZB/W mice age rapidly, indicating that autoimmunity may be a cause of aging. Interestingly enough, at least one of the three gene systems responsible for NZB/W disease resides within the major histocompatibility complex.

The vast majority of gerontologic investigations center on comparing old with young animals. These studies can be either what is termed cross-sectional or longitudinal. A typical cross-sectional study would be to compare several dozen persons born in 1900 with an equal number born in 1960. Such an analysis can be misleading in so far as intrinsic age changes are concerned, and particularly in relation to brain function. Environment certainly influences funtion too, and those persons born in 1900 experienced a very different environment, life-style, education, and social organization during their first twenty years compared to those born in 1960.

In a longitudinal study, on the other hand, the same group of animals or persons are followed over a long period. The two most extensive longitudinal investigations in humans are the Baltimore Longitudinal Study of Aging, outlined in the last chapter, and the Framingham Study in Massachusetts. In 1949, 6,000 Framingham residents aged 30 to 59 underwent various laboratory tests and were examined by a physician. Persons free of vascular disease were reexamined every two years to detect any evidence of newly developed heart disease, and all deaths and their causes were recorded. From statistical analysis Dr. William Kannel, director of the study, determined that an individual's chance of dying from any cause, as well as the chance of developing heart or vascular disease, was strongly influenced by nine risk factors besides just age: sex, blood pressure, serum cholesterol, cigarette smoking, weight in relation to ideal weight, pulse rate, lung capacity, history of diabetes, and abnormal electrocardiogram. How two of these factors predict the risk of cardiovascular disease and death (from any cause) for a 45-year-old man over the next ten years is shown in Figure 3.1. More recent studies have proved that determination not only of cholesterol but also triglycerides (a kind of fat) and high-density-lipoproteins (HDL = Fat-carrying proteins) provide more reliable risk measurements for arteriosclerosis and heart disease. The range of values in a normal population for different ages is given in Table 3.1.

Risk of arteriosclerosis is much less if one is on the low side for cholesterol and triglycerides, and high for the HDL. Any ratio of cholesterol to HDL greater than four is serious enough that an attempt should be made to lower it with diet, exercise, or other means. While the average HDL is around forty-five, for those who jog more than fifteen miles per week it's about sixty-five. HDL impede cholesterol accumulation by cells, and

If you are 45—
and male...

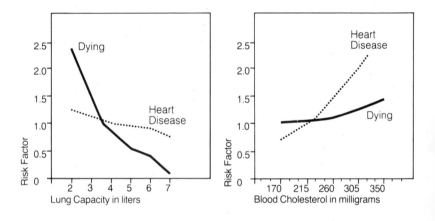

this is the relationship of two different risk factors to the chance of dying (——) or developing heart disease (·····) within ten years as calculated in the Framingham Study. (A lung capacity of only 2 liters means the chance of death is 2.4 times normal; a cholesterol of 305 milligrams means the chance of heart disease is 2 times normal.)

Figure 3.1

Table 3.1

Age-Range	Cholesterol	Triglycerides	HDL
20–29	120–240	10–140	35–70
30–39	140–270	10–150	35–80
40–49	150–310	10–160	40–95
50–57	160–330	10–190	35–85

may pick up or remove already-absorbed cholesterol from cells, possibly leading to reversal of arteriosclerosis.

With arteriosclerosis, the main age-related disease in humans, raised fibrous fat-containing plaques form on the insides of arteries, smooth muscle cells proliferate in the arterial walls, and elastic fibers split and fray. The plaques are like toxic waste heaps, created by diet. Beginning about age 30, by age 70 they typically cover 25 percent of the inner surfaces of arteries. Nevertheless, one may attain great age and possess coronary arteries scarcely affected by arteriosclerosis. An autopsy study of thirty persons more than 69 years of age revealed eight persons over age 80 who had only minimal arteriosclerosis.[3] Except for whales and pigeons, the disease does not occur in other animals under natural conditions. When fed a diet high in cholesterol and saturated fats, monkeys and pigs will develop arteriosclerosis, but it is rapidly reversed when they are returned to a diet of vegetables, fruits, and cereals. Conditions or disease which are largely confined to man and for which few or no animal models exist are not features of intrinsic aging, and therefore ought to be avoidable.

Probably the most feared ravage of age, but again not an inevitable consequence, is senility or dementia, i.e., being constantly short-circuited and out of contact with reality like the old man in the following brief simulation of early senility by writer Wells Teague, entitled "Senile."[4]

I remember my parents. Dad had sugar diabetes, and they didn't have any help for it in the twenties. We had to let them take his leg off, and he gave up after that. After he died, Mama went to stay with my brother Hath. She lived with him nineteen years. That like to have driven him crazy. He shot himself, finally, but that was long after she died. What I'm afraid of is that the crazy is inherited and that she will have it too. It didn't show up until she was seventy, and I had that spell several years back, though I'm all right now. There is some around here that seems to have caught it. Some of them I won't have on the place. There is an old man lives beside the water tower who comes by here. Said he just wanted to see if there was anything I needed, that he knew I was by myself. He wanted to know if I wanted to go into town. You know what he wanted? He wanted to get me out of the house so his gang of thieves could do their dirty work. You read the papers, you know it's happening all around. McBride is his name, or what he calls himself. He has put wires in my attic to listen to what I'm saying. He has radios set up so that he can contact any of this gang that is close by and someone will be here the minute I leave to steal everything I own. I haven't left the house in over six months.

Forgetfulness, disorientation, severe loss of memory, intellectual confusion, emotional disturbances, senility of one type or another afflicts about 1,500,000 Americans. Some of mankind's greatest intellects have lapsed into senility with age: the foremost German philosopher Immanuel Kant, Jonathan Swift who wrote *Gulliver's Travels* (and who alas, became a Struldbrug himself when he grew old), Winston Churchill, and Ralph Waldo Emerson.

Is senility of one form or another to be everyone's lot if we live a very long time? The answer is clearly "no." It's true that at peak age of onset (80 to 81 years), between one birthday and the next, one of every twenty persons will develop senility, but not everyone does and only one-third of all persons who die over the age of 80 display any of the telltale signs. About 20 percent of senile dementias are caused by multiple small hemorrhages or blood clots in the brain due to arteriosclerosis or hypertension—both preventable and to some extent even curable diseases.

But the cause of 50–60 percent of senile dementias is an

entity called Alzheimer's disease, named after the physician who first described it. People with Alzheimer's disease slide rapidly into mental oblivion and mercifully more than 95 percent die within five years. On microscopic examination the brain displays tangles of threadlike nerve filaments in the outer layers, and many small plaques of a protein precipitate called amyloid. The cause is unknown but might be infectious (viral), degenerative, or autoimmune. A person's brain functions both electrically and chemically. The electrical impulse travels along the wire-like projections of the nerve cell, but for the message to jump to the next cell in the circuit a chemical, called a neurotransmitter, must flow across the short gap between the sender filament of one cell and the receiver of the next. When the neurotransmitters are deficient, the brain malfunctions. The brain in Alzheimer's disease suffers a great decrease in an enzyme needed for manufacture of the neurotransmitter substance, acetylcholine. Not all humans are afflicted with any degree of senility, even at ages 90 to 100. And what is perhaps equally important in convincing us that senile dementia is not a necessary part of advanced age is that there is no animal model for it.

More negative myths endure about the aging brain than all other organs combined. The Baltimore Longitudinal Study indicated that while the mental processes involved in logical reasoning generally decrease after age 70, not everyone shows the decrement. In research at the National Institute of Mental Health, persons 60–92-years-old were divided into two groups. Both groups had been selected as free of disease, but one was classified as extremely healthy, and the other as having only minimal vascular disease, i.e., to be still much better than average for their age. The extremely healthy oldsters displayed a cerebral blood flow and brain oxygen consumption equivalent to normal persons fifty years younger, whereas the merely healthy group tested significantly lower. Also, the healthier oldsters showed only minimal decline in mental abilities and perceptual functions compared to the younger controls.

Much built-in bias beclouds the issue of mental testing. Most such studies are cross-sectional and fail to reconcile the different backgrounds of old and young test subjects. Whereas cross-sectional studies have shown I.Q. declines, longitudinal tests have generally reported I.Q. maintenance and in some cases I.Q. gains throughout the life cycle. Bias may also be introduced because young people are accustomed to being tested. Since their future depends on doing well, they are competitive by habit. Old persons tend to be less motivated in taking a test, so may do less well, but not because they are less intelligent. The older person may also not see or hear quite as well as a young competitor, and so do less well even though these sensory impairments are not major health problems. Environmental effects may also be considerable. Socially disadvantaged children tend to do poorly on intelligence tests, but are not basically less intellectually endowed. By the same token, a 70-year-old man retired for five years and put on the shelf by a neglectful society is apt to test below his true potential. It's a lot like the nursery rhyme,

> And nothing he had
> And so the old man
> Was said to be mad.

Finally, a rapid decline in intelligence scores does occur in persons nearing death or within four-to-five years of dying. Unknowingly including these in the test scores makes it appear that all older people in general decline in intelligence.

Different kinds of intelligence can be measured in relation to age: fluid intelligence, crystallized intelligence, and memory. Fluid intelligence means tests of reasoning. A simple test would be:

> Some peaches are spoons,
> All spoons play baseball,
> Therefore, some peaches play baseball.
> True or false? The answer is, True.

Crystallized intelligence refers to the use of judgment based on experience. A simple test would be:

The Hieroglyphs of Aging

Change the order if necessary:
(a) clay brick wall house
(b) sheep yarn wool sweater
Answer: Yarn should follow wool in (b)

Figure 3.2 shows how several tests of intellectual function vary with age up to 59 years in a highly educated population (Parisian schoolteachers) and in a less educated population (random French). The decline is minimal among those whose work is largely cerebral.

Neurologists have recently recognized the existence of what they term "plasticity" of the brain. The impression that the adult brain is like a finished complex machine which can run nowhere but slowly downhill is no longer tenable. "Plasticity" can go in either direction, better as well as worse, and the potential of the aging brain under optimal conditions is better than most people suppose. In an enriched, stimulating environment the thickness of the cerebral cortex (the outer layer of the brain) will increase at *any* age. Rats at ages equivalent to about eighty human years exhibit some ability to grow fresh nerve circuits within their brains, albeit less so than young rats. In the January 1982 issue of *Science,* Drs. G. Jonsson and H. Hallman of Stockholm describe a protein substance which serves in part as a chemical messenger between nerve cells, i.e., as a neurotransmitter, but also looks promising as a treatment for cell degeneration in the brain. The chemicals hydergine, piracetam, and derivatives of choline may all lead to some recovery of deteriorated brain function. Both our knowledge of preventive health measures and the bright outlook of the developing neurosciences signify that the fear that superlong life might be compromised by significantly deteriorated mental function is unnecessarily pessimistic. And in any case, if we prolong maximum life span and at the same time square the new survival curve (by curing disease), then the 150-year-old person will merely suffer the same mental decrements from his one-hundred-and-fortieth year that the present 90-year-old suffers from his eightieth year. Most chronic diseases responsible for secondary aging are largely

Use it or......

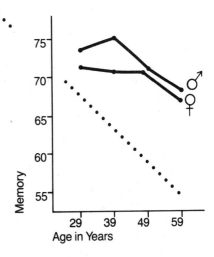

Intellectual performances
in relation to age of a group
of Parisian schoolteachers
(——) compared to an
average French population
(····).

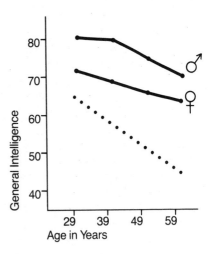

Figure 3.2

due to modifiable factors such as diet, life-style, self-destructive habits, addictions, and exposure to harmful environmental agents.

As anti-aging therapies prove effective in animals, it becomes important to test whether they will also be effective in humans. We need tests of "functional" or physiologic age in humans, to determine whether, over the span of a few years, a certain treatment has slowed the aging rate.[5] These tests are referred to as "biomarkers" of aging. A representative battery is that of Dr. Richard Hochschild of San Diego, who devised a thirty-minute computerized examination to estimate "functional" age. His H-SCAN involves spending thirty minutes with an ingeniously programmed table-model computer which measures twelve physical and mental functions. These include two mental functions:

(1) Picture recognition as a kind of fluid intelligence test: twenty-one incomplete pictures of common objects appear at eight-second intervals on the computer screen and the subject indicates proper or improper recognition by pressing one of six buttons. Thirty to 40-year-old persons average sixteen correct recognitions, 70-year-old people about ten.

(2) Memory: A symbol moves on the computer screen above the buttons in an unpredictable manner. The subject tries to repeat the sequence by pressing the corresponding buttons in correct order.

The physical tests in H-SCAN include the followoing:

(1) Hearing: Measured as auditory pitch ceiling. How high a tone (pitch, not loudness) can you hear? A 30-year-old person can hear up to about sixteen kilohertz, a 70-year-old person only up to ten. The decline impairs the perception of speech by older persons. They may hear the overall loudness but not the higher tones of spoken words.

(2) Reaction times: Both auditory and visual. You push a button as quickly as possible after you hear a sound through earphones. The test estimates slowing of transmission across the nerve junctions, and possibly a loss of nerve cells with age. In the visual test, an image on the computer screen jumps at unpredictable intervals from a start button to a goal button,

and you try following it with your finger at maximum speed. A 30-year-old person requires about 0.25 seconds to react, a 70-year-old person 0.34 seconds.

(3) Lung function: One of the best biomarkers of age.[6] With an instrument called a spirometer, you can measure vital capacity, which is the maximum volume of air you can blow out after a deep breath. A five foot seven inch woman, 30 years of age, can normally exhale a total of about 3.8 liters of air; at age 70, 3.2 liters. The forced expiratory volume is an even better biomarker. It's not the total volume that is tallied, but the rate at which air is blown out during the first second of a maximum expiratory effort. The 30-year-old woman could exhale at the rate of seventy-three liters per second, but only fifty-three liters at age 70. These declines in lung function are caused by changes in the rib cage, chest musculature, and in the lung structure itself.

(4) Visual accommodation: The distance over which your eye can focus falls from about eight dioptres at age 30, to six dioptres at age 40, then sharply to two dioptres at age 50 with a much slower falloff thereafter. One of the first age changes that people notice in themselves is their need for bifocals. This is caused by alterations in the lens protein of the eye.

A simple test for functional age you can do on yourself concerns skin elasticity. Pinch the back of your hand and measure in seconds how long before it's smooth again. From youth to age 45 about two seconds are required, then the time increases rapidly, to twenty seconds by age 65, and fifty seconds by age 75. The time will vary somewhat depending on past exposure of the skin of your hand to sunlight, which ages the skin severely. The wrinkles, dryness, and other changes in the skin whose prevention or disguise occupy so many pages of *Vogue* and *Glamour* are due to thinning of the superficial epidermis, deterioration of the tiny skin glands, and damage to the connective tissue (collagen and elastic) fibers deeper down. Collagen and elastin are inert, elongated proteins which undergo relatively little turnover with time. Once fully formed, they stay with you the rest of your life. You don't lay down more, absorb them, and lay down a fresh supply—the one exception being the uterus, which forms new connective tissue during pregnancy, then resorbs it after birth to shrink back to nearly its original size. If we knew how the uterus performs this feat, we might be able to do more about the wrinkled skin, osteoporosis, reduced strength of tendons, stiffening and loss of elasticity with age, susceptibility to bruising, and blood vessel fragility that afflict old people. The connective tissues all over the body become stiffer and chemically immobilized with age, due to the formation between parallel collagen fibers (you see these fibers most purely in tendons) of so-called crosslinks, wherein a by-product of metabolism containing two highly active chemical groups combines one of its groups with one collagen fiber and another group with another, so the two fibers can no longer slip past one another or stretch. The contractility of old collagen when a small weight is hung from it decreases with age, and its solubility in weak acid also decreases. These simple tests are among the best biomarkers of aging available for studies on live rodents because one can readily obtain a single collagen fiber from the many in the rodent's tail, and without much injury to the tail.[7]

Other organ systems also show decrements with age, and a synopsis is given in Figure 3.3 from the Baltimore Longitudinal Study. Complex functions (such as breathing capacity) tend to vary more with age than simple functions (such as the amount of a particular substance in the blood). Complex functions summate all the smaller changes. However, the biologist must dissect the smaller changes to understand and control the complex ones. The decrements illustrated in Figure 3.3 are average values, not immutable accompaniments of age. Indeed, healthy men in their fifties who exercise vigorously show a maximum exercise and oxygen uptake capacity 20–30 percent *higher* than those of young sedentary men, and maximum oxygen uptake capacity is an excellent indicator of overall cardiovascular function.

Complicated interacting upswings and downswings in many hormone levels occur with age, a notable example being the decrease in estrogens in women at time of menopause, leading by a circuitous biochemical route to the thinning of

Loss of function with age.

Loss of function with age does not occur
at the same rate in all organ systems.

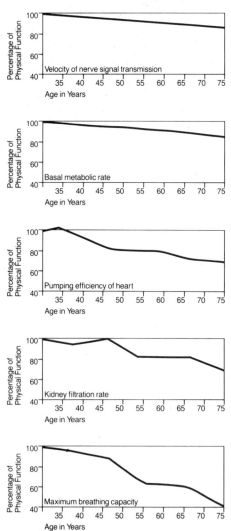

Figure 3.3

the bones known as osteoporosis. This skeletal disorder is the main cause of hip fracture in the elderly, which will strike 25 percent of women and 15 percent of men by age 80, and leads to 50,000 deaths each year in the United States alone.

One large class of hormones transmits its message to the cells of the target organs by striking "receptors" on the cells' outer membranes. Monoclonal antibodies prepared by the new hybridoma techniques have fostered the discovery that the number of membrane receptors for many hormones declines with age. An intricate hormonal and receptor problem causes old people either to contract overt diabetes or at least to reveal abnormal glucose tolerance curves, suggesting that even "normal" aging is slightly diabetic. After a standard amount of glucose (sugar) is taken on an empty stomach, its level in the blood rises, whereupon the pancreas releases enough insulin to stimulate uptake and use of the sugar for energy production by the various organs, or storage in the liver until needed. The height reached by the blood sugar and the length of time it stays elevated comprise the glucose tolerance curve. In a normal young person the sugar level returns to its original value within two hours, in an old person four to six hours. The elevated blood sugar leaks through the kidneys into the urine, making it slightly sweet. In the Middle Ages a class of practitioners concentrated their diagnostics on examining the urine. Popularly called "piss prophets," they knew that sweet urine, to which ants would be attracted, spelled diabetes.

The form of diabetes that requires insulin injections displays important features of accelerated aging. Immune biomarkers indicate that such diabetics are functionally 15–20 years older than their given age. As a group they suffer from an increased amount of autoimmunity. And if their cells are allowed to divide and grow and divide and keep dividing in tissue culture in test tubes, they undergo fewer divisions than cells from normal persons of the same age. Interestingly enough, the risk of developing insulin-dependent diabetes is greatly influenced by the major histocompatibility complex or

MHC. People with certain MHC profiles are thirty times more susceptible than other individuals.

Most diseases showing accelerated aging in humans, like the dramatic, somewhat misnamed malady *progeria*, are quite rare. Only eight to ten cases of progeria now exist in the United States. While progeria sufferers, whose wizened white-haired birdlike appearance makes them look like strange little old professors, almost invariably die from advanced arteriosclerosis before age 20, the malady falls short of being a full copy of accelerated aging—no mental deficiency, no cataracts, and a normal glucose tolerance curve. No single disease shows *all* the features of premature aging. But perhaps this is fortunate because the genetic influences operating to produce different restricted parts of the picture of aging are automatically isolated and brought into focus by these diseases.

Two additional common diseases showing parts of accelerated aging are systemic lupus erythematosus (SLE), an autoimmune disease afflicting about 300,000 persons in the United States, and Down's syndrome (mongolism) which occurs once in every 1,000 births even though the abnormality can be detected early in pregnancy by a special test. Characterized by anti-DNA antibodies, SLE is the human counterpart of the autoimmune disease of NZB/W mice, and susceptibility is once again under the sway of the MHC.

Down's patients rarely live beyond 50 years of age and show early senile dementia of the Alzheimer's type added to their original Down's dementia. Down's syndrome originates from accidental partial duplication of part of the embryo's twenty-first chromosome (the twenty-three pairs of chromosomes in the nuclei of human cells carry the DNA embedded in a protein covering). Other diseases with specific chromosomal abnormalities are far rarer than Down's syndrome but usually also lead to accelerated aging.

To the gerontologist these maladies represent "experiments of nature." A sizable share of modern medical discoveries have arisen from painstaking investigation of such "experiments of nature" in which the genetically based lack of, say, a particular enzyme has caused a particular disease state. By studying that disease we can figure out the function of the enzyme in normal persons. Similarly, diseases of accelerated aging are teaching us about normal aging.

Two experimental procedures are known which definitely slow or "decelerate" the rate of aging: caloric undernutrition, and lowering internal body temperature. If rats from time of weaning are fed a diet relatively low in caloric content, but supplemented with vitamins and minerals so they are not actually *mal*nourished (only *under*nourished), then maximum life span stretches 25 to nearly 100 percent longer, and they stay functionally young. A similar or even greater extension can be obtained in cold-blooded animals by keeping them in a slightly colder environment. I've devoted two later chapters to these important age-decelerating procedures, both of which, but definitely the first, may be applicable to human use.

What else can we do to promote our surviving into that not so far-off period when the span of life will be two or three times what it is today? Before entering that practical realm, and now that we have briefly surveyed a selection of the major phenomena of aging—what I call the hieroglyphs of aging— we ought to inquire into the principal biological theories about what causes aging, and what these theories portend for the future of life-span extension? How soon will it begin to happen?

4

Theories of Aging
I Love Best

G erontology, the science of aging, is alive with prerevolutionary fervor as we plunge into the 1980s. Many signs
of a major breakthrough are evident. As pointed out by
Thomas Kuhn in *The Structure of Scientific Revolutions*, prerevolutionary periods are characterized by a proliferation of sound
but competing ideas about a series of phenomena—in this
instance, the observed and experimental facts about aging.
Although different from one another, most of the hypotheses
explain the facts pretty well. I can explain most things about
aging from the many observations that with age the immune
system goes haywire.[1] It not only fails to protect the body, it
destroys the body. Another theory builder might equally well
explain aging as being due to imperfect DNA repair mechanisms, which can't quite repair the genetic machinery (the
DNA) in the cells as fast as it slowly breaks, frazzles, and sticks
with metabolic time. If repair were absolutely perfect, there
would be no mutations, no natural selection, no evolution.
Nature's plan for evolution includes death for dessert, or as T.
S. Eliot put it, "Birth and copulation and death. These are the
facts when you get to brass tacks."

Each idea or hypothesis—and we shall learn of other good
ones besides the above—can be shown more or less to satisfy

those criteria which it both dictates for itself and uses to sit in judgment on the common facts. The advocates of the different hypotheses tend to talk past or through one another, in part because the languages of the various sciences are different. The biochemist and the immunologist may not quite understand one another. In the prerevolutionary period a number of investigators or schools of investigators compete for domination of the field. Nobody is decisively winning at this stage, but the existence of the competing hypotheses, all rather well developed, self-contained, and seeming to explain the same body of facts, imposes a substantial strain upon the scientific community within the particular discipline. So many paths, and all of them so inviting! Does the elusive answer lie down this one or that? Everybody is exhilarated by the tension of choice. Finally some special achievement illuminates one area, or more likely a synthesis suddenly joins what had looked like separate avenues. Then the revolution is over, the way temporarily shines clear, and we are back to one of the longer periods of so-called "normal" science, in which puzzles are solved according to the newly arrived-at orientation, the new "paradigm."

A paradigm is a kind of model or example, a way of looking at things, an agreed-upon set of values. Man's most treasured paradigm is that the world is real. The great paradigm of science is that the world can be explained in terms of chemistry and physics. Another big one is that what is not repeatable does not exist. Most top scientists today don't quite believe these last two any longer, but insofar as they act within the disciplines of science they must assume the paradigms or they won't progress at all; they'll be bogged down in intangibles. In science there are no final causes, no ultimate solutions. It's a game you can only play as long as you never try to reach for the end.

One famous illustrative paradigm derives from the theory of evolution, which replaced the earlier one of the creation. I say "derives from" because a paradigm is more than a theory, it's an orientation toward a subject matter and can be binding as well as liberating. The "creationist" faction of the Moral

Majority are still caught in the cage of an old pre-evolutionary paradigm, like the monkeys they are. Progress within a paradigm, like slowly finding all the links in the ascent of man from the other apes, is normal science: hard work, nobody too up tight, and reputations once made are secure.

> While paradigms are "young," they are exciting fields of discovery; but as they grow "older," they tend to discourage new ways of seeing things, new approaches to defining and solving problems, new understandings and meanings. They ultimately end up as the enemy of their own purpose —the attempt to better understand the world.[2]

Change of paradigm in science constitutes scientific revolution. The work is sometimes less difficult technically than in normal science but it always requires more imagination, faith, and risk; fine reputations are apt to be ruined, their owners quickly demoted from noble chapter headings to embarrassed footnotes. George Stahl was one of the great chemists of history and father of the long-respected phlogiston theory of combustion, but Lavoisier overthrew his paradigm. Few people today have even heard of George Stahl.

Paradigm changes occur at various levels in science. The change does not have to be on quite such a combustible plane as those dominated by Lavoisier or Darwin. I am thinking of Pasteur's idea that microbes cause infectious disease, Paul Erlich's proposition of "horror autotoxicus" whereby the immune system of the body is not supposed to be able to react against itself, and, to take an example close to the gerontology we shall presently be discussing, the metaphorical paradigm of "program," i.e., that the body is organized like a computer and growth, development, and aging just run clickety-clack off the genetic code in the DNA tape. In planning experiments we tend to be conceptually limited by the confines of the paradigms of our times.

Change of paradigm signifies a new view of reality. It can be major or minor. The prerevolutionary stage of the change is often characterized by warring theories, all well documented and all reasonably likely. Synthesis of these may consummate the revolution, or a sudden, successful working out of one of them may establish that it is correct, and the others are dropped. Ostwald T. Avery's careful series of experiments with bacteria showed that the hereditary material was not protein, as had been thought, but DNA. The deciphering of the double helical structure of DNA by Watson and Crick completed the paradigm and gave us the major orientation of present-day biology.

In this chapter we shall focus upon six equally challenging theories of aging. Each can explain most of the facts of aging. We don't know which, if any, is primary, or quite how they fit together. Herodotus, the first great historian, wrote, "Of the cities which were great, many are fallen, and of those which were small, many are risen. I shall therefore discourse equally of both, convinced that human happiness never continues long in the same place." I shall deal with these six theories of aging in the same way.

Dr. Alexis Carrel and his famous fibroblasts are a good example of how reputations fade when paradigms change. Fibroblasts are the connective tissue cells which form the bundles of fibers made of collagen, enfolding and supporting the cells in most organs. One of the foremost biologists of his time, Carrel commenced growing the fibroblasts of chickens' hearts in flasks in his laboratory at the Rockefeller Institute in 1912. Fed with a special medium containing extract of chicken embryo, they grew well in his flasks. They kept dividing and forming additional cells. The excess cells had to be periodically discarded or they would have performed one of those 2^n multiplication feats and covered the earth. The cells, in what we now refer to as a "tissue culture" system, kept dividing for thirty-four years. By the time his co-workers discarded the culture two years after Carrel's death, the performance of the cells had prompted the formulation of one of the first paradigms of modern gerontology: cells are inherently immortal if given an ideal environment, and the aging of organisms we see in the laboratory and in the mirror must be due to interactions between cells, or to some central mechanism, hormonal perhaps, whose influence reaches everywhere.

In the early 1960s, however, Dr. Leonard Hayflick observed that human fibroblasts in tissue culture wouldn't divide more than about fifty times.[3] He exposed bits of embryonic lung tissue to digestive enzymes to dissociate the tissue into individual cells. The cells were washed free of the enzymes, put into bottles containing a nutrient solution, and kept at body temperature. They proceeded to divide regularly. When there were too many cells for the bottle, half were discarded and the remainder allowed to keep dividing, the same as Carrel had done. Each refill of the bottle by the growing cells was called a "doubling." As the fiftieth doubling approached, the cells divided more slowly. Microscopically visible senescent changes developed within the nuclei and fluid space (cytoplasm) of the cells. Finally, they wouldn't divide at all. Fibroblasts from young people underwent more doublings than those from old persons before dying out. The results were clear. It became equally clear that Alexis Carrel had been wrong. He had probably committed the unpardonable sin of being derelict in his laboratory technique. Embryos too have fibroblasts. Carrel had allowed a few of these to escape crunching when he periodically made up his nutrient embryo extract, and so inadvertently added fresh cells to his precious cultures. Fresh young cells! For thirty-four years! Nevertheless, because Carrel had won the Nobel prize for earlier, unrelated work (how to sew blood vessels together end to end), and was colorful and enthusiastic and an accomplished if narrow-minded writer, his well-publicized study of supposedly immortal fibroblasts gave an early, strong impetus to gerontology. And much of it, unlike Carrel's own work, was very sound gerontology. The publicity surrounding the Rumanian doctor, Ana Aslan, and her Gerovital gave a similar impetus to gerontology a few years later.

In due time Leonard Hayflick's observations overthrew the Carrel paradigm. The Hayflick paradigm is that aging is fundamentally an intrinsic cellular process. Look within the cell for the riddle of aging, at the nucleus which guards the genetic secrets, the tiny folded tubular factories (called mitochondria) within the cytoplasm which provide the energy, or the membrane-enclosed bags (lysosomes) which house the dangerous digestive enzymes and sometimes the unexpurgated refuse of the cell. A genetic clock ticking away within each cell determines when old age sets in. It keeps physiologic rather than Greenwich time.

Hayflick found that if he froze his cell cultures after, say, twenty doublings, they would "remember" that they had thirty doublings left to go when they were thawed and refed. Fifty doublings is called "the Hayflick limit." Fibroblasts begin looking old as they approach the limit. They become larger and accumulate an increased amount of the yellowish age-pigment (lipofucsin) seen, for example, in splotches on the skin of old people, and in old hearts and brains if you look at ultra-thin slices of these tissues under the microscope.

The Hayflick reorientation has led to much useful work. Some cellular enzymes increase, some decrease, and some remain the same as the fibroblasts undergo what Hayflick calls "aging under glass." The clock keeping time for the aging changes probably resides in the cell's nucleus. When a cultured cell is treated with a certain drug (cytochalasin B), it extrudes its nucleus, leaving the rest of the cell (the cytoplast) behind. By taking advantage of this sundering of the cell's two main parts, it's possible to reinsert an old nucleus into a young cytoplast, and a young nucleus into an old cytoplast. Experiments with these reconstructed cells have indicated that the physiologic age of the cell, the number of doublings it has left, is determined by the nucleus. A programmed synthesis of a "senescence factor" occurs in old cells; the factor inhibits DNA formation.[4]

It's not a cause for alarm or even surprise that Hayflick's paradigm may prove ultimately false, or be replaced by a better but ultimately equally false paradigm. Everything is true for its own time. Science periodically reorders the framework of Nature so that she can be properly entertained within the mind, otherwise the dominant overview of the world would become, as in the distant past, chaotic, magical, or theological.

Dr. Faro Naeim and I initially found that human lymphocytes, the white blood cells of the immune system, may reach a limit after only fifteen-to-twenty doublings, but later experiments are less certain and we are not sure whether all varieties of normal cells conform to the Hayflick model. David Harrison at Jackson Laboratories in Maine has transplanted bone marrow cells from old mice into young mice whose own bone marrow had been destroyed by irradiation. He allowed the young recipient mice to grow old, then retransplanted the marrow into a new set of irradiated young mice, and so on. He found that marrow from the original old mice could survive these repeated transfers and sustain four or more successive generations of mice, apparently exceeding the Hayflick limit by a considerable margin. Two British scientists, Doctors Robin Holliday and Tom Kirkwood, have advanced a so-called "commitment theory" which tries to explain the Hayflick experiments without concluding that all cells possess an internal program of aging and death.[5] According to them, early in development and in some cases throughout life, each organ system contains a mixture of primitive cells, partly mature cells, and the fully mature (differentiated) cells which have particular functions, like the function of skin epithelium or of the nerve cells in the brain. These differentiated cells do the work of the body, and all arise by maturation from the primitive cells. According to the commitment theory, when the primitive cells divide, a certain fraction stay primitive and uncommitted while the rest begin the path of maturation which leads to useful function but ultimately to the Hayflick limit. If this certain fraction is less than three-fourths, then upon long-term growth and the necessary, continuous discarding of excess cells, the primitive cells will be diluted out, leaving an increasing number of cells in the culture that are partway along the differentiation pathway. This sequence would result in the Hayflick phenomenon but with a different interpretation —that, after all, not every variety of cell dies out, and there are no absolutely immutable inside clocks ticking away like Mafia bombs under the hoods of our bodily runabouts. We just have to stop diluting our primitive cells!

Cancer cells make their own rules. In tissue culture they

don't pay any attention whatever to the Hayflick limit. They'll divide forever as long as you feed them and give them enough room. It's true they're not normal cells. They've learned something normal cells don't know, or forgotten something best forgotten if they want to stay uncommitted. Even so, they represent a perfectly legitimate form of life. Although we don't like them personally, cancer cells possess a full complement of cellular machinery. A normal cell can be "transformed" into one of these immortal (cancer) cells by various methods, by repression of a gene that inhibits DNA formation in old cells,[6] or by insertion of just a few extraneous genes, like certain viral genes.[7] Fundamentally, it's not that big a change, just a few more genes, but *voilà*—outside the Hayflick limit and heading for the end of time! The enigma of the bust-out immortality of the cancer cell has not received enough attention from gerontologists.

Despite these exceptions, which are perhaps mere eccentricities, the Hayflick paradigm remains the accepted view today, with much additional supporting evidence which I have not detailed here. Nevertheless, you can see what I mean by a strain in the material of the discipline. Hayflick built a strong, high dam. It holds a lot of water, including some of my own, but I'm not building my house downstream. Not that we would be back to Carrel if the dam burst. Science doesn't necessarily work like that. Except for the really main events, everyone is apt to be partly right, which makes it difficult to understand why they are so frequently apoplectic over the minutiae of differences and the claims of priority for the smaller discoveries.

All paradigms must inevitably confront contradictions or anomalies—either internally or externally, or both. Ironically, these anomalies are "uncovered" by the very people who wish to preserve the paradigm. Their efforts to prove the paradigm lead them to expose the external limits and contradictions which they themselves may not "see" or accept, but which may be seized upon by others who have not invested themselves in the paradigm, and so are free to challenge it."[8]

A generalizing biologic hypothesis or theory must attempt to explain all the facts and phenomena pertinent to its realm. I restrict myself to pertinence because there are innumerable data about aging, and it is critical in theory-building to know which data must be encompassed within the structure of the theory, and which can be left as, for the present, merely neutral. The fact that a few liver enzymes are somewhat increased or decreased in relation to age needn't be explained by either limit or commitment theory, or any other theory for the moment. However, life-span extension by caloric undernutrition definitely has to be explained. Why are those hungry rats hanging around so long?

Other pertinent gerontological observations which anybody's theory had better explain include the following: (1) Each species has a characteristic maximum life span, some much longer than others: for example, a mouse's 3 years to man's 110. (2) As shown by its "biomarkers," aging is a downhill run. The capacity for physiologic function declines with age, measured, for example, by how long a rat can swim before sinking, the amount of air a person can inhale and exhale in one breath (his "vital capacity"), the decline with age in degree of visual accommodation (the distance over which the eye can focus things sharply, like newsprint), the auditory pitch ceiling (the shrillness of sound beyond which you can no longer hear it—like a dog whistle), how fast your kidneys can filter out foreign material from the blood (called "renal clearance"), or the time required to run the New York Marathon (Figure 4.1). (3) After adulthood is reached, the percentage of the population dying at each age increases exponentially, like one of those 2, 4, 8, 16, 32, 64 series of doubles which are heaven if you're riding the winning color at roulette, but hell if you're very far out on the doubles where the body's ability to withstand stress, to bring everything back to the middle again until it's in normal working order, falls off. The boundaries of change, beyond which we cannot correct the imbalance and once again reach physiologic equilibrium, grow narrower with age. (4) Aging is accompanied by an increased susceptibility to a number of diseases at characteristic older ages. Arthritis,

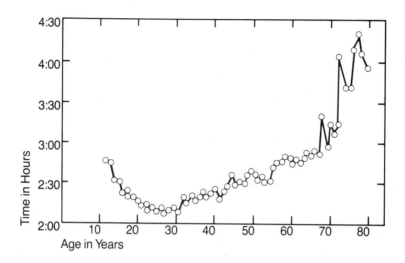

The fastest times in the New York marathon according to the runner's age.

Figure 4.1

cancer, cataracts, arteriosclerosis, heart failure, and maturity-onset diabetes are six unpleasant but familiar examples. In addition to these large-scale phenomena, an aging theory must encompass quite a number of smaller more specific ones if it's going to have any chance of becoming a new paradigm: (1) The Hayflick phenomenon. (2) The rate at which different species of animals spontaneously repair damage to their own DNA is related to the maximum life span of the species. (3) With age a decrease in the protective immune response occurs, together with an increase in the anti-self-destructive activity of the immune system. (4) Certain diseases, as we have seen, show striking features which look like accelerated aging.[9] These include the horrid malady progeria (stunted growth, taut, wizened skin, death from arteriosclerosis before age 20), Werner's syndrome (like progeria but with onset a bit later in life), diabetes, Down's syndrome (mongolism), and systemic lupus. None of these diseases manifest *all* the features of aging; each is like a part thereof; thus all aging syndromes are lopsided. (5) The connective tissue fibers—the collagen and elastic fibers—undergo deteriorative changes with age, among these, the change known as cross-linking. Other materials also undergo cross-linking with age. (6) Biochemical alterations do occur with age which cannot be left in the neutral category. These include variations in the second messenger system within cells (the chemicals called the cyclic nucleotides, which carry information from the cell's outer membrane into the nuclear headquarters), hormonal changes, alterations in some (but not all) enzymes and in the rates at which they are formed,[10] the accumulation of the yellow pigment lipofuscin inside aging cells, and damage within the chromatin complex. (The DNA in the cell is not naked; different proteins are wrapped around it and stuck to it. They serve to stabilize the whole structure and to turn genes on and off. "Chromatin complex" is the name given to this whole three-dimensional mystery maze, in which one can sometimes hear the faint cries of lost biochemists.) (7) The existence of a similar "specific metabolic rate" for almost all creatures. Nearly all animals, you see, use up approximately the same amount of chemical energy in a lifetime—about twenty-five-to-forty million calories per pound per lifetime. A mouse burns the same number of calories per pound in his two-to-three year life span as an elephant in his fifty-five-to-sixty years. Man is the luckiest of species in this regard. An exception to the general rule, he is allowed to consume eighty million calories per pound (more than any other animal) before the alarm goes off and he awakens unto aging and death.

These are among the fundamental gerontologic observations which can be arranged to fit within two major classes of aging theories, the damage theories and the program theories.

Damage theories require a greater subtlety than simply postulating that with time you get brittle, your molecular lights grow dim, and you wear out. Such "wear and tear" interpretations of aging are no longer tenable. The damage theories I prefer are based on the idea of inadequacies in the restorative systems within the cells, or between organs. In a classic experiment performed in the early 1970s, Professors Ron Hart and Richard Setlow[11] measured the DNA-repair rates in fibroblasts from a number of animals, from mouse to hamster to cow to elephant to man. They exposed fibroblasts in tissue culture to strong ultraviolet light, stimulating the formation of unnatural unions between adjacent molecules on the same DNA strand. Fortunately each cell has a collection of enzymes which recognize and repair such damage. The enzymes remove the damaged segment and rebuild the gap with newly added material. One can measure how much of the newly added material is consumed after a few hours of exposure to the DNA damaging agent, and thereby estimate the rate of repair. The rate is much greater for long-lived man than short-lived mouse. The splendid relation between maximum life spans of different species and their DNA repair rates is illustrated in Figure 4.2.

The genetic material, the DNA, is responsible for transmitting the characteristics of a species from one generation of animals to the next, and from primitive or embryonic cells to fully differentiated, mature cells. The DNA can be envisaged as a computer tape written in the language of the genes and programmed with all the information needed to build and run the whole organism. Every cell has a complete copy. So, theoretically, the cloning of a whole Hercules would be possible from a single Herculean cell. However, the cell reads only that section of the copy which pertains to the kind of cell it is struggling to become. Genes for skin cells are also present in fibroblasts but are turned off, repressed.

It's important that damage to the genetic tape be kept minimal, or repaired correctly if it occurs. Damage occurs spontaneously during normal metabolism, and secondarily by contact with a large number of environmental agents: cigarette smoke, pesticides, nuclear fallout, downtown Los Angeles air.

There are many kinds of damage which can strike DNA besides the unnatural unions (called dimers) caused by ultraviolet light, and Dr. Edward Schneider of the National Institute on Aging has shown that old cells respond differently than young cells to DNA damage.[12] In Figure 4.3 we see the two strands which normally form the double helix of DNA laid out as straight lines, one line having a little bubble or blister where it was pulled together by a dimer. Composed of strings of

DNA repair as a function of life span.

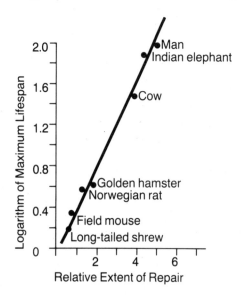

Figure 4.2

sugar and phosphate molecules, the two strands are bound together by base pairs, shown as  and  in the figure. Each base pair consists of two out of four possible specific organic molecules. Attached to the sugar portions of the DNA strands, these base pairs (whose sequence on the strands forms the much-heralded genetic code) extend across the gap and share hydrogen bonds, more or less like shaking hands. For a gene to be turned on and become functional, the hands in that small stretch of the DNA must let go. For the DNA to replicate its whole self, as in cell division, all the hands have to let go. In DNA damage one strand can break ("single strand

DNA Damage.

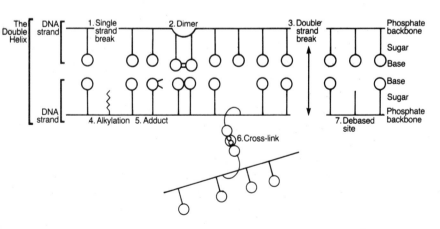

Seven types of DNA damage. The two strands are held together by hydrogen bonds across the space between the bases. In the native state the strands are twisted around each other to form the double helix.

Figure 4.3

break" in Figure 4.3) or, more disastrous because more difficult to repair, both of them can break; two adjacent base pairs
on the same strand can form a dimer (⃝⃝) as happens after
ultraviolet light damage; cross-links much tougher to break
than the handshaking hydrogen bonds can form across the gap
between different strands (⑧), extraneous protein or other
material can get stuck to a base, and so forth, as illustrated.

Different repair systems exist for all these types of damage.
But we won't ask right now who repairs the repair systems. We
must take one thing at a time, for if we get too far ahead of
reality we may never catch up with it. In any case, those damage theories which deal with DNA repair look promising to
me. At one time scientists thought DNA was very stable, that
it was maintained without change throughout the life of the
cell and from generation to generation except for occasional
mutations which were smiled or frowned upon by the incor-
ruptible judgment of Evolution. It was a big surprise to learn
that the DNA in every cell is constantly being damaged and
repaired. If all repair processes worked perfectly, there would
be no mutations, because a mutation is simply an unpro-
grammed DNA alteration that manages to persist. If natural
selection finds the change slightly advantageous, the mutation
is allowed not only to persist but to join with others until finally
the mutant-evolving apes swing right down from the trees,
become men, and start writing books. If repair were perfect,
none of this could be happening. Nature has set the rate of
repair of DNA at less than the rate of damage, so that animals
can accumulate mutations and evolve. Aging is simply a by-
product of the repair deficit. Notice how the clever repair
theoreticians have performed the legerdemain of pulling a
program theory out of a damage theory. Hayflick's cells stop
dividing when the accumulated, unrepaired DNA damage
reaches a certain threshold value. The level of the repair rate
is what is programmed.

The DNA repair theory holds the promise that we might be
able to extend life span reasonably soon and very substantially,
by finding out how to increase the level of the repair processes
inside the cells. Dr. Joan Sonneborn of the University of Wyo-

ming has accomplished this for the one-celled organism, *Paramecium*.[13] She exposed her *Paramecia* to ordinary ultraviolet light (which caused dimers ⌒=⌒ to form in the DNA), then to "black light," which stimulates a so-called "photoreactivation" process that repairs the unnatural dimers. In addition, the photoreactivation tuned other, not well-understood repair processes to a higher level, repairing not only the ultraviolet-caused damage but a part of the damage accumulated during normal aging. The *Paramecia* lived considerably longer than if nothing had been done at all. They had been rejuvenated by the interplays of the double whammy of light.

We don't yet know how to induce higher levels of DNA repair enzymes in animals closer to us, but no great conceptual leap seems to be required. It may be more like puzzle solving —the normal business of science. How do cancer cells handle accumulating DNA damage so as to escape the limits of the Hayflick phenomenon? And what about the germ plasm, the basic hereditary material which, except for the mutations selected by evolution, is passed down intact through all the endless generations of mice, elephants, and men? How does the germ plasm avoid accumulated DNA damage over this long time? Evidence does exist that at fertilization, when the winning sperm enters the ready egg, an enormous burst of DNA repair activity takes place,[14] and when everything has been fixed and no strand breaks or other defects remain (Fig. 4.3), the fertilized egg divides and development proceeds.

Most human diseases which show features of accelerated aging also manifest defects in one or more DNA repair systems: for example, the fortunately rare disease, xeroderma pigmentosum, and the more common Down's syndrome (mongolism). In xeroderma the system for repairing the DNA damage caused by ultraviolet light doesn't work well. Any exposure to sunlight is bad for xeroderma sufferers. As some exposure can't be avoided, their skin ages rapidly and they tend to develop multiple skin cancers. In fact sunlight is bad for anybody's skin. The more of it any portion of your skin receives, the faster that portion ages, which is why the youngest part of a person's package is the part he sits on.

People with Down's syndrome or mongolism age faster than normal. They rarely live more than fifty years. As we have seen in Chapter 3, all of them develop true senile dementia on top of the dementia that comes with their Down's syndrome. In addition, they display premature graying of hair, degenerative changes in different glands, age-like alterations in their second messenger cell membrane $\rightarrow$ nuclear headquarters communication system, an increase in the yellow age pigment (lipofuscin) in their cells, and an earlier than normal decline in their immune system. In tissue culture their cells succumb to a foreshortened Hayflick limit. Dr. Kathleen Hall and I at the UCLA Medical Center have found that the capacity of their lymphocytes to repair DNA injured by either ultraviolet light or regular X ray is defective.

Those damage theories which postulate that cross-linking and free radical reactants are involved in aging will invite our attention next. The damage caused by these agents can sometimes be metabolized away, but it cannot be repaired in place. We are not dealing here with a balance between rates of damage and repair, but just with the rate and extent of damage. A cross-linking agent is a chemical with two reactive groups with which it seizes hold of two otherwise separate molecules or parts of the same molecule and binds them firmly together. The tanning of hides is a good example of an extensive cross-linking process, and indeed it was an expert in the chemistry of tanning, Johan Bjorksten, who first suggested the cross-linking theory. Cross-linking agents are churned out as products or by-products of normal metabolism (malondialdehyde is a hot cross-linker, for example). Whether they be the collagen and elastic fibers of the connective tissues of our bones and bodies, or even the DNA in our cells, cross-linked organic structures become rigidified, immobilized, and their function declines. The theory has an intuitive appeal in that most people as they grow older feel more and more like they were being cross-linked.

Another and equally destructive class of damage agents produced during metabolism but present in the environment as well are the free radicals, introduced to gerontologic scrutiny by Dr. Denham Harman of the University of Nebraska.[15] These immensely reactive chemicals differ from conventional molecules by possessing an extra electrical charge, a free electron. They trigger processes which are characteristically "once-only," irreversible, and energetically wasteful. Most free radicals in the body are oxidants, their free electron whirling around a super-activated oxygen atom, as in the hydroxyl free radical, which can be written as OH· (the little extra dot is the unpaired free electron, which rarely holds still long enough to be seen), or singlet oxygen and hydrogen peroxide. Great white sharks in the biochemical sea, these short-lived but voracious agents oxidize and damage tissue, especially cell membranes. Free radical shark attacks on polyunsaturated fats yield lipid peroxides, which in turn decompose to yield chemicals known as aldehydes, which cross-link proteins, lipids, and DNA.

Not everybody realizes that the oxygen of our atmosphere is a highly poisonous gas. Alien entities arriving from a methane planet would choke and die on the stuff we breathe so casually. It rusts iron, is involved in the decay and crumbling of granite boulders, and participates in every fire in town . . . yet we live in it and love it. That's probably why the galactic aliens have not revealed themselves to us. They come to Earth exploring and take one sniff. Zounds! All that oxygen! Better leave those tough Earth devils alone!

Life on earth has had to devise ways of handling the dark side of the oxygen surfeit. From bacteria all the way up to human cells certain enzymes function to degrade, neutralize, or detoxify the free radicals: enzymes with such heroic names as superoxide dismutase, catalase, and glutathione peroxidase. These enzymes are the free radical "scavengers." Dr. Richard Cutler at the Gerontology Research Center of the National Institute on Aging has found that the amount of superoxide dismutase in relation to specific metabolic rate increases proportionately with maximum life spans in different species. Thus, longer-lived species enjoy relatively higher levels of protection against the by-products of oxygen metabolism, against the free radicals. But if any free radicals do surge past the defense system of scavengers, the damage may not be repairable. You just have to live with it, a little stiffer in the A.M., a little cloudier in the P.M. Certain things can be injected or taken in the diet which have free radical scavenging effects. These are the antioxidants: vitamin E, selenium, vitamin C, a number of food additives such as BHT, BHA, and others. The subject will engage us further in Chapter 7 when we consider what can be done right now to counteract aging.

The above are my favorite damage theories. They are rather straightforward in concept. Program theories, by contrast, tend to be more mysterious, more intricate, more metaphorical. The most general program theory says that aging is part of development, like childhood, adolescence, and mid-adulthood. These are all genetically controlled. Somehow the genes turn on which are appropriate to whatever period in life comes next, and others turn off, are repressed, until gradually next is now. In such a program the onslaught of aging deals primarily with the regulation of gene expression and repression. Fortunately the regulatory gene game is being actively played today by many biologists, and we may soon learn how to cheat and how to manipulate the unfolding sequence of expression and repression. Repressed genes in adult nuclei of frogs can be reactivated by being inserted into frog eggs.[16] Tadpoles can be developed from nuclei of transplanted skin cells of adult frogs. Thus the "program" can be switched back to an earlier stage, at least in some instances. Experiments by Dr. Sinan Tas and I indicate that gene repression may involve the formation of bonds between the sulfur atoms in protein molecules tightly associated with DNA in the chromatin complex.[17] These are the disulfide (meaning two sulfur atoms) or S-S bonds. We think it might be possible to break these bonds, and indeed Dr. Takashi Makinodan of the Veterans Administration Hospital in Los Angeles has rejuvenated the immune responses in old mice with the chemical, 2-mercaptoethanol, an S-S bond breaking agent.

While we are breaking bonds together, we must not overlook the possibility that a purely developmental theory of aging could be missing the point if, as many think, evolution loses interest in our well-being when the childbearing time slips past. Our life-support systems simply lapse into "uncoordinated" and we jiggle ourselves apart. That's "program," if you like, but different from the steady, controlled, turn-off turn-on which brings on childhood, puberty, and other ordered phases of development.

Another program theory maintains that the initiating event in aging is the programmed appearance of some destructive agent. Aging in a few species is clearly caused by a sudden massive outpouring of deleterious hormones. That's what finally overtakes the Pacific salmon. Hatched in streams from the Columbia River and up the west coast of Canada and Alaska, the salmon spend six months in gravel river bottoms, a year or so in lakes, then drift downstream and head out to sea. Two to four years later they return, making their miraculous swim-jump-swim upstream to the precise place they were born. Arrived home, they spawn. Immediately thereafter their adrenal glands release a massive amount of corticoid hormones into their bloodstreams, and the salmon grow old almost as rapidly as She in Rider Haggard's novel of the same name where the 900-year-old, still beautiful, wicked queen bathes herself once too often in the preservative flame and becomes a hag before the astonished eyes of the explorers.

The dreaded but actually very shy octopus also ages suddenly and dramatically following massive hormone release. At a certain stage in life, after the shy octopus mates, its optic gland releases the hormone overdose. Remove the optic gland and the octopus lives five times its normal life span.

Aging in humans may be partly secondary not to the sudden outpouring of a particular hormone as in salmon and octopi, but to a slowly developing hormonal imbalance. Hormones within the brain are particularly suspect. One theory holds that the "clock" of aging lurks in the hypothalamus, a pea-sized area of brain a bit posterior to a spot midway between your ears. It regulates hunger, rage, sleep, sexual desire, and to some extent development and aging. Dr. Caleb Finch at the University of Southern California has detected significant decreases in neurotransmitter chemicals in the hypothalamus from old compared to young animals. Released at a nerve ending and picked up by receptors on the adjacent nerve cell's surface, the neurotransmitters are a class of brain chemicals which transmit impulses from one nerve to the next. The hypothalamus and its transmitters regulate the pituitary gland hanging nearby from the base of the brain. When instructed to do so by the hypothalamus, the pituitary releases a bevy of important hormones such as growth hormone, ACTH, thyroid-stimulating hormone, and others. Hormonal variations programmed by the hypothalamus and carried out by the pituitary may induce the onset of aging, just as other variations within the same axis bring on puberty.

A programmed decrease in neurotransmitter secretion serves to initiate what Dr. Finch calls an "endocrine cascade," in which changes in the secretion of one hormone alter other endocrine hookups and responses. The neurotransmitter called dopamine declines with age in a number of regions of the brain, leading to such age-related neurological disorders as the disease Parkinsonism with its fixed stare and shuffling gait. To some extent these disorders can be treated by the drug L-dopa, which is converted into dopamine in the body. The mean life span in mice has been considerably extended by including large amounts of L-dopa in the diet.[18]

The picture that we see emerging from these studies of the aging brain is one of imbalance among neurotransmitters rather than specific alterations in a selectively vulnerable system. It's a complicated puzzle but again it's one that we can progress toward solving without having first to make any enormous conceptual leap into a new domain of science—at least until paradigm change time, which cannot be precisely predicted except in terms of its gathering momentum.

The endocrine system is altered with age not only in its primary hormone levels but in the numbers of receptors located at the surfaces of cell membranes, and within the fluid space inside the cell.[19] Many hormones must first react with cell receptors in order for their message to influence the program of the cell. In Figure 4.4 the fat-soluble hormones are seen to penetrate the membrane to combine with a receptor on the membrane itself, causing the release, just inside the membrane, of the "second messenger." The sequence is: hormone receptor → second messenger → cell nucleus → turning on of the appropriate genes. The loss of many types of receptors from the cells of old animals interferes with this progression.

Notice that we are gradually progressing from a molecular level (like DNA repair) to a systems level. There may well be two kinds of aging clock, one in the brain's hypothalamus orchestrating growth and development, another in each indi-

How hormones act on cells.

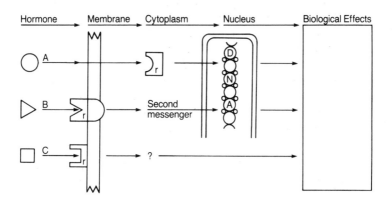

Hormones act on cells in three ways. A: the steroid hormones, such ACTH, cortisone, and the sex hormones, pass through the cell membrane and unite with a receptor *(r)* in the cell's fluid interior. This receptor-hormone complex goes to the nucleus and activates a portion of the cellular machinery (according to the type of hormone). B: some hormones, such as adrenaline, attach to a receptor on the outer cell's membrane, and then a "second messenger" (specifically, a cyclic nucleotide) is produced, which activates the cell machinery. C: other hormones, such as insulin, also attach to a cell membrane receptor, but we do not know the later steps in the cell activation.

Figure 4.4

vidual cell, the two clocks roughly synchronized and providing what is designed to be a fail-safe system. I shall be outlining experiments at the systems level involving either the endocrine or immune machineries that lead to rejuvenation of many features of aging . . . but not to extension of maximum life span. A two-clock model might explain the reason for what appears at first sight a stubborn paradox.

At a systems level the neuroendocrine and immune systems have been regarded, not necessarily as clocks, but as pacemakers for aging. The cause of aging is at a deeper, molecular level, but the way the molecular disarray manifests itself in sagging tissues, wrinkled skin, gray hairs, and declines in nearly all bodily functions is via the hormonal or immune systems, and probably both.

The theory of aging I love best and am inclined to be more faithful to than the others is the immunological theory, which posits a double dose of doom arriving with the years, one part decline of function, the other part active destruction.[20] Due to popular press reports about organ transplantation, most people know by now that if you receive an unmatched kidney or heart graft from another person, your immune system recognizes it as foreign, as "non-self," and reacts against it. All the hearts Dr. Christian Barnard transplanted some years back were ultimately rejected in part because tissue typing, whereby donor and recipient can be genetically matched to ensure against rejection, was still at an early stage of development. Equally important to the integrity of the self/non-self recognition process, your immune system must not react against your own heart, kidneys, or other organs, but must recognize them as "self" and leave them alone. It must only react against non-self, whatever form that non-self takes.

Two things therefore happen to the immune system with age. First, its normal response declines so that it can no longer react effectively not only against other peoples' donated parts but also against aberrant cells that may arise in its own body, cancer cells for example. The policeman-like immune system ought to be recognizing them as foreign and therefore killing them. We could hardly take the immune system as a desirable political model because it is in fact an organic totalitarian ministate where anything that's different, that does not carry the markers of "self," is apt to be isolated and dispatched. The surveillance against aberrant cells, bacteria, other invading organisms, foreign proteins, and viruses protects the integrity of the body. This normal, protective response is high in youth and low in age, hence with age we grow more susceptible to cancer and many infections. With age those cellular instruments which are playing off-key in the orchestra of the body are no longer silenced, the music becomes gradually more discordant, and the other musicians give up. The fundamental reason for the decline and switch-over in the immune response is not precisely known—although we can sometimes slow down the change, even reverse it for a while—but immune dysfunction is one of the pacemakers of aging.

Now for the other dose of immunological doom: with age the immune system begins to act against the very "self" of which it is a part. I suppose the analogy with the totalitarian state holds up pretty well here too. On an experimental level, if you transplant or graft the white blood cells (the lymphocytes, which are the enforcers of immunity) of an adult mouse to a newborn one, the newborn mouse's immune system, being not yet mature enough, fails to recognize the grafted cells as foreign, but the grafted adult lymphocytes will consider the newborn as foreign and react against it in the classical "graft-versus-host" reaction. Taken as a model for the anti-self response that I think plays a significant role in normal aging, a chronic graft-versus-host reaction shows many features resembling accelerated aging: failure to thrive, loss of hair, vascular and kidney disease, a foreshortened life span. Human bone marrow is sometimes transplanted in the course of treatment for leukemia and certain other diseases. The patient is first given total body X ray to destroy the leukemia. Unfortunately this heroic treatment also destroys his own bone marrow, so he must be injected with genetically matched marrow from a normal individual to sustain him. The principal danger is that the match is rarely quite perfect and about half the time a graft-versus-host reaction ensues, with disastrous consequences for the patient. Until better perfected, the treatment remains a chancy resort for a few incurable diseases.

Out of control, an immune system can be a two-edged sword: it not only fails to protect, it actively destroys the body. Much of this complicated system is regulated by a collection of genes located, in vertebrates like mice and men, quite close to one another on a single chromosome. The collection is called the major histocompatibility complex (the MHC, for short). Organized like a super blood group system with an enormous number of different types, its unraveling has been one of the main Nobel prizewinning events in modern biology (given in 1980 jointly to Drs. Jean Dausset of France and the Americans George Snell and Baruj Benacerraf). The MHC has among other responsibilities that of self-anti-self recognition; hence, organ grafts survive best if donor and recipient are the same MHC type. Susceptibility to a wide variety of diseases, including many diseases of aging such as Alzheimer's disease (senile dementia), is influenced by the MHC type of the particular person.

A few years ago Dr. George Smith and I were able to show a direct effect of the MHC on maximum life span of mice.[21] We compared maximum survivals between many strains of congenic mice. These are mice which have been bred by brother-sister matings through multiple generations until all the individuals of any one strain are just like identical twins, except (in our experiments) for those genes clustered about the MHC. With such strains, any life-span differences could be attributed to differences at the MHC alone. Our demonstration of these differences provided the first direct evidence that the MHC is an important regulator of the rate of aging. Dr. Ed Yunis at Harvard University quite elegantly confirmed our findings.[22]

It must be more than chance that a number of other genes regulating aging besides those directly controlling immunity are also associated with the MHC and reside on the same chromosome. These include superoxide dismutase certainly, and possibly catalase, two of the body's own, intrinsic free radical scavengers. It includes also the level of the second messenger substance involved in the response to many hormones. And Dr. Kathleen Hall and I have found that the level of DNA-repair may be influenced by the MHC.

The disease systemic lupus shows many features of accelerated aging as well as DNA-repair deficiencies. It has been found recently that the blood of patients with this disease contains a substance which is activated by ultraviolet light and causes breaks and other damage to DNA.[23] This substance is inhibited by SOD, the free-radical scavenger, so it must be some new form of free-radical producing material which hits directly at the DNA. Since susceptibility to systemic lupus is in part controlled by the MHC, we see again an association between the MHC, aging, DNA-repair, and free radicals.

Recall now from our first chapter that the increase in life span from early to modern man happened so fast in geologic time that mutations of only a few genes could have occurred and been selected for, hence the idea, championed especially by Drs. Richard Cutler and George Sacher, that aging is regulated not by the whole shebang of thousands of genes along the double helical DNA ladder, but by relatively few. My associates and I think the MHC is one of these key gene systems. Because of its multiple protective influences, many of which are non-immune, it might better be called the life-support complex, or LSC.

I suspect the MHC or LSC represents a very ancient gene cluster having to do with protection against damage from free radicals, and which has had things added to it and been modified during evolution. After all, the free radical scavengers like superoxide dismutase were a very early necessary invention for the evolutionary transition to life forms that could survive in the presence of oxygen. Superoxide dismutase bears some chemical resemblance to the MHC gene factors. We know that aging of the bread mold *Neurospora* is greatly influenced by a single gene system which also controls the free radical scavengers.[24] My guess is that during the course of evolution the MHC ultimately evolved as an additional part of a widespread self-protective complex already existing in very early life forms.

All the theories I've described so far may be classified as reductionist theories. They clearly attribute aging to what may be termed "local failure" of a part or parts of the body or the individual cell. The failure then leads to decline in other parts or in the whole. A completely different and nonreductionist approach might view aging as a "global failure" primarily involving interactions *between* systems rather than *within* any one system. Although it seems paradoxical, engineering studies teach us that global failure can occur before or without complete local failure, which may be why reductionist aging theories, all based on local failure of one sort or another, have not been wholly successful. Within each bodily system—the immune system, the nervous system—reigns a hierarchy of balance. I have elsewhere designated this concept as one of "hierarchical homeostasis."[25]

Here is a simple example: at the level of the whole organism one of the highest requirements is to keep enough blood flowing to the brain so that it doesn't lack oxygen, because oxygen lack soon kills the brain. Under stress, such as after blood loss, other organ systems may undergo vascular spasm in order to reduce their blood supplies, so that the brain can have a larger share of what blood remains. At the cellular level, the highest requirement might be to conserve and maintain the cell's energy system. Therefore the readjustments within the organism, the cell, or a subcellular system required to maintain the respective hierarchies may finally result in an out-of-control disharmony at the interfaces *between* systems—the immune and the nervous systems, for example—with progressive aging and, at last, the global failure we recognize as death.

We've seen that a number of respectable theories exist which at different levels of biological organization interpret the aging process in ways that seem concrete and appealing to our sense of order. But perhaps something is still missing. The theories are merely parallel and each has a school of adherents. Notice, however, that much is known, otherwise such reasonable theories, many of them susceptible to the test of predicting experimental results, could not be constructed at all. We are no longer wandering in the dark of total guesswork which surrounded gerontologists until quite recent times. The outlines of what actually goes on during aging are becoming visible. The theories are beginning to coalesce, to make sense as parts of a whole process. When this happens we shall have a new paradigm.

Meantime, as a kind of illustrative summary, let's attempt a synthesis of the various ideas. Development (program) and damage and repair of damage underlie aging at the most fundamental level. All of these involve the genetic material, the DNA within the chromatin complex. Some portions of the DNA, i.e., some gene systems, are more important for aging than others, one such being the MHC. The nature of development still eludes us (perhaps here is where the new paradigm must enter), but we know a fair amount about damage and repair, and are learning more each year. How these fundamental processes lead to the outward features of aging with its organ and tissue changes is mediated through the pacemakers of aging, namely the immune system and the brain/hormonal interplay. We are definitely learning how to interfere with these pacemakers.

5

Undernutrition Now

Information is already available to enable one to live to be more than 120 years old if he begins early enough and adheres religiously to a lifelong regime of dietary restriction. Clive McKay's classic caloric undernutrition experiments, performed at Cornell University in the mid thirties, in some instances approximately doubled both 50 percent survivals and maximum life spans of rats. The undernutrition regimes could almost certainly be adapted to human use. Notice carefully the word *undernutrition* here rather than *malnutrition*. In an undernutrition regime the total intake of calories is sharply limited but there's no lack of critical nutrients such as vitamins, essential amino acids, fatty acids, and minerals. "Undernutrition without malnutrition" is the key concept in dietary modulation of the life span. It was once thought that such a regime would only be effective if started early in life, not long after the time of weaning, but dietary restriction studies performed in my laboratory at the University of California Medical School in Los Angeles by Dr. Richard Weindruch and myself[1] showed substantial life-span benefits in mice even when the restriction was begun in mid-adulthood. So humans could do it without having to start when they are babies.

With regard to human application, however, my distinguished colleague, Dr. Leonard Hayflick, has typified a more conservative position: "In the 40 years since we have known about undernutrition, no one has consciously chosen to do it, even the biologists, and even though it's widely known that it works and that it's not dangerous. Any method is unacceptable if it affects the enjoyment of life." We have to deal with this not uncommon viewpoint even though it's misconstrued and not quite historically correct.

First, for most of the forty years during which we've known about the effects of undernutrition on aging, i.e., since McKay's work in the thirties, it was thought on the basis of animal experiments that it would have to be started at the time of weaning, or at least in early childhood. Indeed, earlier attempts to extend life span in rodents by dietary restriction starting in adulthood actually shortened survival. We know now that in these initial attempts the restriction was too suddenly and too severely begun. Gradual restriction of calories has been our own key to success in the adulthood experiments.[2]

Second, it's not quite true that no one has ever voluntarily chosen a lifelong nutritionally restricted existence. Luigi Cornaro, who we recall wrote one of the four most famous autobiographies of the Renaissance, *The Art of Living Long,* was born in Venice in the year 1464 and died in 1567. A member of the minor Italian nobility, he followed a dissolute, gluttonous life leading to dangerous ill-health by the age of 37, at which time he voluntarily adopted a rigidly temperate, dietarily restrictive regime. This he stuck to for the rest of his life. Despite his unrestrained earlier years, he lived to be 103. As serious fasters know quite well, long-term restriction gives you an energetic clear-minded "high." It's obvious from reading Cornaro's exemplary autobiographical treatise that he was "high" from the age of 37 on, or for sixty-six years. Professor Hayflick to the contrary, undernutrition may augment the enjoyment of life, particularly those joys which the alert mind enhances.

Not until many centuries after Cornaro did McKay[3] initiate his long and famous series of studies by feeding experimental rats, on a daily basis and beginning at weaning, about 60 percent of the caloric intake of rats allowed to eat as much as they wanted. The restricted diet was supplemented with extra vitamins and minerals. On this 60 percent regimen the animals' growth rate was greatly retarded although in other ways they were super healthy. They could be held in a growth-retarded state for up to 1,000 days, by which time all the normally fed rats had died. When the retarded rats were allowed a full diet, they began to grow again. They were also sexually active and could reproduce at a far more advanced age than normally fed rats.

In the nineteen sixties and the seventies a long series of incisive experiments by Morris Ross[4] of the Institute for Cancer Research in Philadelphia yielded a maximum life span of 1,000–1,099 days in fully fed rats and 1,600 to 1,699 days in dietarily restricted rats, a 60 percent increase. These experiments also involved daily feedings of enriched diets, but in less than normal amounts, thus the typical "undernutrition without malnutrition."

In the 1940s Professors A.H. Carlson and F. Holzel had added a new wrinkle by studying the effects of intermittent fasting on life span in rats.[5] They fed rats a high-quality diet, and as much as they wanted, but fasted them completely every second day; another group were fasted every third day; another group, every fourth day. The maximum life span of unfasted animals was 800 days, but in all three intermittently fasted groups it was 1,000 to 1,100 days. This amounted to a 20–30 percent extension of maximum life span. A very recent study of the effect of intermittent fasting (in this case, feeding as much as desired but only every other day) by Dr. Charles Goodrick[6] of the National Institute on Aging's Gerontology Research Unit is illustrated in Figure 5.1A. Maximum life span was increased from the 875 days of the normally fed rats to 1,295 in the restricted ones, and 50 percent survival from 630 days to 980 days.

All of the above experiments started with weanling animals. In my laboratory we have used gradually induced intermittent fasting in adult mice, beginning at a mouse age equivalent to 30–35 years in a human, to achieve the significant life-span extension shown in Figure 5.1B.

With some species of animals even greater extension can be achieved than with rodents. When the carnivorous microorganism *Tokophyra* is allowed to feed freely, its maximum survival is ten days; with feedings cut down to only twice daily, survival increases to eighty days—an 800 percent increase (see Figure 5.1C).[7]

Do people who are just naturally thin live longer than those of average weight? One might think so from what I've said above, but the matter is not quite so simple. An enormous study of the relations between mortality and body weight among 750,000 men and women was recently published by Drs. Lew and Garfinkel of the American Cancer Society.[8] The overall mortality of people who were more than 10 percent lighter than average was actually increased. This seems a paradox and out of line with the whole Cornaro, McKay, Ross, Goodrick, and our own evidence cited above. The answer can be found in some of McKay's work on variables affecting the last half of life in white rats.[9] Up until middle life these rats were kept on a good stock diet. Then some were given protein rich diets, others moderate or low protein diets, some were allowed to grow fat, others kept thin. None were subjected to a genuine calorically restrictive regimen. McKay found that the degree of body fatness in later life was more important than such variables as protein intake or even exercise. Fat rats lived shorter lives. However, and here's the answer to the 750,000 men and women question raised above, rats that were unable to fatten on a totally permissive diet, and tended despite the diet to remain of less than average weight, also lived shorter lives. The message here is that being "naturally" thin is not the same health-wise as thinness induced by dietary restriction. People who remain underweight despite excessive food intake have a slightly increased metabolic rate and increased body temperature, both of which reduce life span. People who are underweight because they eat very sparingly, but don't carefully select what they do eat, are apt to be somewhat malnourished. The human population data about life span and body weight are affected by these additional variables, which have

Survival curves for animals subjected to "undernutrition without malnutrition."

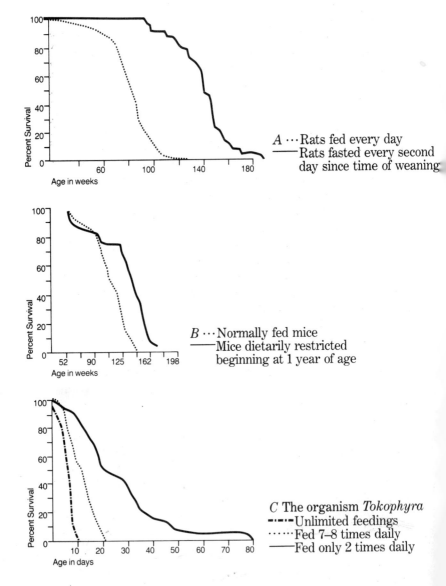

A ... Rats fed every day
—— Rats fasted every second day since time of weaning

B ... Normally fed mice
—— Mice dietarily restricted beginning at 1 year of age

C The organism *Tokophyra*
–-–- Unlimited feedings
····· Fed 7–8 times daily
—— Fed only 2 times daily

Figure 5.

been largely avoided in the animal studies. So there is no necessary paradox. If you are the type of person who gains weight easily by overeating but you elect to lose weight by dietary restriction, then you have a survival advantage. You are able to use and conserve food more efficiently. This tendency probably evolved to allow better use of a limited food supply under primitive conditions. Naturally thin people may well live longer by becoming even thinner so long as there is no malnutrition.

Intermittent fasting, by the way, with no restriction of intake on the eating days except that the food must be highly nutritious, does not lead to growth retardation although it does extend life span. The regimen I personally follow and recommend is total abstinence from food two successive days each week, and a healthy supplemented diet the other five days. What such a five-day diet might include will be covered in a later chapter.

What other effects does caloric undernutrition have besides life-span extension? It's important to know how it affects susceptibility to disease, as well as the biochemical status, physiological performance, mental alertness, and intelligence of restricted animals. The answer seems favorable to all of these questions. Cancers, cataracts, discoloration and matting of hair, dryness of skin, kidney disease, and heart disease are all less frequent in restricted animals than in normal ones. Furthermore, the smaller numbers of the restricted animals which do finally develop these maladies do so at a substantially later age than their unrestricted partners.[10] There's less disease and what there is, is postponed.

Let's take some specific examples. In a study conducted at my laboratory about 50 percent of fully fed mice ultimately developed cancers of one sort or another, but only 13 percent of restricted mice.[11] In a similar experiment with rats in Australia, the figures were 64 percent and 15 percent.[12] These are composite values covering many types of cancer. The effect varies with the type. In rats, tumors of the pituitary gland occurred in 60 percent of unrestricted animals by 800 days of age but not in any of the restricted ones. By 1,200 days (by which time all unrestricted rats had died), only 10 percent of the restricted animals had the pituitary tumor. Thus the frequency is less and the age of onset much later.[13]

Spontaneous breast cancer can be reduced from an incidence of 60 percent in some strains of mice to zero by very long-term underfeeding. (Note that this is prevention of occurrence, not cure of established cancers.[14]) The incidence of cancer in the lymphatic tissues amounts to thirty times greater in normally fed than in restricted animals. The incidence of kidney disease (nephritis), vascular disease, and heart disease at 800 days of age has been respectively 100 percent, 63 percent, and 96 percent in normally fed rats but only 25 percent, 10 percent and 26 percent in dietarily restricted rats. A high incidence of arteriosclerosis occurs normally in certain strains of pigeons but can be greatly diminished by undernutrition.[15]

A number of biochemical measurements indicate that restricted animals are chemically younger than their chronologic age would indicate.[16] Blood cholesterol increases with age in normally fed but not in restricted rats. The contractility of heated collagen (the main chemical component of connective tissue) is altered with age. This alteration affords one of the best means of making a chemical estimate of the age of an animal. It's a good "biomarker" of senescence. The change in collagen is less severe in diet-restricted animals. They are biochemically younger.

The amounts of different enzymes in tissues, in liver for example, are in many instances characteristic of the age of the animal. Enzymes are of critical importance in metabolism, because they regulate the rates at which most cellular events are happening. Their mode of action may be likened to the eighteenth camel in the classic Arabian tale. An Arab died leaving seventeen camels plus a will, which read, "I leave half my camels to my oldest son, a third to my next, and a ninth to my youngest." Nobody knew what to do with these divisions. How can you take a half of seventeen camels? Everyone was stumped. Along came a wise man who said, "I own a camel which I'm lending to the estate. Now there are eighteen camels. Give the oldest son 9 camels, the next son six camels, the youngest two camels. That's a half, a third, a ninth, and it comes to seventeen. There's one camel left over. That's my original camel. Give it back to me."

That eighteenth camel was an enzyme. An enzyme makes a reaction possible without itself being changed. It enters the reaction but comes out unaltered at the end. Enzymes therefore "catalyze" reactions and allow them to run much faster than they otherwise would.

Instead of an eighteenth camel, the liver uses adenosine triphosphatase, alkaline phosphatase, and dozens of other enzymes. The level of adenosine triphosphatase in the liver of a normally fed rat reaches peak value at 200 days of age, then gradually declines with further age. In restricted rats the peak and beginning of decline do not occur until 600 to 700 days.

The fat cells of rats whose caloric intake is restricted are significantly more responsive to certain hormones which release the stored-up material from the cells and carry it to the blood so that the body's tissues can convert it to energy. This response ordinarily declines with age, but less so in restricted animals.[17]

At UCLA Dr. Richard Weindruch and I and other colleagues have extensively evaluated the functional ability of the immune system in restricted compared to fully fed mice. Recall that the immune system's job includes combatting invading organisms, neutralizing a wide variety of toxic substances, and surveying other cells of the body and destroying any which have become abnormal or cancerous. The latter function is delicately tuned and discriminative. Your immune system recognizes the difference between "self" (your own kidney or any other organ) and "non-self" (someone else's grafted kidney, or one of your own cells which has become aberrant or malignant and so achieved a kind of "non-self"). Your immune system rejects non-self by sending armies of antibodies and killer lymphocytes against it.

While it is not supposed to attack "self," the ability to make the distinction between "self" and "non-self" becomes blurred with age, and aging is characterized by anti-self reactions. With advanced age, the ability to combat invaders and handle toxic materials declines to 10 to 20 percent of its peak value in youth; at the same time anti-self or auto-destruct processes make their appearance. Aging involves not only passive wearing out or failure to repair damage, but active self destruction.

Dietary restriction counteracts both the above trends. Restriction from time of weaning greatly slows the age-related decline in response to foreign materials. Restriction beginning in adulthood actually leads to substantial rejuvenation of the immune system. At the same time, the signs of anti-self reactions are markedly reduced.[18] In humans, part of senile dementia may be caused by antibrain auto-antibodies which occur with aging. These are greatly reduced by dietary restriction.[19]

In terms of potential human application, it is critical to know whether severe caloric undernutrition affects mental development or activity.[20] A widely publicized opinion in health circles holds that malnutrition in early life jeopardizes mental development. Animal experiments have indeed shown that protein-calorie *mal*nutrition during the period of rapid brain growth (which in man would be up to two years of age) both retards body growth and leads to permanent reduction in brain weight and in the number of brain cells. In vigorous caloric undernutrition instituted at the time of weaning, overall body growth may be decreased by about a third. The animals are definitely smaller and lighter than fully fed animals. By such a regimen in rodents, are we producing long-lived idiots? That would hardly be a feasible option for man.

Fortunately we are not producing idiot mice. Even though the rate of general growth of weaning-restricted animals may be much reduced, the brain weights increase at the same rate as in fully fed animals. Thus, *under*nutrition is quite unlike *mal*nutrition: brain weight is preserved irrespective of body weight. In rats sufficiently restricted in food intake to extend their average life spans by 40 percent, the normal age-associated loss in certain cell receptors in the brain was greatly retarded.[21] Furthermore, pilot experiments from my own laboratory and ongoing collaborative work with Dr. Raymond

Bartus of Lederle Laboratories involving intelligence testing (so-called passive avoidance tests as well as others) suggest that the smaller, restricted mice are just as smart as the big, fully fed fellows. And thirty-eight-month-old restricted mice tested as highly as twenty-four-month-old regular mice, so the rate of brain aging itself seems less on a proper restrictive regime. These results are with weaning-restricted animals; therefore adult-initiated undernutrition would certainly not adversely affect the brain. Very possibly the opposite.

Unfortunately, modern academic nutritionists have learned little from the various gerontological truths outlined above. Most nutritional scientists, like the members of the American Dietary Association, the Food and Drug Administration, the Department of Agriculture, and the American Society of Nutrition, are seriously misdirected because their science of nutrition has gone off on a dubious foot, opting to optimize two things. Using rats as the main experimental animal, nutritionists have sought to maximize both growth rate and ultimate body size, to create the fastest growing, biggest possible subjects. The regimen which does this for rats is then adapted to human nutrition. That's fine if you just want big kids who are sexually developed at a younger age so they can breed like rats. But such measures unfortunately *reduce* life-span potential and *augment* the frequency and number of diseases, including cancer, and allow these diseases to occur at a younger age. Settling for a slower growth rate and slightly smaller body size under a regime of caloric undernutrition would secure a longer life with fewer diseases, and very possibly increase intelligence. The diet you want to select depends on what you want to optimize.

Both Cornaro, the Venetian, and Sir Francis Bacon, who praised abstemiousness, knew better than modern doctors. This isn't surprising. According to the Government Accounting Office, federal spending on health programs between 1972 and 1979 totalled fully sixty-three billion dollars; of that, only three million was dedicated to nutrition education in medical schools, and half of that was withheld in an effort to reduce federal spending. My own experience in research and education supports the view that nutrition is the most neglected of any major area in the nation's medical schools. This neglect is due not only to a lack of funding but also to the pigheaded irresponsibility of some educators. Nobody doubts that nutrition needs more exposure in the curriculum, but nobody is willing to give up a portion of the time allotted to his own particular subject during the four-year medical school course to allow this to happen. Higher education tends to be built around what professors want to teach rather than what students need to know.

A few of the nonacademic dietary advocates are clearly ahead of the schools. At least three popular modern diets are worth discussing in terms of what we now know about survival curves in general: The Nathan Pritikin program, the Scarsdale Medical Diet, and the high-protein regimen of Dr. Robert Atkins.

Pritikin's dietary and exercise programs are excellent.[22] They will certainly increase life expectancy (50 percent survival) of whoever graduates from and thereafter sticks to the twenty-six day course given at his Longevity Institute in Santa Monica, California. Despite his claims, however, his recommendations are not likely to increase maximum life span. The regimen will, I believe, inhibit the development of a number of diseases, but not retard the rate of aging. Pritikin makes much of the heartiness of people like the Tarahumara Indians of Mexico who still live on a primitive diet rich in grains and seasonal vegetables but low in meat and fat, and argues that his diet ". . . is probably the most feasible method of attaining an extra 20 to 30 years of vigorous life." Particularly aimed at preventing arteriosclerosis, the diet calls for 10 percent calories from fat, 10 percent from protein, and 80 percent from complex carbohydrates. It prohibits refined sugar, honey, and molasses as well as alcohol, caffeine, tobacco, and table salt, and is comprised chiefly of whole grains, vegetables, legumes, and fruits. The claim is made that it will not only prevent arteriosclerosis, heart disease, diabetes, and other forms of degenerative illness but that patients can be "returned to normal functions," which means normal blood pressure and normal levels of cholesterol, glucose (sugar), and triglycerides (fats) in the blood. There is medical dispute about such "cures"—not denial that they occur but about the nature of the documentation, which is largely anecdotal. My own impression is that a reversal of actual blood-vessel lesions might well occur on such a diet. We do know that arteriosclerosis can be brought on and then made to regress in monkeys, that it's not necessarily irreversible. The Pritikin diet resembles "Diet D" of the American Heart Association, its "extremely low fat" diet, which derives only 10–15 percent of calories from fat. Pritikin claims that a low fat diet can actually eliminate the fatty deposits which have built up within the walls of aging human arteries.

The Scarsdale Diet, devised and popularized by the late Dr. Herman Tarnower,[23] averages 1,000 calories per day with 43 percent protein, 22.5 percent fat, and 34.5 percent carbohydrates. This is a higher protein intake than in the typical American diet of about 15 percent protein, but lower in fat. (The American diet is around 40–45 percent fat.) Nevertheless, because of the low total intake of calories, the body must supplement its energy needs by burning fats, both those in the food and those already piled up in the fat depots of the body. The burning of fats yields by-products known as ketones. (Acetone, for example, is a common ketone that most people are familiar with.) Ketones curb the appetite, which makes the diet easier to follow. In the Scarsdale diet the 1,000 calorie regimen is alternated every two weeks with a more moderate, non-ketonic intake of 1,500 to 1,700 calories (depending on body size). This 1,500–1,700 calorie regimen is a maintenance level. Whenever you get four pounds above a certain weight (charts are given showing what your weight should be for your sex and height), you return to the 1,000 calorie diet until the four, pounds are off.

Dr. Atkins Diet Revolution[24] begins with a high protein, high fat, and *zero* carbohydrate regime, with gradual reintroduction of carbohydrates but always at a low enough level that the dieter remains in ketosis as determined by testing the urine with Ketostix obtained from the drugstore. According to Atkins, ketosis of this nature is harmless, as opposed to the ketoacidosis of diabetes. The zero or low carbohydrate diet supposedly works by stimulating the body to produce a fat-mobilizing hormone, although there's some doubt as to whether adult fatty tissues are in fact very susceptible to such a hormone.[25] Producing dramatic weight loss without hunger and without the necessity of significant caloric restriction, Atkins's diet works because it reduces or controls appetite, to some extent mobilizes and degrades fat, and has a strong diuretic effect. The maintenance diet remains a relatively high protein, high fat, relatively low carbohydrate formula. If any lost weight returns, you step back into the first weeks of the zero carbohydrate regime.

These are among the most popular, most talked about, and most written about diets of today. Let's consider them from the standpoint of ease and effectiveness at inducing weight loss (the reason most people go on a diet) and from the standpoints of probable effects on general health (i.e., 50 percent survival) and maximum life-span potential.

The Scarsdale and the Atkins diets are both effective ways of achieving prompt weight loss, the Atkins diet being somewhat easier to follow but more controversial from the health standpoint. The Pritikin regime is more difficult to follow because it does not evoke the hunger-diminishing effects of mild ketosis.

In terms of long-term health and maximum life span, we are forced to derive our opinion from what we know from animal experiments, because appropriate published long-term studies in human beings with these diets are nonexistent. We know from results with animals that the key element in prolongation of maximum life span must be caloric restriction, in fact quite servere caloric undernutrition, so long as it does not coexist with malnutrition. The overall caloric level is more important than the relative amounts of protein, fat, and carbohydrate, but once that level has been achieved, proper protein, fat, and carbohydrate ratios may allow some additional benefits. Within these limits, animal experiments indicate pretty clearly that a high protein diet is best during the early growing years, with a progressive reduction in protein intake through middle age, and a relatively low protein regimen in late life. In mice or rats this means about 25 percent protein in youth and down to 6–8 percent by 50 percent survival time. The shift should be balanced between proteins and carbohydrate, with the fat content being relatively low at all times. (Our longevity mouse diet is about 13 percent fat, and we think even that may be excessive.)

When started near the time of weaning, severe caloric undernutrition, while it prolongs maximum life span of survivors, leads to a slight increase in mortality in early life. Thus it would not be acceptable to begin by severely restricting very young children. Those who survived would live to be 140 or more years of age, but some would not survive the rigor of the initial course, and would die quite young. If the restriction were instituted later in life, an increase in mortality would occur only if the reduction in caloric intake were too abrupt. If the reduction were instituted gradually enough to induce major weight loss over a long period (three months in the mouse = four to five years in man), mortality at all stages should be decreased, 50 percent and maximum survivals significantly increased, and the incidences of various diseases, including cancer, sharply curtailed. Those diseases which still occurred would do so at a later chronologic age.

Judging from animal studies, it seems quite clear to me that while it is probably the easiest and most effective diet for inducing prompt weight loss and keeping slim thereafter, the Atkins high protein, unrestricted caloric, relatively high fat refreshment is a gerontological catastrophe. It's almost exactly opposite in essentially all respects to the results of forty years of nutritional gerontologic studies. However, one must be fair in saying that Atkins's precise regime of zero carbohydrate provender has not really been studied in animals.

While I believe it has serious drawbacks, the Scarsdale diet comes closest to the practice preached from the age of 38 by our pioneer friend, Luigi Cornaro. While the chance of any single person living so long is less than one in ten thousand, a single person's experience doesn't constitute an experiment.

(However, Dr. A. Guenoit, president of the Paris Medical Academy, followed a somewhat less restrictive Cornaro-type regimen,[26] and died in 1935 at the age of 102.) According to Cornaro's own account, his daily diet consisted of a little meat, one egg yolk, bread, and soup, all amounting to twelve ounces per day. This would yield around a 1,500 calorie diet or less. For a five foot six inch man the Scarsdale diet calls for 1,690–1,860 calorie daily maintenance intake and a protein, fat, carbohydrate ratio roughly resembling Cornaro's. However, the Scarsdale "desired weight" of 130–143 pounds for a five foot six inch man is too much to lead to extension of maximum life span. That weight for that height does not add up to a fat man, but it exceeds our caloric goal of "undernutrition without malnutrition."

The Pritikin regime is without doubt closer to the successful animal diets than are either of the others, and might certainly be expected to decrease incidences of degenerative diseases and to increase 50 percent survival. Maximum life span is not likely to be increased because Pritikin places no restriction on food quantity so long as only "permissible" foods are consumed. Also, his recommendations against supplemental vitamins and other items such as antioxidants are gerontologically uninformed, as we shall see in the next chapter.

It's curious to note that Pritikin thinks his diet, which is low in protein and heavy on complex carbohydrates, "revives the types of food available when our physiology evolved to its present complexity," whereas Atkins believes that his high protein prescription corresponds to that of prehistoric, supposedly largely carnivorous man. Atkins may be closer to being correct in terms of very early man, man the hunter and flesh-gatherer, and Pritikin in terms of somewhat later societies, those near the dawn of agriculture, and also for modern primitive socieities like the Tarahumara Indians of Mexico and the Hunza of India. The Hunza diet is relatively low in protein, calories, and fat, and the protein eaten is mostly derived from vegetable rather than animal sources.

The fact is, however, that both Pritikin's and Atkins's arguments relating to "evolutionary" man are largely irrelevant since evolutionary pressure tends to decline in late middle and old age. Some may remain, as suggested by the fact that the leader of an elephant herd is typically a post-reproductive female. Where there is a long period of childhood dependency and a low reproductive rate, as in elephants and man, there may have occurred a degree of evolution of post-reproductive survival. For the most part, however, the strategy of evolution has been to postpone inherited disease susceptibilities until beyond the childbearing age, thus neutralizing their genetic influence. The major degenerative diseases occur in late life because they've been postponed to that period. People with the genetic tendency to get cancer at, say, age 25 are likely to be weeded out early and no longer contribute to the genetic pool. Therefore, this particular age-specific trait tends not to be passed on but to be eliminated by the natural selective forces of evolution. But the susceptibility to develop cancer at age 65 will not be eliminated from the genetic pool because the afflicted person will generally already have accomplished all his or her potential procreation.

Since primitive man had a far shorter 50 percent survival than modern man, except for rare individuals, he would not have lived long enough to develop degenerative diseases. The best possible diet for early man would have depended on what was evolutionarily best to ensure his survival under prehistoric conditions. I suppose that would have been to be bigger, swifter, stronger, and as soon as possible—precisely what modern academic nutritionists generally do tend to strive for in their dietary recommendations. These goals may have been fine for primitive man's situation, but as we've seen the food intake that leads to them is suboptimal for maximizing life span and minimizing late-life diseases. In this sense modern academic nutritionists are about fifty thousand years out of date.

6

Keep Cool, Methuselah

It has been known for some time that fruit flies live longer at a temperature slightly reduced from what they normally experience. This fruit fly information would be more interesting to us if we also, like fruit flies, were insects, if we had therefore divided the great animal kingdom into insects and non-insects, and had convinced ourselves that we fruit flies were evolution's crowning achievement. But we're not fruit flies. We're vertebrates. We have divided the animal kingdom into vertebrates and invertebrates.

Fence lizards are also vertebrates, with hearts, livers, and guts roughly similar to ours; so when it came to my attention that fence lizards enjoy a life span of two years in the cold climate of New England compared to only one year in palm-frolicking Florida, I was more interested than I had been in the effect of temperature on the life span of fruit flies.

To me, it seemed probable that lowering internal body temperature might also prolong life span in those other vertebrates that, like lizards, are poikilothermic, that is, those whose temperature is the same as their surroundings, because they have no automatic mechanism for controlling internal temperature. The idea needed experimental verification in the laboratory. Once it was verified, it was necessary to inquire whether the longer life span of the chillier fence lizards and other coldbloods was due simply to a general metabolic slowdown. That would be the most straightforward guess, but it might be wrong. It would have to be wrong for the whole phenomenon to be of major interest to the longevity seeker. After all, who would want to creep through a longer life at only half speed? People would stop you in the street and try to wind you up out of sympathy.

The cause of the increased life span of coldbloods at lower temperatures could easily be more complicated than general metabolic slowdown. In coldbloods the speed of many of the chemical reactions involved in metabolism is independent of temperature over a wide range. Or at different temperatures the animals may simply use different metabolic pathways: they may "metabolically reorganize."

In a quest for answers to these intriguing questions, I found myself some years ago in an airplane heading from Los Angeles toward the frontier separating Brazil from Argentina, passing high over the rain forests of the north central Amazon, the Guaporé River, and the scrub forest of the Mato Grosso, flying southward with the change of seasons. I was on a special kind of fishing trip.

The shortest-lived, evolutionarily advanced coldblooded vertebrate in the world is the annual fish, and several large species of annuals can be found in the province of Buenos Aires, Argentina. I planned to study them in the field, catch some, bring them back alive to my laboratory in Los Angeles, and establish an experimental colony.

When the plane landed in Buenos Aires, I retrieved my gear: a suitcase, two large styrofoam boxes containing fish nets, plastic bags, chemicals for measuring the status of the habitat, tablets that would dissolve slowly in water while giving off oxygen, and other materials. The next morning I went to the Museum of Natural History, joined my host, fish expert Dr. Rogelio Lopez, and set out with him on a series of splendid fishing days.

Annual fish have apparently evolved a short life span because they live in small ponds or water holes that dry up during the summer. A spawning pair wriggle head down together into the soft mud. She lays eggs, he fertilizes. They do this a number of times, with many partners. As the water evaporates, the fish die, but the eggs survive in the slightly damp earth of the dried-up pond and hatch with the next season's rains in the revived ponds. You might even find the hatchlings in the eighteen-inch deep hole made by a cow's hoof the year before in soft mud which dried to become the cast of a hoof, then was filled by the rains to become a marvelous receptacle of life. In such a hole later that year in Brazil I would find specimens of *Cynolebias melanotaenia,* an annual popularly known as the fighting gaucho. The eggs which hatched into these gaucho fish had doubtless been carried there from another water hole on the hoof and fur of the cow who, making her imprint, drove the eggs into the mud.

Fifteen miles south of Buenos Aires, extending along both sides of the highway and between the highway and wide flat cattle fields, Rogelio and I found long wide shallow ponds, muddy, wholly opaque, half-choked with floating vegetation and containing two separate species of annual fish, including *Cynolebias bellotti,* the Argentine pearlfish with which I would do most of my temperature experiments over the next several years. The male *bellotti* is a bright speckled green, the female a dark speckled brown. Fully grown, both are an inch and a half long.

We donned chest-high rubber waders and unlimbered Rogelio's seine net, eight feet long, three feet broad and laced at either end to wooden poles. Each of us grabbed a pole. Standing about six feet apart and holding our poles end down in the knee-deep water in front of us, we charged forward side by side with the net stretched between us like a giant scoop. Using this seining technic, if you haven't fallen on your professorial bottom at the end of the charge, you will have caught some fish. From this bottoms-up adventure sprang the gerontological colony of fish I established in my laboratory back at UCLA: *Cynolebias elongatus, bellotti, adlophi,* along with *Trigonectes strigabundus* scooped from a single pool near Forte Principe, Brazil, in the deep jungle of the Mato Grosso itself. Batches of fish from these various collection points were shipped by air freight to Los Angeles, with oxygen tablets bubbling in their semi-sealed containers; but those which survived best I carried home with me on the adjacent seat on my return airplane, dousing them with oxygen from the plane's own tank, courtesy of Pan American World Airways.

At UCLA my colleague, Dr. Robert Liu, and I raised many successive generations of the handsome fish, allowing them to spawn in peat moss at the bottoms of tanks whose water was carefully controlled to match the original South American habitats as closely as possible. I had been careful to determine the hardness, degree of acidity, and other characteristics of the fishes' native waters. In the laboratory they lived their short life spans of about one year even if the water was not allowed to dry up, and they did indeed reveal signs of true aging before they died. Old annuals developed humped backs, they decreased in length, just as a human's stature decreases a few inches with advanced age; they showed microscopic changes in the thyroid gland and the liver and had arthritic degeneration of the spine.

But we found all these changes could be delayed and life span prolonged by keeping the temperature of the water, and hence of the fish, a few degrees colder. At a lower temperature their maximum life span would actually double. Furthermore, fish reared at 59°F grew faster and wound up bigger than those reared at 68°F, sure evidence that the colder temperature had not exerted its influence simply by a general metabolic slowdown. Finally, the chemical structure of the fishes' connective tissue—collagen—indicated that the aging process had been truly decelerated. Thus, the information about coldblooded animals suggested by the natural history of North American fence lizards had been verified in the laboratory with the South American fish.

We were fascinated to discover that the life-span-prolonging effect of lowered temperature was most operative during the last half of life. During the first half it was much less influential. Dietary restriction, on the other hand, as shown in the last chapter, is most influential during the first half of life.

We found the effects of the two regimes to be additive. By dietary restriction during the first half and temperature reduction thereafter, the life span of fish could be increased threefold. During their greatly extended life spans the experimental fish remained just as active and as sexually busy as fully-fed younger fish kept at a normal temperature.

But what about mammals and humans, the so-called "homeothermic" or warm-blooded vertebrates? Except for the special situation of hibernation, scientists have no data at all on long-term effects of reduced internal body temperature in warm-bloods. Data from short-term temperature reduction are available, for instance, from packing anesthetized people in ice for open heart surgery. Some reports describe adverse physiological effects of hypothermia (reduced core temperature) in humans when temperature falls below 95°F, but other studies have found that patients undergoing hypothermia down to 86–90°F, as part of a clinical regime, remain rational, their mental states varying from fully alert to mildly drowsy. In 1973 Dr. L.K. Kothari and colleagues of the Ravindranath Medical College, in Udaipur, India,[1] carefully monitored a yogi named Satyamurti who underwent an eight day foodless confinement in a sealed underground pit. According to their measurements, the yogi brought his temperature down to 85°F, far below the normal value of 98.6°F, and without suffering any ill effects, a self-induced hypothermia hitherto unknown in man.

The above information is admittedly scant, and it refers not to long-term but to short-term (acute) hypothermia, during which the body would not have had time to adapt to the lower temperature, to "metabolically reorganize."

What indeed is the ideal body temperature for humans? This is the same sort of question we've asked about growth rate and body size in relation to dietary restriction. The question is, ideal for what? Our temperature of 98.6°F was set by evolution as optimal for what we were all doing back in our pleistocene days 100,000 or 200,000 years ago; trapping mastodons and dodging sabre-tooth tigers on grueling hunting trips. But 98.6°F is not necessarily optimal for today, when we're taking the great trips of intelligence and imagination. Perhaps we can't depend on evolution any more. We have to adjust our nature all by ourselves.

Although lowering the temperature of the environment causes fish and fence lizards to live longer by lowering their core body temperatures, it is not possible to do this with warm-blooded mammals. We mammals possess a complicated internal mechanism for maintaining our core temperature at or near a fixed, preset level.[2] Changing the outside temperature alters only our superficial skin temperature.

Our primary controlling thermostat is located in a primitive portion of the brain, near the base of the skull, an area known as the hypothalamus. After sensing the temperature of the blood, the hypothalamus fires off the appropriate regulatory commands. If the blood is slightly cooler than the hypothalamus reference set point, shivering results, and this builds up internal body heat. If the blood is warmer, humans begin to sweat and dogs to pant. Body temperature can also be altered by information from peripheral nerve sensors. If we enter a cold room, for example, we begin shivering long before our blood runs cold. A peripheral nerve reflex has served to raise the reference set point in the brain, which now senses blood of normal temperature as being cold. By these delicate bodily arrangements our internal temperature is kept within a narrow range, hovering around 98.6°F regardless of what's outside. So for humans there is no life-span advantage to living in cold Canada instead of in hot Africa.

If we could control the reference mechanism in the hypothalamus, however, we could control body temperature. Hibernation involves such control. It does not abandon temperature regulation but it precisely lowers and resets the central thermostat's set point to conserve energy for lasting through the winter. The fact that hibernation is indulged in by a number of higher vertebrates physiologically similar to us, like bears, squirrels, and hamsters, who can take their body temperature down to a point half way toward freezing, does suggest that any deleterious effects from lowering core temperature in man might result from an unreset hypothalamus firing off last-ditch commands—in other words, going into frenzied stress as it tries to counteract the fall in temperature. In short the harmful effects of cooling are not necessarily due to any intrinsic inabilities of human cells and organs to function at a lower temperature. But we do not yet know how the hibernators adjust their central thermostats.

If silver rods, which are good conductors of heat, are surgically placed in the hypothalamus of a rodent and allowed to project out through the skull, the hypothalamus can be cooled or warmed by cooling or warming the external portions of the rods. If the rods are cooled, the animal will shiver and raise its body temperature even if the actual environmental temperature is already quite warm. If the rod is warmed, an opposite effect occurs. Some of the NASA scientists have suggested to me that implantation into the human hypothalamus of an electrical device whose temperature could be raised by radio wave transmission might achieve a similar result. Still, this surgical technic would not be the same as resetting the central setpoint, as hibernators do.

The hypothalamic mechanism can also be influenced by drugs. In experiments with mice Dr. Liu and I found that THC, the active ingredient of marijuana, and also the tranquilizer chlorpromazine could either lower the set point or turn the switch completely off, depending on dosage.[3] High doses of THC, for example, allow mice to drop their body temperature to the temperature of the environment. Because of their extremely low toxicity, THC or less purified marijuana derivatives might be excellent drugs for lowering body temperature for certain types of surgery, but they would not induce chronic hypothermia. We found that upon repeated exposure to the drugs (two to three times in the same month), animals become resistant to the temperature lowering effects. It's unfortunate, some might think, that one cannot stay cool by staying high all the time, because the potential reward in terms of life-span extension could be remarkable. Calculated on thermodynamic principles by Dr. B. Rosenberg and co-workers from Northwestern University, the curves of Figure 6.1 show what survival for humans might look like if the hypothalamic switch were reset at various levels below present levels in each of us.[4]

Since drugs capable of resetting the switch are not yet available, one wonders whether biofeedback and/or yogic techniques such as Yogi Satyamurti undoubtedly employed in his sealed underground pit might be more successful. To a certain extent you can learn control over the autonomic, or involuntary, nervous system. You can slow your heart rate, cure headaches, render your skin temperature hotter or colder, decrease acid secretion by the stomach, and make your brain waves beat out the alpha rhythm of transcendental meditation . . . all by biofeedback. Gaining control through biofeedback requires an appropriate indicator system that will increase the brightness of a light or change the pitch of a sound when your mind is going in the right direction to obtain the desired response, as illustrated in Figure 6.2. Making the mind

Predicted survival curves of humans

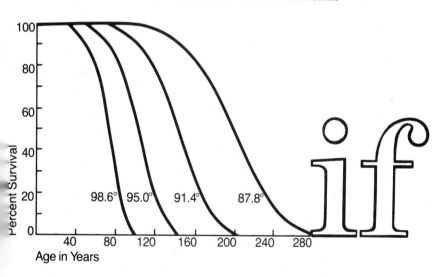

the thermostat in the brain which controls body temperature could be reset from 98.6° to lower levels.

Figure 6.1

How biofeedback works.

correct mental direction or condition

indicating and reinforcing   leading to

external light bulb to glow brighter   decreased gastric acid secretion

causing   which is

recorded by acidity measuring device which you have swallowed

correct mental direction or condition

indicating and reinforcing   leading to

you hear your heart rate slow down   decreased heart rate

so that   which is

made audible by a stethoscope

These flow charts illustrate how two biofeedback techniques allow control of physiologic functions by enabling you to symbolically see, or hear, and control them. The quicker you can sense a change, the easier you can learn to control it. If time from a slight decrease in gastric acid secretion to a slightly brighter glowing of the bulb is more than one minute, biofeedback control is difficult to learn.

Figure 6.2

go in the right direction is tricky, but we are constantly doing it, at least for voluntary responses. If you raise your arm, your mind is telling your arm to go up, but you've no real sensation of mental activity. As Wittgenstein put it, "This strange thing, thought, but it does not seem strange while we are thinking." Your arm just goes up, that's all. In this case the indicator system is immediately visual and sensorial. Critical to the learning of even these ordinary voluntary responses, as well as the autonomic ones, is that the feedback must be immediate or almost so. If ten minutes had to elapse for your arm to go up after you thought "Up, arm!," you would never raise your glass to your lips. (Some of the larger dinosaurs apparently had an "extra brain" down around the pelvis just to compensate for huge size and cope with the problem of conduction time within a very elongated nerve network.) If feedback time exceeds even one or two minutes, control of bodily functions can be very difficult to learn.

And even if you could switch the regulatory thermostat in your hypothalamus completely off, quite a bit of time would be required for the internal body temperature to fall substantially. As a pathologist I can tell you that under normal conditions a dead human body cools off at the rate of only about one degree per hour. That's clearly too slow (and you can't set the hypothalamic switch any lower than by dying). It's not likely therefore that lowering internal temperature could be learned by the usual biofeedback approach. Might there be other methods, I wondered.

Just to help set goals within a region of established possibilities, I thought it would be helpful to know if any of the skilled yoga masters could manipulate their internal temperatures by methods less drastic than trancing out in underground isolation chambers. Tales of surprising physiological feats are continually coming out of India, Tibet, and the Arab lands of the Sufis. Therefore, a few years after my South American fishing trip I found myself once more in an airplane, but this time heading eastward from Los Angeles toward the great shark-toothed subcontinent that hangs off the underbelly of Asia: India, the Land of Many Parts, None of Which

Fit, the Land of Surprises. My intention was to measure body temperature regulation in Indian yogis.

Having arrived in New Delhi, I watched airport customs pick through the gear from my blue Wilderness Experience backpack, gear less plentiful and less varied than I had taken to South America—mainly personal effects and a sensitive electronic telethermometer with dermal, oral, armpit, and rectal probes. After exiting from the airport into the hot October Indian sun, and escaping the throng of drivers of three-wheeled minitaxis clamoring to take the visitor somewhere, caught up in the first press of the street scene of India, I wrote in my journal, ". . . the image of being out in the bush and coming to a store, but it's another language, I mean entirely another language, not even Indo-European, and you try to tell them that what you want is a rubber band."

This is the best way to enter India.

I was feeling footloose in my choice of directions. Other than to give a few lectures, I had made no prearrangements about what to do or whom to see. I had been informed that the ablest yogis—including those yogis grouped under the generic name of *sadhu,* derived from the Sanskrit *siddha* (he who has attained miraculous power)—were not likely to be hanging around universities. Where therefore should I look for a certain Ramana Maharshi, who it was said could take you inside the hollow hill where the *sadhus* of all ages meet? Perhaps on the old Poona Mahableshwar road near the big stone belonging to Kamarli Dervish which can only be lifted by the fingers of eleven strong men. I allowed one foot to follow the other.

A few weeks later I found myself in Bombay entering the Kolaba district to visit a wealthy Parsee. He opened the embossed door to his apartment and conducted me into a huge living room carpeted with rich oriental rugs upon which rested wide brass stands and teakwood chairs.

The Parsee smoked cigarettes and we drank iced rum. Only a few miles away, I knew, were the massive, squat, circular Towers of Silence where the Parsees after death are picked clean by vultures. Zoroastrianism, one of the world's oldest religions, founded by the Persian prophet Zoroaster in the seventh century B.C., survives today mostly only among these Parsees of India. They are sun and fire worshippers, and at death their bodies are laid out above ground until the flesh is entirely eaten by the great birds; then the skeleton is retrieved. At the last analysis they believe that the whole creation will enjoy eternal bliss in the presence of Ohrmuzd, the Lord.

I told my gracious Parsee host what I was doing in India and he conjectured I'd have trouble getting cooperation from the yogis, who would want to put me on another track, their own. We discussed Gurdjieff and Ouspensky and ceremonial magic, whose works the Parsee had explored heavily at one time. He advised me to seek out the half-naked *sadhus* around Hardwar and Rishikesh to continue my yogic studies. But that would take enormous stamina on my part as the *sadhus* often march twenty miles a day and are pretty crazy. I thought the Parsee was pretty crazy himself, although there was much half-truth in what he foretold, and I was half grateful.

Leaving him, I proceeded to the nearby hill town of Poona, where the huge, upstairs, partially roofed-over balcony of an old gray mansion was filled with domestic and foreign devotees of the famous Swami Rajneesh. Most of the devotees wore bright orange cotton cloth, as sarees, lungis, dhotis, or pyjama tops and pants. Nodding to and fro like a field of poppies, they waited patiently for the Swami himself.

At last he appeared through a side door. Clad in a white sheet wound togalike around his well-proportioned body, he mounted the two-foot-high carpeted platform at one end of the room, relaxed into an overstuffed chair, and tapped his index finger on the microphone next to him.

The instrument clicked audibly. The current was definitely on. The poppies popped to attention.

Swami Rajneesh, the Sage of Poona, began the morning's lecture, which was about Jesus.

Jesus asked his disciples, "Who am I?" Then Peter answered, "Thou art like a righteous angel." This in fact says nothing about Jesus but everything about Peter. It was because of Peter that the Church became self-righteous and moralistic. Then came Matthew's turn. He said, "Thou art like a wise man of understanding." From Matthew the Church derived its obsession for fine-spun theology. Then Thomas said, "Master, my mouth will not be capable of saying whom thou art like." Thomas came closest, therefore his answer was excluded from the Authorized Version of the Bible. But Jesus replied to each of them, "I am not thy master": for what Jesus and all great people like him are about is BEING.

The Swami's lecture at this instant was punctuated by an audible drawing-in of breath by his devotees, the equivalent of "Right On" in other times and places.

I tiptoed out. It had been a wonderful sermon but I could not imagine I would be allowed to put my electronic telethermometer up Swami Rajneesh's respectable rectum.

Most of the big-time or even locally well-known and accessible yogis I met for the remainder of my trip were on quite resplendent ego trips, and were not generally able to come off them enough to be very helpful. Swami Rama, who had visited the Menninger Clinic in Topeka, Kansas, boasted that he could boil water in his naked hand. He held his cupped hand out but poured no water into it. In New Delhi Mrs. Ghandi's personal yoga master, Dhorendra Bramachara, proudly showed me how he could swallow his tongue, and back it went into his posterior pharynx, after which he was speechless. In the Patiyala House in Hardwar, Swami Ashish reclined on a raised pink platform under an embroidered pink canopy, while a young man whom the Swami whisperingly identified as a Cleveland lawyer was performing *Kapalbhati* or vigorous hyperventilation in and out 120 times a minute. That's fast. I could see the lawyer was really comin' round the bend.

I finally decided to follow the Parsee's suggestion and seek out the *sadhus* who roam in packs or live on buffalo milk and fruit in little thatched huts in the open air in the forests and bush on the banks of the upper Ganges. These gentlemen were more to my taste and utility. It is alleged that among their ranks dwell malefactors and fugitives who hide out by assuming the pretense of holiness, but most of the *sadhus* have simply left their homes in order to concentrate on physical and spiritual disciplines. To become a *sadhu* is to be set apart: hermits following vows of poverty and celibacy and depending largely on the charity of householders for their food. I spent several days among them, sleeping at night under a blanket beneath a tree, but nothing positive came of the experience for my experiments.

My companion and interpreter, orange-robed Swami Vasant whom I had met on the street in the nearby holy city of Hardwar, a small, thin old man who whenever I had taken him to dinner ate enough to last through the interregnum, confirmed what I had been learning, that one major characteristic of the most advanced yogis in terms of mastery of techniques is physical inaccessibility and few or no followers. Look for them in the high mountains, in caves, in the deep forests, and not near a town or on a podium or a dais. A good place for saints and advanced practioners is the area of the Jhilmil caves fifteen miles from Hardwar. Led by my guide, I tramped up there. The yogis of the caves are a better educated lot than the *sadhus* living along the river banks. Involved in heavy spiritual and isolation trips, with daylong periods of meditation, they were receptive once they realized that I was also on a serious quest.

Some could lower their internal body temperature as much as one degree by a combination of meditation and breathing methods. In several days' testing of two of them, Swamis Udasin and Ram Dayal, I recorded average internal or rectal body temperatures of 94 to 95°F. Thus a few yogis, those who live in the Himalayan caves or forests and with much meditation and (as I also observed) subsistence on very low calorie diets, seem to be permanently three or four degrees colder than normal. Theirs must represent a steady-state adaption, but not a type of hibernation, because they were not apathetic or slowed down. Referring to Figure 6.1, we see that my demonstration of low body temperature affords some biological rationality to the stories of yogis who claim extremely long lives, although these claims cannot be authenticated by reliable

birth records. Furthermore, while becoming a full-time isolated yogic practitioner is hardly feasible for us in the West, my
evidence does indicate that successful adaptation to a lower
body temperature, if we could find an easier way of lowering
it, would by physiologically possible. This was the main question I had set out to answer.

To meet as a final experience the great yoga master, Indra,
whom author Elwyn Chamberlain later used for a model in his
novel *Gates of Fire*, required half a day's journey through ever
smaller, filthy backcountry villages, followed by a five-hour
walk into tiger, wild pig, and monkey-filled jungles. Finally I
arrived at Indra's acre of cleared land planted with rice and
corn. He was living in a small mud-brick enclosure with a
six-foot high wall, all open above the wall except for corner-
posts, and a high thatched roof, a habitation called an *akara*.
Nearby were several straw lean-tos for visitors. Visitors were
few and sometimes none. That night Indra, who plays excellent harmonium, tintar, conch, and an assortment of drums,
gave a concert for his visitors, of which there were only three,
including me. Ritualistically sharing his chillum of grass, he
sang these songs in the deep jungle night, as we sat around a
sacred dunhi fire and tigers coughed off someplace outside the
light: Song to Ganesh, Lord of Obstacles; Song to Maha Kali,
the Divine Mother; The 110 Names of Kali; The River Ganga;
Song about a bird called Chakur who goes mad when he sees
the moon; Hail to Auspicious Kali, who wears a necklace of
skulls and holds a skull-bowl; Praise to Durga, the World
Mother, who destroys all the Demons of the Kali Yuga; a song
asking for a boat to cross the sea of existence.

I was unable to persuade Indra to do any temperature
experiments with me, but it didn't matter much anymore. I
found that India, and Indra, had cooled me out. And during
my stay with Indra my instruction took a fascinating historical
turn. In the ancient medical text, *The Charaka Samhita*, I found
written:

It came about that in the course of time the Rishis became,
by taking to an urbanized diet and drugs, luxurious and

leisurely in their habits and for the most part deficient in health. Finding themselves unequal to the observance of the code of obligations which the order entailed and realising that the blame lay with their urban residence, these Rishis returned to their original dwelling, remote from the evils of city life, namely the Himalayas which are auspicious, holy, majestic.

One of the original elixirs of life, *Soma*, came from these regions, and forms a principal nostrum of the branch of Aryuvedic or Hindu medicine known as Kaya Kulp, the science of rejuvenation. *Soma* itself belongs to Rasayana, the science of potions, and is made from "sovereign herbs growing in the Himalayas, ripe with potency." These include climbing asparagus, yam, ginkgo fruit, wild dill, wild fennel, plus others and at least one secret one; but the trick is in the making as much as in the ingredients, and the secret of how to make *Soma* is not as clear to us today as it must have been to the Rishis.

We would know how to use it, however, if we could ever get any. Its use and benefits are described in another health and medical text, *The Sushruta Samhita,* where we are instructed that the gods created *Soma* to prevent the decay and death of the body.

An inner chamber in a comfortable site protected on each side and provided with all kinds of accessories and attendants should be first secured before taking the juice of the *Soma.* Then at an auspicious hour on an auspicious day marked by favorable astral combinations and lunar phase, the person desirous of using the *Soma* should enter the inner chamber after having his system cleansed with the proper emetics, purgatives, etc. and having had his diet in the proper order. The bulb of the *Soma* plant should be pricked with a golden needle and a quantity of the secreted milky exudation collected in a golden vessel. The patient should drink off a measure of the secreted juice at a draught without tasting it, and the remainder, if any, should be cast into water. Then, having controlled his mind and speech with the vows of *Yama* (paramount duties) and *Niyama* (minor duties), he should stay in the inner chamber. He may, after taking his meal in the evening and hearing benedictory words, lie down on a mattress of grass covered with a black deer skin and thus pass the night, and may take cold water when thirsty. Then, having got out of his bed in the morning, he should hear benedictory words recited and have benedictory rites performed unto him. Vomitings mark the digestion of the *Soma* juice and after he has vomited blood-streaked worm-infested matter, milk boiled and cooled should be given him. Worm-infested stools follow on the third day, which help the system in purging off all filth and obnoxious matter accumulated in the organism through errors in diet and conduct.

Swellings appear on the body on the fourth day and worms creep out from all parts of the body. The patient should lie down on a bed strewn over with dust and in the evening should be made to drink a potion of milk as before. He should pass the fifth and sixth days in the same manner, but milk should be given him in the morning and in the evening instead of only in the evening. The muscles become withered by this time and on the seventh day the patient is found to be a mere skeleton covered with skin only, the vital spark being retained by the potency of the *Soma.*

On the morning of the eighth day, the body should be washed with milk and plastered with sandal-paste. From now on the muscles of the body begin to show signs of fresh and vigorous growth, the skin becomes cracked, and the teeth, nails and hair begin to fall off. New teeth, well-formed, symmetrical, strong, hard and as clear as a diamond or crystal will appear on the seventeenth and eighteenth days. Fixed, glossy and coral-coloured fingernails resembling the new rising sun in lustre and possessed of auspicious marks will be found to be growing and hair will begin to grow. The skin will assume the soft hue of a blue lotus or of a ruby stone. Then the person should stir out from the innermost chamber, and stay in the second chamber for ten days. He should not contemplate himself in a mirror during this time owing to his enhanced personal beauty, and should renounce all passions and anger for a further period of ten days.

Keep Cool, Methuselah

The use of the *Soma* plant, the Lord of all medicinal herbs, is followed by rejuvenation of the system, and enables its user to witness ten thousand summers on earth in the full enjoyment of a new and youthful body. Such a person bears a charmed life against fire, water, poison and weapons, and develops great muscular energy. The presence of such a beautiful person gladdens the heart, and the entire *Veda* with all their allied branches of knowledge instinctively dawn upon such a consciousness.

Ten thousand summers with *Soma* sounds better than Coca-Cola or Heinekens to me; but alas, the *Sushruta Samhita* also informs us, "The *Soma* plants are invisible to the impious or the ungrateful, as well as to the unbeliever in the curative virtues of medicine, and to those spiteful to the Brahmans."

So it's not going to be so easy after all. But at least I had learned two things from this brief excursion into ancient texts and modern India. The quest for rejuvenation was an important part of a very old system of medicine, the Aryuvedic system of India; and that a human can induce and adapt to a lowered body temperature and still remain mentally alert and active. This suggests that by keeping cool, you would not be creeping through a longer life at half-speed, but would keep going at normal speed, for a much, much longer time.

7

Practical State of the Art of Life-Span Extension

Many ancient and magical nostrums and procedures are recorded for extending life span and achieving the rejuvenation of old peoples' dreams. We learn from Ovid in his *Metamorphosis* that the sorceress Medea "plunged her dagger into the old man's throat to draw his blood; then in his gaping veins instilled her magic brew, which filled his feeble age with strength he had not known for forty years." In ancient Rome aged men and women sometimes tottered into the arena to drink the fresh blood of dying gladiators, so to prolong their own fast ebbing lives. The major medieval alchemical therapies for rejuvenation involved the use of gold, the withered flesh of mummies, viper meat, and human blood. Count Dracula was a highly successful practicing gerontologist, and Pope Innocent III is credited with having drunk on one occasion the blood of three boys to rejuvenate himself.[1]

Gentler, bloodless remedies have also had their adherents. King David, the ancient physician Galen, Paul of Aeginata, and "the great clinician" Hermann Boerhaave all prescribed the inhalation of the breath of virgins. The German Emperor Frederick Barbarossa is said to have taken their advice, although we cannot judge whether it worked because the experiment terminated when Frederick at age sixty-seven drowned while crossing the Saleph River en route to the Third Crusade. Arnald of Villanova, the renowned fourteenth-century physician, prescribed a rejuvenation treatment to be used every seventh year and consisting of brews, plasters, baths, and fabulous concoctions. I suspect he was writing for an earlier version of *Vogue* magazine. In his *Book of Marvels,* John Mandeville tells of a Fountain of Youth deep in the Asian jungles, while the sixteenth-century German painter, Lucas Cranach, placed his own vision of "The Fountain of Youth" in a verdant European countryside. In Cranach's painting in the Staatliche Museum in Berlin, we see elderly wrinkled ladies (No wrinkled men here, as though men ne'er grew eld!) limping or being drawn in carts down to a Versailles-like garden pool. They enter the pool. They are transformed. They emerge on the other side where robust, youngish gentlemen in buskins and bodkins and jerkins and sloppy expensive hats wait to disport with them among the bushes. Referring to this painting and to these sporting gentlemen, Alex Comfort has remarked in lecture, "Here are the gerontologists."

Perhaps still there in their hearts, but one hopes less chauvinistic in their visions, the gerontologists are now happily arrived at the even greater magic of our own today, an interesting time when old and new dreams as well as nightmares are beginning to be materialized. Therefore, what precisely can we moderns do that promises to stretch our lives beyond our set genetic times, since we can no longer drink the blood of dying gladiators, nor so readily inhale the breath of virgins?

What is practical to do today?

Chopping off the head of the questions as a kind of historical sacrifice, we divide it in two: What is now known and/or available which may extend average human life span (50 percent survival); what may extend maximum human life span?

Regarding the first question, consider the following: Over forty years ago at Jackson Laboratories, Bar Harbor, Maine, Dr. Charles Little and later Dr. George Snell, who won the Nobel prize in 1980, began developing our now familiar inbred strains of mice by mating brother mice to sister mice and from their progeny selecting another brother and sister and mating them, and so on down through the incestuous rodent generations until at fifty or more generations every mouse descended from an original pair became genetically exactly like every other, and each separate succession constituted a separate inbred strain. Consider next that if a cell were taken from my own forearm or my own blood stream and successfully cloned and raised to manhood, there would be hundreds of exactly identical Roy Walfords (except perhaps the original one who would stand out as being astonished and perhaps unnerved to see himself so doubled and redoubled).

Now look at Figure 7.1. Curve A represents the survival of a particular inbred strain of mouse, or of a Roy Walford clone, and curves B, C, D the survivals of other strains or other persons' clones. We see that mouse strains A and B do not enjoy as squared a survival curve as strains C and D. Doubtless there are ways the A and B curves could be further squared, enhancing their strains' average life expectancies (their 50 percent survivals), without necessarily influencing maximum

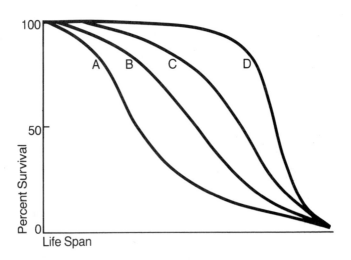

Representative survival curves for four different inbred strains of mice (*A, B, C, and D*), or clone populations from four different humans.

Figure 7.1

survivals. On a genetic basis, however, the shorter-lived A and B mice are stuck with having greater susceptibilities to various diseases than C and D have; but even so, A and B do not necessarily age more rapidly, since maximum life spans are seen to be the same for all.

The situation would be similar for clones derived from different people. Each would be like an inbred strain. If the Roy Walford clone be represented by curve A and, let us say, a Frederick Barbarossa clone by D, then I as a single Roy Walford am apt to live less long than a single Frederick Barbarossa (A is less than D). I may or may not be able to do something about my own chances to achieve a life span greater than the ordained maximum for our species. To increase maximum survival is hard. However, I can with greater confidence undertake to move my personal chances for survival from curve A to B to C to D. To increase 50 percent survival is not so hard. As individuals we don't know how our clone would behave, because each of us is merely the first member of an uncloned clone. We don't know what curve we're potentially on. Only the fortunate minority are already on curve D. Our first question therefore can be framed by asking how to get onto the next higher curve; and the second question, how to extend the endpoint of the curve. In so far as we can answer either or both of these, most of us can live longer than we're supposed to, which is why we all sneaked into the devil's gerontological kitchen in the first place.

Much evidence exists that your 50 percent survival may be extended by combinations of antioxidants like vitamins C, E, the food preservative BHT, the element selenium, and several sulfur-containing amino acids; by certain B vitamins; by a number of brain-reactive drugs; by a regular program of the right exercise; perhaps by thinking right thoughts like the Buddha told us to do (I shall not, however, elaborate on this aspect, not in *this* kitchen); and possibly by having the pituitary gland removed from your head (an interesting but purely experimental procedure only recommended for rats).

The antioxidants neutralize free radicals. We recall from Chapter 4 that free radicals are highly reactive chemical substances with an unpaired electron whirling around a super-activated oxygen atom. They attack membranes, DNA, and other parts of the tissues. Rancid changes in fats and oils result from a series of free radical reactions in which each step is activated by the uptake of an oxygen molecule to yield an auto-oxidation, a potential anti-self reaction besides the immune type and in your own bodily butter. The free radicals within us may originate partially from the environment but are mainly produced spontaneously like sparks from the metabolic machine. The body produces enzymes (examples: superoxide dismutase and catalase) which quickly break down or, in the parlance of the chemist's profession, "scavenge" free radicals. That's why we don't go completely rancid ourselves. All the ingredients for massive free radical oxidation are present in living cells. Cells are impregnated with iron and other metal complexes, drenched in oxygen, enveloped in and shot through with highly unsaturated fats and oils. We would instantly set solid if these became saturated, as they do do and we do in rigor mortis, and as we would do if we were not protected by our scavengers. Without our scavengers we would plasticize. In fact free radical technology forms the basis of the plastics and polymer industry.

Dr. Denham Harman of the University of Nebraska has shown quite convincingly that supplementing the diet with free radical scavengers will substantially increase 50 percent survival, particularly in animal strains like A and B of Figure 7.1. In principle the same happy result ought to accrue for man.

In rodents the amount of free radical scavengers that must be included in the diet to prolong 50 percent survival is much larger than an animal would get in any ordinary diet. In transposing the animal data into possible human application, we shall not get far unless we are bold enough to part company with the Food and Drug Administration, the nutrition moguls of the National Academy of Sciences, and many experts occupying academic chaise longues, because we must in some instances considerably exceed a sacred quantity, the Recommended Daily Allowance (RDA). Experts arrive at the RDA by first considering how much of the vitamin, amino acid, or other material is required to keep people free of specific nutritional deficiency diseases.[2] How much vitamin C do you need to avoid scurvy? Well, it's not much. How much niacin to keep from getting the dermatitis, diarrhea, and dementia which comprise the famed "3D's" of the disease pellagra that once afflicted the people as well as the reputations of the southern United States? Again, not much. Those not-much amounts receive first consideration in arriving at the RDA. Second, the experts determine how much of the material is found in what they consider a healthy diet, one that includes helpings from the four categories of food: dairy goods, meats, vegetables, and fruits. Next the disease prevention miniquantity and the healthy-diet quantity are subjectively judged and juggled to arrive at the RDA. The RDA is therefore never more than and may in some instances be less than that found in a so-called healthy diet. Furthermore, the RDA gives allowances for two age-groups of adults: those aged 25–50 years and those over 51. It is unrealistic to assume that a 50-year-old and a 75-to-85-year-old person have the same requirements.[3] Except by gerontologists, experiments are rarely conducted into the effects of widely different and perhaps quite high dietary levels of RDA materials on life span, the incidence of late-life diseases, and the rate of aging.

The basic conflict is whether food can serve as more than simple nourishment, whether desired reactions can be reinforced by unnatural alimentary means. There is little doubt, however, that at least some such reactions can be reinforced: for example, large amounts of certain amino acids can modify brain function.[4] At the center of the conflict is our old question of optimization. Nutritionists have taken it for granted that what a good diet should supply is just what we needed when we were back in the forests and caves, where the optimum was to be big and strong and fast—and quickly so. Nobody lived long enough to fall victim of late-life diseases anyway in those mighty mastodon days. Today, however, we want to optimize intelligence, life span, and perhaps other things (sexual prowess, if you simply must!) by what we eat, and these could require a different food orientation than what would make you the top slayer of mastodons in Los Angeles. Standard dietary recommendations are designed to help us slay mastodons, but the mastodons were all slain long ago.

The RDA is not slanted toward optimizing modern desires. The great differences we hear among nutritional experts, holistic healers, gerontologists, body builders, aficionados of the cuisine and connoisseurs of fitness often reflect different optimization choices. It's at least refreshing in a too-much me-too world that such an intelligence as Nobel prize-winner Linus Pauling is at World War III with the FDA, the AMA, and the NAS over vitamin C, especially since another biologist, also a Nobelist, Roger J. Williams, wrote in 1976, "Convincing evidence has come to light in recent years that young guinea pigs (whose metabolism is similar to that of man's) need *at least 200 times as much vitamin C for good health* [his italics!] as they do to protect them from scurvy. Accumulating research indicates that the same may be true for human beings."[5] Part of Pauling's semi-ostracism reflects what Dr. Jim Goodwin has termed the "Galileo effect." It wasn't so much Galileo's ideas about the earth's not being the true center of the solar system that landed him in hot water with the Inquisition, as that he wrote in Italian rather than Latin, and ordinary people could understand him. You're not supposed to do that in either religion or science until the "authorities" have determined what the official line should be.

There's an enormous resistance on the part of establishment nutritionists and physicians to recommending more of anything than is present in the daily mastodon diet. In part this resistance comes from honest umbrage at the fads and fallacies that have always plagued the longevity movement, driving establishment experts into demanding almost absolute proof before they will recommend anything purporting to have an anti-aging affect. However, in other health matters this same establishment will rely on merely suggestive and incomplete evidence, or even the mere presumption of authority. From 1930–1960, medical opinion remained ultra-conservative about the benefits of vigorous exercise, regarding it as a form of "stress" that would wear out the body. There was no evidence for this presumptive view, and we know now that in contrast to machines which wear out the more they are used, the organs and tissues develop an adaptive increase in function with use that runs counter to the changes which occur in aging.

Not many years ago it was accepted practice to remove teeth, tonsils, and appendices under the notion that these might be "septic foci" responsible for a wide range of skin rashes, headaches, and vague ailments. That particular craze has subsided.

The dogma dating from about 1950 that diets low in saturated fats and cholesterol and high in polyunsaturated fats would decrease serum cholesterol and check the rise of heart disease was well accepted by clinicians and nutritionists, but on rather incomplete evidence. What has been the effect of twenty-five years of this nutritional policy? Heart disease remains the number one killer. Two of five dietary regimes substituting vegetable oils for butter and animal fats have shown an increase in cancer in humans.[6] In mice, Drs. Gabriel Fernandes, and Robert Good, then of the Memorial Sloan-Kettering Cancer Center although now at the Oklahoma Medical Research Foundation, have shown that several types of cancer are greatly increased by diets high in polyunsaturated fats. There appears to be an increased number of noncardiovascular deaths among people whose blood cholesterol levels have been lowered by a diet high in polyunsaturated fats. Gerontologists know that eating polyunsaturated fats is a good way to increase free radicals. The nongerontological experts have simply remained unaware of this serious potential drawback. The point is, there is easily as much evidence that antioxidants will extend 50 percent survival as that unsaturated fats will help prevent arteriosclerosis, yet the "experts" have enthusiastically embraced unsaturated fats and not antioxidants. The refusal to look without prejudice at the strong presumptive evidence that a number of anti-aging therapies are beneficial is in fact a form of agism on the part of health professionals. Faced with the various inconsistencies outlined above, we shall allow ourselves to embrace what seems good to us.

Deciding what to take to increase one's survival chances

requires extrapolating experimental evidence from rodent to man on the basis of their biological similarities. As they're mostly similar, I shall set down what I and those who follow my advice do in hopes of extending life span. It's guesswork but I believe I can say informed guesswork, and probably sounder than the polyunsaturated margarine fat jumping-to-conclusions story. *Nevertheless, you should not adopt mine or any similar regimen except after consulting with your personal physician.* You should undergo appropriate fitness tests, plus others your physician may suggest, to rule out specific diseases as well as a number of genetic tendencies which might be aggravated by selected dietary excesses, additives, or restrictions. Carefulness extends life span too.

The best free radical scavengers for potential human use include vitamin E, the element selenium, the food additive BHT (bis-hydroxytoluene), possibly vitamin C, and amino acids containing sulfur in the -SH form, specifically cysteine and methionine. All these inactivate free radicals and theoretically could avert damage if delivered to the cellular sites that need protection. Potentially beneficial effects would depend on the animal strain or the uncloned clone that one belongs to. If I personally am a unit of the short-lived A clone (Fig. 7.1), scavengers can move me to a longer-living clone curve. If I'm already so genetically fortunate as to be in clone D, scavengers will probably do me neither good nor harm.

The following list extrapolates for men and women sizable but not megadose quantities of various radical scavengers and antioxidants which have extended the life spans of rats, mice, or other animals. Not an exhaustive list, it's part of what I take daily in divided doses:

Vitamin E	600 International Units
Selenium	160 micrograms
BHT	250 milligrams
Cysteine	300 milligrams
Methionine	120 milligrams
Ascorbyl palmitate	600 milligrams
Vitamin C	1000 milligrams
Bioflavinoids	300 milligrams

The first six are taken just before or during meals and the last two after or between meals. Vitamin C is an acid and best not taken in large doses on an entirely empty stomach. Ascorbyl palmitate is the derivative of vitamin C having the strongest antioxidant properties. Like BHT, it is used as a food preservative. Some of these materials are excreted rapidly by the body once a certain threshold is reached. Thus, to take all the vitamin C at one time, instead of in divided doses throughout the day, would lead to a peak in concentration for a few hours after the one big dose, but only the normal level the rest of the day. Hence the daily divided dosages.

The list includes substantial but not excessively large or megadose quantities of the antioxidants. One might choose to take megadoses, with their unlikely but possible toxic side effects, and seek to be forewarned of these effects by means of frequent laboratory tests in time to lower the doses. Unfortunately the warning system is not necessarily good enough to forestall damage. For example, you could gradually increase your alcohol intake, at the same time running periodic tests of liver and brain function, and reach quite large prolonged alcohol imbibition resulting in damage to yourself, before the warning tests turned positive. The body's organs have too much reserve, and considerable injury may be done before the reserve is overreached and the tests turn positive. Also, a great deal of individual variation exists in response to drugs, and perhaps even to nutrients in large enough quantities. So while they are very probably safe, I am not yet ready to recommend megadose amounts of the various antioxidants.

I'll not describe the spectrum of physiological effects of all the above agents, or of other agents coming up later. That's been done enough already by every minor copyist on the bookshelves of the health food stores. Suffice it to say that the antioxidants extend life span in longterm experiments and doubtless accomplish this mostly by scavenging free radicals.

Vitamin E has been shown to have a slight positive effect on life span in fruit flies and rats, with an increase in 50 percent survival of about 10 percent. In some cell components (microsomes and mitochondria, for those who know their anatomy), it's the only naturally occurring fat-soluble antioxidant. The antioxidant properties of the vitamin E family (the tocopherols) are said to be the reverse of their biologic potency in other kinds of tests: thus, for antioxidant properties d-delta > d-gamma > d-beta > d-alpha tocopherol.[7] Commercial brands of mixed tocopherols, made from wheat germ oil, contain mostly the d-alpha form, and also a fair amount of the female sex hormone estrogen. Among pure tochopherols, only the d-alpha form is readily available. The situation is not perfect but our information allows us to navigate.

Where accessibility within the cell is not restricted, the effectiveness of two or more antioxidants is probably greater than the sum of their individual actions—vitamins E and C in the preservation of meat, for example,[8] and vitamin E and selenium, which together help prevent damage to cell membranes. Vitamin E inhibits the formation of the radicals called hydroperoxides. In the energy factories of the cell (the mitochondria) strong additive effects are evidenced by formulas incorporating vitamin E, BHT, mercaptoamino acids, and the so-called Aging Control Formula 223 devised by the Swedish Institute of Gerontology.[9] As a componet of an important enzyme, glutathione peroxidase, the element selenium converts whatever hydroperoxides slip past the vitamin E into alcohols, which are less damaging to cells.[10] Some prefer taking the yeast-bound form of selenium because mammalian systems can convert certain mineral forms into a toxic product.[11] However, there is evidence that inorganic selenium is preferred for incorporation into the enzyme glutathione peroxidase, which is the actual antioxidant.[12] More information is needed on this important point, but most animal studies reporting beneficial effects from addition of selenium to the diet have employed the inorganic form, sodium selenite. I personally take eighty micrograms each of organic and inorganic selenium.

Too much selenium, in whatever form, may be toxic. In soils with excessively high selenium contents, grazing animals may suffer from "blind staggers," a malady characterized by lameness, loss of hair, and blindness. The quantity in human food varies widely from one source to another. The amount in eggs and milk from two different regions of Oregon differed by tenfold. Too little selenium is as bad as too much. Death rates for several types of cancer are lower in areas of the U.S. where crops take up larger amounts of selenium.[13] In a study involving 45,000 Chinese, the occurrence of Keshan Disease, a form of heart disease characterized by an enlarged heart, fast pulse, low blood pressure, and high death rate was found to bear a distinct geographical relationship to the amount of selenium in the soil.[14] Where it was low, Keshan Disease was common. In the United States the area called the "stroke belt," a section of the southeast coastal plains of Georgia and the Carolinas having the highest stroke rate, has also the highest incidence of heart disease, and is a low selenium area.

Most fruits and vegetables are quite low in selenium, although broccoli, cabbage, celery, cucumbers, mushrooms, onions, and radishes are reasonable sources. Brewer's yeast contains a lot. Fish are a rich source, as are organ meats (liver, kidney), bread, and cereals. The 160 micrograms supplemental amount of my list is not large, but I don't exceed it without knowing what I'm getting in my daily food intake.

BHT has been approved by the Food and Drug Administration and is found in the typical American diet in the amount of several milligrams per day because of its use as a preservative in processed foods. Denham Harman demonstrated that BHT is one of the most effective agents in increasing average life span in long-lived strains of mice. The increase was as much as 30 percent.[15] In a shorter-lived mouse strain BHT led to a 45 percent increase in life span.[16] In another experiment it helped suppress the development of skin tumors.[17] BHT cause a 64 percent reduction in the damaging breaks induced in DNA by a cancer-causing chemical.[18] In the same study, selenium decreased the damage by 42 percent, vitamin E by 63 percent, and vitamin C by 32 percent. Admittedly I am being selective in my citation of a vast and not always agreeing scientific literature, but most of the news is either good or neutral, quite like what Pascal said about the effects of prayer.

A number of antioxidant chemicals containing sulfur in the

reduced form (the sulfydryl or SH-group of drugs) have been tested for their influences on aging. These include the amino acids cysteine and methionine, of which the levels in the blood decrease with age. Mice and guinea pigs injected with cysteine every other day for forty days beginning at one year of age showed an increased survival.[19] In another experiment, 53 percent of cysteine-fed mice were alive at eighteen months of age compared to none of the control animals.[20] Cysteine and methionine are present in many edible proteins, gelatin for example. They are precursors of another amino acid, glutathione, which is used by the body to combine with and eliminate deleterious foreign substances. Depletion of liver glutathione allows increased binding of toxic chemicals to DNA and to protein.[21] Glutathione exists in the body in an oxidized form in which its sulfur atoms are bridged, written as S-S, and in unbridged reduced form, where the sulfur atoms are free groups, -SH and -SH. The two hydrogens (the H's) are eliminated when the sulfur atoms bridge. The more of one form in the tissues, the less of the other.

Many important chemical reactions in cells require the reduced form, glutathione-SH. Aging involves a decrease in -SH groups and an increase in the S-S bridges in those proteins wrapped around the DNA itself, as shown at the University of California by Drs. Sinan Tas, C.F. Tam, and myself.[22] This S-S bridge, or disulfide bond as it is called, is also a cross-link (it even looks like one when you write it). Agents which tend to increase the quantity of -SH groups in tissues, and particularly the levels of glutathione-SH, extend average life span in some animals, and in older animals tend to alter the levels of biomarkers toward those typical of a younger age.

Beside its free-radical scavenging effect, cysteine may have a role in some forms of DNA repair,[23] but too much cysteine can be harmful. It may potentiate the toxicity of monosodium glutamate in susceptible individuals, causing the well known "Chinese Restaurant Syndrome" (headache, burning, and pressure about the face and chest, and an aversion to calligraphy). It should not be taken except in the presence of at least twice the amount of vitamin C or it may be transformed into its cousin, cystine, and form kidney stones.

The natural antioxidants and free radical scavengers operate in different compartments of the cell because the sites of free radical formation are themselves compartmentalized. The fat-soluble vitamin E scavenges free radicals in the membranes; superoxide dismutase mops up free radicals in the cell fluid, and the enzyme catalase degrades radicals in those parts of the cell where many nutrients are oxygenated.[24] Extra antioxidants taken to prolong survival must cover many compartments and might not be able to penetrate all of them. That's why I take several kinds.

The controversy over whether vitamin C abets cancer and aging has achieved the status of a national pastime. Vitamin C deficiency causes one of the historically important diseases, scurvy, the plague of early-day British sailors on long voyages without citrus fruits, until in 1747 James Lind cured them with lime juice—hence the name "limeys." Even so, as many as thirty thousand people died from scurvy during the Civil War more than 100 years later. In 1912, having just lost to Amundsen the race for the South Pole, explorer Robert Scott forgot his orange juice and lost his life as well, lying scorbutic and hardly able to walk, with his two remaining men in a tent eleven miles from the safe return base while a polar blizzard howled outside for nine days.

The degree of vitamin C deficiency leading to scurvy can be cured by very small doses. The real question is whether large doses, megadoses on the order of one half to ten grams, do any additional good. Nobelist Linus Pauling has claimed that large doses will increase average life span by sixteen to twenty-four years. Such an increase would be getting close to a maximumn life-span extending effect for the species, and there's no evidence any antioxidant or vitamin will do that. Nevertheless, Pauling's general position is to my mind sounder than his critics give him credit for, although it is not to his credit that he hasn't so far conducted direct animal studies—in guinea pigs for example, which, like men, cannot manufacture their own vitamin C. In a study reported by Davies,[25] megadoses of vitamin C in fact decreased the life span of guinea pigs; however, the adverse result might have reflected the possibility that high doses of vitamin C are ineffective unless enough essential fatty acids, vitamin B_6, zinc, and vitamin E are also present in the diet.[26] The fatty acids should include especially linoleic acid and dihom-mogammalinoleic acid, both abundant in the oil of the evening primrose. In doses of one to three grams or more, vitamin C is said to stimulate the immune system;[27] decrease blood cholesterol,[28] protect against cross links, possess poorly understood antioxidant properties, and perhaps extend the lives of cancer patients.[29] Most of Pauling's opponents have probably overstressed certain potential toxicities of megadoses of vitamin C which are in most cases limited to genetically susceptible persons; they include two rare kinds of kidney stones, possible alterations in metabolism of the fetus in pregnancy, and diminished tolerance to a rapid increase in altitude.[30] So vitamin C could be bad news for competition balloonists.

Excess vitamin C is cleared from the blood within three to four hours, so that at least 200 milligrams must be taken four times daily to maintain blood levels at maximum.[31] This amount is far higher than the forty-five milligrams of the Recommended Daily Allowance. The RDA'ers have never attempted to find the "optimum" amount, which ought to include analyses of life-span and overall disease patterns throughout life, and not just resistance to scurvy. Even though blood levels cannot be changed by megadose vitamin C intake, recent investigations indicate that levels in the tissues can be raised.[32]

Ascorbyl palmitate is included among my supplemental vitamins as it has potent antioxidant properties and is the fat-soluble form of vitamin C. It penetrates into cellular compartments not reached by the water-soluble form. Bioflavinoids are added as they serve to inhibit destruction of vitamin C by oxidation, and potentiate the body's ability to use it.

The most recent work on vitamin C does add a note of caution,[33] and recommendations to take it in excess of several grams per day may be premature. Very large quantities may cause dietary copper (important in cholesterol metabolism) to be less available, and so lead to an increase in serum cholesterol.[34] While moderate doses seem to be antioxidant (antifree radical), larger amounts may exert the opposite effect, in part by inhibiting the function of catalase, unless accompanied by a greatly increased intake of vitamin E.[35] This interplay illustrates that an appropriate balance between intrinsic or administered antioxidants must be striven for to achieve positive effects. The duplicated twenty-first chromosome of Down's syndrome is the one carrying the gene for the free radical scavenger SOD (superoxide dismutase), so SOD is in excess in Down's, which nevertheless shows accelerated aging. Dr. Pierre Sinet of the Laboratory of Biochemical Genetics, Paris, thinks this selective increase in SOD over the other antioxidants is in fact partly responsible for the faster aging in these patients.[36] Experiments in progress measuring actual rate of production of free radicals in the presence of different combinations of antioxidants should clarify what balances are optimal.[37]

Besides antioxidants, a number of other substances, both dietary and medicamentous, have been shown to increase 50 percent survival in at least some strains of mice, rats, or other animals. As I am not here writing a general health advice book, I won't discuss vitamins A, D, many of the B vitamins, or minerals and trace metals. Adequate studies of their effects on life span and long-term disease patterns have never been done, so there's no information. Those substances which have given positive results in life-span studies include pantothenic acid (part of the B complex), several brain-reactive drugs such as DMAE, and possibly procaine or Gerovital, which was sufficiently discussed in the first chapter.

What I personally take among these materials are:

Calcium pantothenate	1 gram per day, in two doses
DMAE (Deaner)	120 milligrams per day, in one dose

Pantothenic acid is the principal constituent of the royal jelly of the honey bee. If fed to a female worker honeybee, who ordinarily survives only a month, it will convert the worker into a queen bee with a life span of six or more years. It would be incorrect to jump from a developmental phenomenon in bees to a metabolic situation in humans; however, in the one and only vertebrate experiment (which certainly requires repeating, but no one has done it), mice fed 300 milligrams of extra pantothenic acid per day lived 18–20 percent longer than control mice.[38] Pantothenic acid and choline are involved together in the synthesis of one of the brain's major chemical neutrotransmitters (acetylcholine), whose decrease during normal aging causes many of aging's mental symptoms.

Large doses of panthothenate augment the ability to withstand stress. In one experiment, when control rats were made to swim in cold water, they lasted thirty minutes before sinking, whereas rats given large doses of pantothenate survived a full hour.[39] Such augmentation could be considered as rejuvenation since a hallmark of aging is a decrease in the ability to respond adequately to various physiological stresses, such as cold or exercise. Pantothenate is essentially nontoxic. Adult monkeys have eaten one gram for every two pounds of body weight for six months and humans up to ten grams daily for six weeks without ill effects.

With the brain-reactive drug DMAE (short for dimethylaminoethanol) Richard Hoschschild increased the life spans of mice by 30 percent to 50 percent.[40] However, as he did not use long-lived strains, it remains uncertain whether more than 50 percent survival was being increased—in other words going from curves A or B to C or D (Fig. 7.1). In a longer-living mouse strain a larger dosage increased survival by only 6 percent,[41] and DMAE may have actually shortened the remaining survival of already aged Japanese quail.[42] DMAE inhibits the buildup of age-pigment in the brain cells of old animals and in tissue cultures of brain cells,[43] a desirable result because age-pigment may decrease learning capacity in elderly rats.[44] (Large doses of BHT and vitamin E given together also decrease the rate of pigment accumulation.)[45] Marketed in the U.S. by Riker Laboratories under the trade name "Deaner," DMAE is used for treating behavioral problems, reading difficulties, and shortened attention span in children. Taken by mouth, it is absorbed, goes from blood to brain and is converted to the neurotransmitter acetylcholine. The toxicity of Deaner is low and there are no known contraindications except epilepsy. It has been approved by the Food and Drug Administration for experimental human testing as an anti-aging drug.

Experiments in the older scientific literature described life-span extension in mice given yeast nucleic acids (RNA). Mice receiving 2.5 milligrams per day beginning at 600 days of age lived an average of 765 days instead of the expected 706 days.[46] The test animals seemed healthier than the controls, fewer went blind before death, and the body weight curves suggested that aging had been retarded. In another strain of mice, animals given 25 milligrams per day since youth lived an average of 706 days instead of the 609 days of untreated animals, a 16 percent prolongation.[47] There is no modern, careful scientific work on nucleic acid therapy in relation to aging. The New York physician Dr. B.S. Frank has treated aging in humans with nucleic acids (*Dr. Frank's No Aging Diet,* a best seller in 1977), but his results are of the nature of testimonial evidence, which in general is not worth much.

Dietary substances or nondietary regimens having to do with overall health betterment might indeed extend 50 percent survival by preventing disease, but most of these approaches have not actually been studied in terms of survival curves. In the early 1970s a striking correlation was reported between fiber content of the diet and the prevalence within different populations of certain disorders, especially diverticulitis and cancer of the large bowel. Resistance to these diseases seemed to correlate with fecal bulk, which in turn correlates with transit time through the gastrointestinal tract. Rapid transit time is desired. At least two ounces of fiber per day are required to increase fecal bulk significantly. This amounts to about one cup of pure bran or two to three raw carrots.[48] In the United States fiber consumption today is only one tenth what it was 50 to 100 years ago.

Animal data lend support to these observations on human populations. In one study the inclusion of 15 percent wheat bran or pectin in rat diets caused a 40 percent fall in number of cancers caused by two different kinds of added carcinogens.[49] In another study animals fed the fibers pectin (from apples) or oat bran showed significant lowering of blood cholesterol, triglycerides, and an increase in high-density-lipoproteins (HDL),[50] changes which if they also occur in humans might inhibit the development of arteriosclerotic heart disease.

But the word "fiber" is too general. The behavior of fibers differs considerably according to their sources. Fibers come from the cell walls of plants and include different varieties of pectin and cellulose. Apples and grapes are rich in pectin, nuts and cereals in cellulose. Pectin has only a mild effect on stool bulk but may be a potent cholesterol-lowering agent, whereas the cellulose containing fiber in wheat bran definitely promotes stool bulk but has little effect on blood cholesterol.[51] One gram of wheat bran will suck up and hold 3.2 grams of water, and is relatively indigestible, which is why it promotes fecal bulk. The carrot fiber has both cellulose and pectin and apparently increases fecal bulk as well as leading to a mild lowering of blood cholesterol.[52]

The right kind and degree of exercise will probably extend 50 percent survival, i.e., jump the A or B clone curve to a higher one (Fig. 7.1). A jump is not easy to demonstrate, however, in an uncloned and therefore heterogeneous human population because of control difficulties. Among 12,000 railroad workers the differences in heart disease between sedentary and physically active men was small.[53] That doesn't sound like exercise does much good. However, sedentary workers tend to belong to a somewhat higher economic class, with different diets and higher educational levels. These advantages might counterbalance the lack of exercise. Furthermore, the physical activity must be of a certain type and duration to benefit the heart and blood vessels. It must be strenuous. The autopsy report on "Mr. Marathon," Clarence DeMar, who had been a highly successful runner for over fifty years, revealed a large heart with widely open arteriosclerosis-free coronary arteries.[54] Marathoners who train by running forty miles each week have more of the beneficial high-density-lipoproteins (HDL) in their blood than ten miles per week joggers, and the latter have significantly higher HDL's than sedentary persons.

Aerobic exercise is what's effective: running, swimming, or bicycling in which the pulse rate reaches 80 percent of maximum for at least twenty minutes. Static exercises, even though strenuous, such as weight lifting or body building, make you prettier but not necessarily healthier. Aerobic exercise adapts the body to taking in, transporting, and using oxygen at an increased rate. The heart can pump more blood with each stroke and the pulse rate is slower both at rest and at any given level of activity. Blood triglycerides and cholesterol decrease, the HDL increase, there is more efficient utilization of carbohydrates and decreased resistance to insulin. Figure 7.2 shows for each age group the level to which the heartbeat should be raised during twenty minutes of exercise at least three to four times per week to achieve measurable benefits.

According to 78-year-old Thomas Cureton, professor emeritus of physical education at the University of Illinois and sometimes called the "father of physical fitness," without at least thirty minutes a day of nonstop exercise, women reach a peak of fitness at age 14 and start to decline by 22; men at 17, and start their decline at age 26. There is even evidence that the organism can, by chronic exercise, substantially postpone the age-related decline in oxidative capacity of the brain, improving the information processing that goes on in the brain.[55] I personally run twelve miles and swim one to two miles per week. Individuals over 30 to 35 should receive an exercise stress test before launching themselves into any strenuous program as your program must be tailored to your health status.

By many of the above means, as well as adherence to obvious health measures like not smoking, not overeating, and not overworrying about our troubled times and selves, one can surely extend 50 percent survival. But the ancient goal of

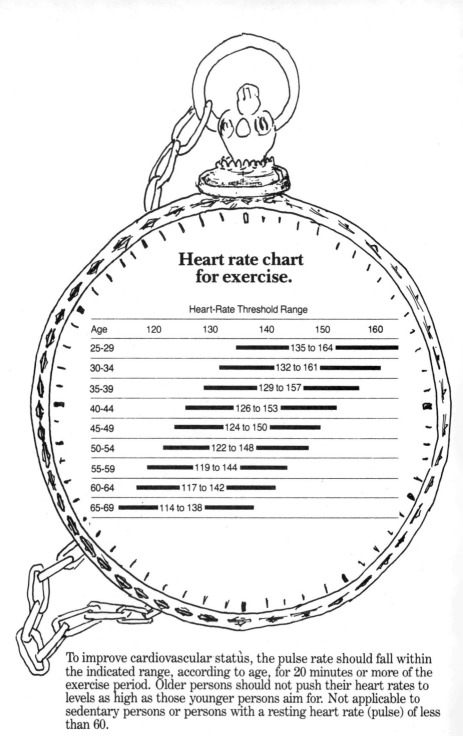

Heart rate chart for exercise.

Heart-Rate Threshold Range

Age	120	130	140	150	160
25-29			135 to 164		
30-34		132 to 161			
35-39		129 to 157			
40-44		126 to 153			
45-49		124 to 150			
50-54		122 to 148			
55-59		119 to 144			
60-64	117 to 142				
65-69	114 to 138				

To improve cardiovascular status, the pulse rate should fall within the indicated range, according to age, for 20 minutes or more of the exercise period. Older persons should not push their heart rates to levels as high as those younger persons aim for. Not applicable to sedentary persons or persons with a resting heart rate (pulse) of less than 60.

Figure 7.2

gerontology since the times of the Tao, pursued with almost mystical fervor and dedication, has been to decelerate the rate of intrinsic aging and extend maximum survival, let's say to 120 to 200 years—enough to be able to peer well into the next century of consciousness from wherever you start now.

The only relatively sure way to extend maximum human life span at present is by severe caloric undernutrition. The scientific background for this approach was reviewed in Chapter 5.

Since a link has been established between low body fat and infertility in females, women who wish to become pregnant should take a hiatus from this program. Similarly, during pregnancy and while nursing it is very important to maintain an adequate level of caloric intake. Pregnant women and nursing mothers should not follow an overly restrictive regimen.

Slowly induced restriction in young or middle-aged animals will rejuvenate the immune system and extend maximum life span. The same method will almost certainly work in humans. The two to three months required for slow restriction in rodents would correspond to five to seven years in man. The amount of weight to be slowly lost for a normal, nonobese person would correspond to about one-fifth to one-fourth initial body weight. A man such as myself, five foot eight inches tall and weighing 148 pounds, might have to lose 20 to 30 pounds to achieve a significant, maximum life-span-prolonging effect. He would undertake gradual restriction of total calories to about 60 percent of his unrestricted intake. For me that would mean gradually decreasing from about 2,500 to about 1,600 calories daily. I could do this in two ways: either eating every day but less, or else by intermittent fasting, which means not eating at all on one, two, or three days a week. According to the animal data, both ways work. I personally find it easier to eat nothing (except water) two days a week, and be less restrictive the other days. Two thousand one hundred forty calories for five days and nothing for two is easier for me than 1,600 daily for seven days. The RDA of 3,000 calories per average man per day and 2,200 per woman given by the UN Food and Agriculture Organization is certainly unnecessarily high. Considerable evidence exists that adaptive abilities will lead to a higher level of metabolic efficiency for a person on a lower calorie diet, say between 1,500 and 2,000 calories per day.[56] Slow reduction in intake is important to allow this adaptation to take place, and you should realize that weight reduction without physical exercise is apt to cause a loss of bodily power.[57]

The absolutely key concept of life-span extension by caloric restriction, again according to the animal data, is "undernutrition without malnutrition." If by simply eating less of the average American junk diet, we reduced from a nonobese 150 pounds down to 110–120 pounds, we would simply be living malnourished, shorter lives. If one is averaging only 1,500 to 2,000 calories daily over a long period, they must be derived from foods superbly high in nutrition. That means cutting out empty calories like sugar, honey, alcohol, and nonessential fats (fats have over twice the calorie content of carbohydrates or proteins). If approved by the FDA, the introduction of left-handed sugar (a form of sugar that tastes sweet but cannot be absorbed from the gut), and of a synthetic substance called SPE (sucrose polyester), which tastes and feels like vegetable oil but cannot be digested, will allow the elimination of all empty calories from a preferred diet, to eat your cake and not have it too.[58]

The food intake must be balanced, high in fiber content, and reasonably low in sodium. Beans, for example, are generally a great source of protein but are low in the essential amino acid methionine, which can be supplied by rice, which contains plenty of methionine but lacks lysine, which is supplied by the balancing beans. Grains (rice, oats, wheat, and corn) and legumes (such as beans, lentils, and peas) balance each other. Tabouli, the cracked-wheat salad, and the chick-pea salad of the Middle East, taken together, constitute an exotic example of good balance. Milk and soybeans contain the only two nearly fully balanced non-meat proteins.

Reasonably low in sodium means no added salt during preparation of food or at the table. In animals, excess of sodium leads to considerable shortening of life span.[59] Man is no exception. He has not been adjusted by evolution or anything else to tolerate the sodium chloride loaded diet that he gets in a typical day's menu in America. The actual amount of sodium required daily is not much over 250 milligrams. Most Americans consume twenty times that much. It's not only what you add in cooking or at the table. The amount in processed foods provides the excess. Salty food may not even taste very salty. A one-ounce serving of Kellogg's Corn Flakes contains nearly twice as much sodium as an ounce of Planter's Peanuts (260 versus 132 milligrams). A eight-ounce serving of Campbell's Beans and Franks contains 958 milligrams of sodium; a Big Mac, 1,510; a tablespoon of Wishbone Italian dressing, 315; an ounce of Breakstone's Low Fat Cottage Cheese, 435; a large Heinz dill pickle, 1,137; Bumble Bee Brand chunk white tuna, 628; the average American cheese sandwich, 1,550 milligrams of sodium. No wonder thirty-five million Americans, or one in every six, have hypertension.

Most processed foods don't fit well with the goal of "undernutrition without malnutrition." An analysis of the sugar content of fourteen nationally distributed cereals, shown in Table 7.1, illustrates the degree of naked calorie addition to what are advertised as highly nutritive foods. The amount of additional sugar or honey ranged from 22 to 32 percent of the dry weight of the cereal. Wheat and other grains naturally contain only ½ to 1 percent or less of sugar, the rest of the sugar in the granola has been added by the manufacturer. As of this writing, among cold cereals only Nabisco's Shredded Wheat is low both in sugar and salt. The average American now consumes a staggering 128 pounds of sugar per year. A twelve ounce can of Coca-Cola contains nine teaspoons of sugar. Manufacturers are adding sugar to foods that hardly need sweetening, like peanut butter, tomato sauce, salad dressing, and chili. In 1910, 75 percent of the sugar consumed came from the family kitchen. Now only 25 percent comes from the home. The rest is supplied by food processors. Just fifty corporations control most of the nation's food industries and products, and they have gone to great lengths to promote the image that factory processing is merely an extension of family cooking, with the

14 popular granola cereals.

Sugar content of 14 popular granola cereals, given as percent of dry weight of the product (letter in parentheses following product name indicates manufacturers: Bio-Familla (BF), General Foods (GF), General Mills (GM), Kellogg (K), Organic Milling (OM), Pet (P), Quaker Oats (QO).

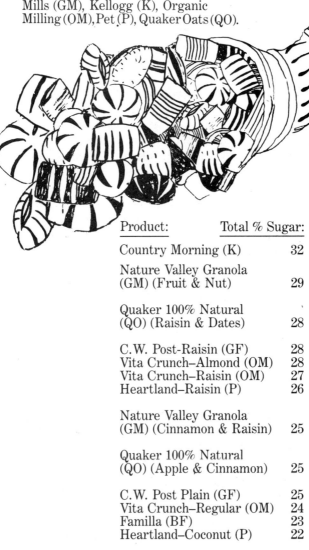

Product:	Total % Sugar:
Country Morning (K)	32
Nature Valley Granola (GM) (Fruit & Nut)	29
Quaker 100% Natural (QO) (Raisin & Dates)	28
C.W. Post-Raisin (GF)	28
Vita Crunch–Almond (OM)	28
Vita Crunch–Raisin (OM)	27
Heartland–Raisin (P)	26
Nature Valley Granola (GM) (Cinnamon & Raisin)	25
Quaker 100% Natural (QO) (Apple & Cinnamon)	25
C.W. Post Plain (GF)	25
Vita Crunch–Regular (OM)	24
Familla (BF)	23
Heartland–Coconut (P)	22
Quaker 100% Natural (QO) (Brown Sugar & Honey)	22

Table 7.1

addition of a few preservatives. The truth is they have transformed the American diet from one based primarily on fresh meats, grains, vegetables, and fruit to a largely synthetic feast of prefabricated foods.[60] The clustering of the offices of their lobbyists about the White House and Capitol buildings, shown in Figure 7.3, looks like a military stratagem, and quite a successful one.

Complete details of an adequate daily intake for the regime I favor will require a separate book, but an outline can be given here. The diet would be for a person of mid-life (age 30–50). Fat content should be less than 10–15 percent, protein 20–25 percent or much less (depending on age), the rest complex carbohydrates. The fat content could be cut even more, perhaps down to less than 2–5 percent before producing a fatty acid deficiency.[61] At later ages the relative protein content should be reduced to 10–15 percent. Self selection experiments in rats have shown that a high protein intake early in life and a lower one later gives longest life span.[62]

Appendix A gives an almost complete breakdown of known nutriments in a number of representative foods. It also shows the official Recommended Daily Allowances, plus what I aim for personally in my own diet or through supplementation. In some instances (pantothenate, for example) there's a big difference. I take a lot more than the RDA. The values given in Appendix A are in most instances for raw food. With care and supplementation for certain items, one can arrange these foods into fully inclusive menus to achieve super nutrition on an average of 1,500 to 2,000 calories per day intake. For personal application I convert this into about 2,140 calories and eat only on five of seven days. If I seem to be losing at an average rate faster than one half to one pound per month, I increase the intake slightly. I should lose 20–25 percent of body weight over four to six years. Not faster. Rapid weight loss will not increase life span.

Using the information of Appendix A, Appendix B gives complete representative menus and recipes for several days. The basic food lists for the menus were put together by what I consider an innovation in nutrition planning: feeding all the

The food lobby in Washington.

1. Anheuser–Busch
2. Armour and Co.
3. Buitoni Foods
4. Canada Dry
5. Carnation
6. CPC International
7. General Foods
8. General Mills
9. Hershey Foods
10. ITT
11. Kellogg's
12. DelMonte
13. Procter and Gamble
14. Ralston Purina
15. Riviana Foods
16. RJR Foods
17. Seven-Up
18. Starkist Foods
19. Swift and Company
20. American Bakers Assoc.
21. American Corn Millers Assoc.
22. American Farm Bureau Federation
23. Whey Products Institute
24. American Institute of Food Distribution
25. American Seed Trade Assoc.
26. Biscuit and Cracker Manufacturers Assoc.
27. Can Manufacturers Association
28. Canned and Cooked Meat Importers Assoc.
29. Cooperative Food Distributors of America
30. Corn Refiners Assoc., Inc.
31. Food Marketing Institute
32. Food Processing Machinery and Supplies Assoc.
33. Hawaiian Sugar Planters Assoc.
34. Independent Bakers Association
35. Institute of Shortening and Edible Oils
36. Milk Industry Foundation
37. Millers National Federation
38. National Agricultural Chemicals Assoc.
39. National Assoc. of Margarine Manufacturers
40. National Assoc. of Meat Purveyors
41. National Broiler Council
42. National Candy Wholesalers Assoc.
43. National Cattlemen's Assoc.
44. National Fisheries Institute
45. National Grain Trade Council
46. National Independent Meat Packers Assoc.
47. National Soft Drink Assoc.
48. National Soybean Processors Assoc.
49. Paperboard Packaging Council
50. National Assoc. of Wheat Growers
51. National Food Processors Assoc.
52. Pickle Packers International, Inc.
53. Sugar Assoc. of the Caribbean
54. United States Beet Sugar Assoc.
55. United States Cane Sugar Refiner's Assoc.
56. United States Tuna Foundation
57. Wheat Flour Institute
58. Food Processors Institute
59. Food Protein Council
60. National Shrimp Congress
61. DelMonte
62. Sugar Assoc., Inc.
63. American Frozen Food Institute
64. International Assoc. of Ice Cream

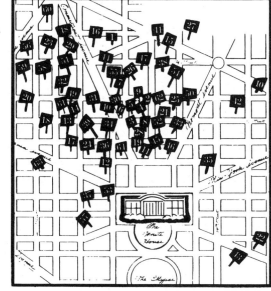

Figure 7.3

information of Appendix A into a computer and asking it the following question, "If I'm restricted to 800, 1,500, or 2,000 calories a day, what combinations of food can I eat so as to be sure of getting enough of all the basic nutrients—in short, of achieving 'undernutrition without malnutrition'?" I have stipulated merely the regular RDA for the various nutrients (the extra amounts I take can only be had in such large quantities by supplementation), and I have also restricted the output to combinations totaling less than 15 percent fat and 25 percent protein. I have also added restrictions on the computer in the way of portions of food—it wouldn't be helpful to have it give me a list which includes a thimbleful of peanut butter, a shot-glass of milk and two pounds of lettuce. Menus and recipes for two 1,500 calorie days, food combinations (with recipes) for six additional days, and two nutrition-complete salads are given. We have also asked the computer the following questions, "What is the combination that gives the minimum possible number of calories but still retains the regular RDA?" Still calling for no more than 15 percent fat and 25 percent proteins, with the listed food stuffs the minimum number turns out to be around 1,500 calories. Fanatics on long fasts sometimes go thirty to forty days on water only. Much longer than that (sixty to seventy-five days) is fatal, and sometimes considerably less can be fatal. Of course total fasting is undernutrition *plus* malnutrition.

On 800 calories per day and without malnutrition (i.e., a supplemented low calorie diet), how long could a person survive? We can make an estimate, assuming the person begins weighing 150 pounds of which 30 pounds would customarily be fat, and that he or she can last as long as the 800 calories per day of food, plus the calories from his own burning fat hold out, and that 2,000 calories per day are needed for his or her activities. Thirty pounds of fat will burn in the metabolism to yield 120,960 calories. That, along with the 800 calories per day in the diet, would last for 100 days. I certainly don't recommend that anybody try this. Too rapid weight loss is detrimental as it does not allow for metabolic adaptation.

Although some may think of it as a mini-disaster, hunger

is not the main difficulty of a restricted diet. Hunger is largely habit. I find the real problem to be social. Eating and drinking are the major forms of polite interaction in society. Our social lives are built largely around the conviviality of food and drink. The meal is accompanied by an emotional atmosphere, conversation, and ideas expressed during a semi-ritualistic event. One is ordinarily not conscious of how adroitly custom forces you to eat, how it throws you into the ritual. How can this be handled? On a restricted diet you will find that it's quite possible to be socially graceful and dietarily frugal at the same time. Let it be understood, for example, that you're a fanatic or eccentric on this point, or that intermittent fasting (or however you style it) makes you "high," as indeed it does. Become attuned to a new life-style and associate it with pleasure, with the pleasure of physical well-being, for example, or clearer thoughts. Then turn noneating into a slightly risqué vice and your host will be charmed and alarmed at your wickedness.

"For years," actress Gloria Swanson was quoted as saying,[63] "people have been asking: 'How is it you're so spritely for your age (82 in March of 1981)? And why is your skin in such good condition?' And I've been asked to write a book about health. But to be honest, I preferred yakking about it to writing. Eventually I got to be too much of a fanatic about health and diet. I don't do that now. I don't bother, I can sit at a table with someone who's chewing broken glass and it won't bother me. If people want to kill themselves by eating the wrong things, that's up to them."

The charming Ms. Swanson was indeed paraphrasing and updating an ancient Greek poet. About 2,700 years ago Hesiod wrote,

"Fools not to know that half exceeds the whole,
How blest the sparing meal and temperate bowl."

8

Future Breakthrough
Possibilities

It's a philosophical paradox that the prospects for a sizable breakthrough fairly soon in extending maximum life span may be better than the prospect for making accurate predictions. In formulating near-term predictions, a specialist like myself enjoys a theoretical advantage over a lay person, but for far-future predictions the advantage subsides. To illustrate why this is so, let's express the amount of knowledge in a scientific field by the year 2050 as fifty units of knowledge. Suppose the specialist of today possesses ten units of that knowledge, and today's layperson two units. Now suppose the specialist of 1990 will have fourteen units. He will have gained four units over today's amount. Then the present-day specialist already has ten-fourteenths of the knowledge that will be available by 1990, and he ought to be able to guess today what will be coming up eight years hence. Today's lay person has only two-fourteenths of the 1990 knowledge, not enough for an accurate guess about the near future.

In the far future of 2050, however, there will be fifty units of knowledge. Our contemporary specialist is only ten-fiftieths or one-fifth of the way there, and today's layperson one-twenty-fourth. Both fractions are small enough that the far-future remains largely fantasy for everyone. The specialist has no significant advantage in imagining what it will be like.

This seemingly neat analysis does fail to come to grips with knowing what is far future and what is near future. The real distance to the future is measured less in time than in events. In predicting future technological developments, the fine bevy of specialists who put together the 1937 National Resources Committee Report to President Franklin D. Roosevelt totally overlooked the discovery of nuclear power, jet propulsion, aviation as a large primary transportation system, and the transistor—all of which were in use within fifteen years and have since transformed the world. In this instance of predictive failure, a mere fifteen years led to a far future, a future lying on the other side of the Atomic Bomb and World War II, which shifted both social and technological paradigms of the age. And just a few years before that shift, munitions veteran Admiral William Leahy commented to President Harry Truman about the Atomic Bomb, "That is the biggest fool thing we have ever done. The bomb will never go off, and I speak as an expert on explosives." In the early 1950s the experts in the new field of computing machines predicted that by 1970 there would be at least 100 sizable computers in the United States. In fact, by 1970 there were 200,000.[1] Experts tend to underpredict and laypersons to fantasize about the future.

I sometimes think it might be equally helpful, as the twentieth century gallops ahead, to proceed by outright divination. In whimsical deference thereto I have cast the *I ching,* that ancient Chinese system of divination in which yarrow stalks are cast and the meaning of the pattern of their fall in relation to the question posed is read from the ancient text, the Book of Changes, which is the *I ching.* As recently as the seventeenth century great Lord Yamaga built the Japanese samurai into the finest fighting force in Asia by teaching them strategy that accorded with a special interpretation of the *I ching.* So let's take a look. In response to my question, "Will significant life-span extension be achieved in the next 5 to 15 years?," the yarrow stalks have fallen into the following favorable hexagram, called

---------------   ---------------

---------------   ---------------

----

the Kuai hexagram, whereof the *I ching* text says, "This hexagram signifies on one hand a breakthrough after a long accumulation of tension, as a swollen river breaks through its dikes, or in the manner of a cloudburst."

The *I ching* seems to describe what we have come to recognize as a paradigm change, either scientific or social or both. With such an auspicious readout added to what we already know about the biology of aging, optimism is in order. Therefore it remains only to inquire into further methodologies for maximum life-span extension, those which are promising but not yet practical or ready for human use, and to realize that these comprise a minimum statement based on our present ten units of knowledge.

In predicting the *far future,* anything goes. Hans Moravec of the Robotics Institute of Carnegie Mellon University predicts eventual immortality through the use of increasingly direct brain-to-computer interface contact in which retrieving information from the computer will be just like retrieving from your own mind. As surgical techniques and equipment improve, parts of the nervous system will be replaceable by computer elements. As your brain is gradually replaced, your consciousness and personality will in effect be gradually transferred to a machine. Such a combination of man and machine is called a cyborg. You will never have the feeling or problem of death or alien change, but will just gradually turn into a living robot or humanoid. The progression is thus human → cyborg → humanoid. The change can be advantageous. You can improve yourself. You can transfer yourself to other machines. You can have everybody else's abilities. It's not a bad prospect but it's so far in the future that the specialist, playing at fantastic futurist, can be as off target as anybody else.

Promising areas for bringing honor to the *I ching*'s predictive abilities by achieving near-future breakthroughs in aging research (say within five to fifteen years) include jacking up the life-maintenance processes and resetting the program clock or clocks.

We've seen in Chapter 4 that the maximum life spans of different species ranging from mice to man are proportional to their abilities to repair injury to their DNA. Indeed the extraordinary longevity of man may have evolved secondary to an increase in the levels of DNA repair and other life-maintenance processes. Repair is brought about by particular enzymes which examine and identify the type of injury and then correct it. As I outlined earlier, Dr. Joan Sonneborn[2] extended the life span of the single-celled organisms called *Paramecium* by first exposing them to intense ordinary ultraviolet light, and subsequently to a longer-wave ultraviolet or "black light." Obtaining a 50 percent extension of overall life span, amounting to a 296 percent increase of residual life span, she speculated that the first dose of ultraviolet damaged the DNA in the cells but switched on or augmented a natural repair process. By a mechanism called "photoreactivation," the second dose of light, in this case black light, eliminated the damage caused by the first dosage, leaving the augmented natural repair process free to mend other damage in the DNA, including the damage involved in aging. It's a good possibility that methods applicable to human use can be devised to increase our own DNA repair processes; for example, the injection of properly altered DNA might act like a vaccine to stimulate the body to increase its level of repair enzymes. Higher organisms like man doubtless possess a reserve repair capacity which we will learn how to enhance. I can easily see this happening in the near future.

Some enzymes necessary to cellular metabolism have the unfortunate additional effect of activating a number of carcinogens; that is, they transform certain otherwise innocuous chemicals into cancer-causing agents (carcinogens) within the body. Dr. Arthur Schwartz of Temple University found an inverse relationship between this ability to activate carcinogens and the life spans of different species.[3] The enzymes of rodents have a greater capacity for activation than the enzymes of longer-living species like man. Because the correlation is with maximum life span, the observation may be as fundamental as that for DNA-repair levels.

Dr. Schwartz then looked for a substance which might inhibit the enzymes. The best inhibitor turned out to be a naturally occurring hormone called DHEA (short for dehydroepiandrosterone).[4] When DHEA was given to mice of a strain prone to develop spontaneous breast cancer, the enzymes and the occurrence of cancer were both strongly inhibited. Furthermore, the development of graying of the fur was inhibited and the treated mice looked more youthful and lived a few months longer. While they ate as much as untreated mice, they did not gain weight as rapidly. On a clinical level the DHEA-treated mice resembled mice on a calorically restricted diet. DHEA inhibits the conversion of carbohydrates to fats in the body. Its level rises in the blood of restricted mice. Because Schwartz's original mice were of a special, very obese, cancer-prone strain having a short natural life span, the results, although highly interesting from the gerontologic standpoint, need to be confirmed in normal longer-living mouse strains. The drug was also effective in preventing the autoimmunity and increasing the life spans in mice of the NZB/W strain, which we recall is a fine animal model of an accelerated aging syndrome.

DHEA is normally present in human blood at a higher concentration than any other hormone. Its level is higher in long-lived man than in shorter-lived species, yet its function in the body is only partially known. Reaching a peak concentration a few years after puberty, it undergoes thereafter a progressive decline to quite low values in advanced age. It is also greatly reduced in women who are prone to breast cancer, in other forms of malignancy, and in persons who have suffered heart attacks. There is as yet inconclusive evidence that DHEA may exert antioxidant properties, and that it may lower blood cholesterol. The blood level of DHEA is higher in persons on vegetarian diets, which might explain the lower frequencies of breast and bowel cancer in vegetarians. Initial studies by Drs. Phil Lipetz and Ron Hart of Ohio State University suggest that the integrity of DNA (as defined by what is termed "supercoiling") is better preserved in DHEA-treated than in untreated mice.

At current writing I don't expect DHEA to be the *elixir vitae* of the alchemists and Taoists, but it might possibly be as effective as severe caloric restriction in extending maximum life span. Its increase in the blood of restricted mice might be the mechanism whereby restriction works to prolong life span. It would, in addition, be a lot easier to take than intermittent fasting—indeed, no trouble at all. Furthermore, if in the next few years DHEA is shown to extend life span in animals, it could be given promptly to an experimental human group. Being a natural hormone of the blood, extensive long-term toxicity studies would not have to be done to win FDA approval.

A commonly expressed position of so-called "basic" scientists is that until we thoroughly understand the fundamental biology of aging—which clearly won't be for a long time—we'll not be able to slow it down. I don't hold with this view at all. Basic, applied, and empirical science leapfrog one another. If any one of them advances, the others follow. We don't in fact know the molecular basis for the life-span extension caused by caloric restriction, yet it works impressively and consistently. If DHEA mimics the effects of that restriction, we'll have a clue to why the restriction works, and a more humanly adaptable method as well. The current DHEA situation adds to the near-term DNA-repair possibilites to illustrate my reason for optimism about the imminence of successful life-span extension in man.

A number of additional substances, regimens, or pay-dirt

avenues have opened to near-future investigation. If only one of them works out, we'll be around long enough to be saying "hello" to forty-five or more great-great-grandchildren in the twenty-first century.

These grandchildren will be fascinated to read in their history books, if events turn out that way, that some of the secrets of aging, the knowledge of which has given them their robust great-great-grandparents, were found by studying a remarkably adaptable microbe called *Micrococcus radiodurans,* which has learned to live in the waste water of nuclear reactors.[5] Radiation is intensely damaging to DNA and also leads to the production of many free radicals. Because of the high level of radiation where it lives, *M.radiodurans* has developed an enormous ability to repair its damaged DNA (including the usually lethal double strand breaks), and to scavenge those notorious free radicals. It is 33 times as resistant to ultraviolet irradiation, 55 times as resistant to X rays, and 4 times as resistant to DNA-damaging chemicals as most other microbes. Although microbes do not undergo aging in the sense understood by us, study of these super systems for DNA repair may have considerable fallout for aging research. In addition, *M.radiodurans* has 3 times as much superoxide dismutase and about 50 times as much catalase (both important free radical scavengers) as other microbes. It's encouraging to know that natural repair systems and scavenging agents can be tuned to such high levels in any life form.

In addition to antioxidants and the other agents already discussed, a rather miscellaneous group of drugs and procedures show distinct promise of exerting potent anti-aging effects, although they have not yet been thoroughly evaluated. I'll discuss a number of these, in part to illustrate the range of imminent possibilities for at least some degree of life-span extensions:

(1) Coenzyme Q_{10}: First identified in 1957, this enzyme is an essential part of the energy factory (mitochondria) of the cell, and declines with age in various tissues. Aging is characterized by an increased rate of degeneration of mitochondria in some cells, and increasing the availability of Q_{10} might

attenuate the processes that give rise to the yellow-brown aging pigment lipofuscin. Treatment of old mice with Q_{10} led to a substantial rejuvenation of their immune system.[6] Effects on life span have not so far been studied.

(2) 2-Mercaptoethanol (2ME): This drug increases the survival of immune cells (lymphocytes) in the test tube in short-term culture. In addition, Dr. T. Makinodan of the Veterans Hospital in Los Angeles has found that weekly injections of 2ME into old mice will partially rejuvenate their immune system.[7] Experiments by Dr. Sinan Tas, C.F. Tam, and myself indicate that 2ME may break certain cross-links which develop with age in those proteins which are tightly wrapped around the DNA in cells. This might allow the genetic material to resume the activity characteristic of a younger age.

(3) The free radical scavenger superoxide dismutase (SOD) is available as an injectable veterinary drug and has been used successfully to treat a number of diseases in cattle. Although its intrinsic level in the body varies in line with differences between metabolic rate and life span between species, it has never been evaluated for anti-aging effects in any species. The form available in health food stores, to be taken by mouth, is ineffective in raising the natural level in the tissues as it is destroyed by stomach enzymes before it can be absorbed into the bloodstream. As we have noted, furthermore, SOD is increased naturally in Down's syndrome, a disease of accelerated aging, which means that increasing the level of only one of the body's free radical scavengers may unbalance the system and be counterproductive.

(4) Oil of evening primrose: We may allow ourselves the romance of admitting this oil to our longevity bower. It contains 72 percent linoleic acid (the most important of the fatty acids essential in human metabolism) and 9 percent gamma-linoleic acid. In the body these fatty acids are converted into a substance called PGE_1. The PGE_1 is the active principle and plays a significant role in the function of the immune and other systems.[8] It inhibits the formation of blood clots in the arteries and veins, and elevates the levels of one of the important second messengers carrying the hormonal message to the nu-

cleus of cells. Treatment of a short-lived mouse strain (our now familiar NZB/W strain) with PGE_1 enhanced its survival. Eighteen of nineteen treated mice were alive at one year, compared to only two of nineteen untreated mice.[9] With aging, the conversion of linoleic acid into PGE_1 may be defective but gamma-linoleic acid can still be converted. However, among available nutritional oils and fats, only evening primrose oil contains gamma-linoleic acid. Thus gerontologists may find one of their longevity edibles at the end of the primrose path.

(5) "Active Lipid": Dr. David Herron of the Weizmann Institute in Israel has observed that aging is accompanied by a decrease in fluidity of cell membranes, and by rigidification of the membranes. Under these conditions the important membrane receptors become less available for interaction with incoming signals. By treating old mice for twenty days with a diet containing 5 percent of so-called "active lipid," a compound prepared from special reprocessing of egg lecithin, Dr. Herron was able to partially reverse the age-related loss in fluidity of membranes and to rejuvenate functional activity, including that of the immune system. Herron's work looks promising but is still at an early stage of investigation.

(6) Thymus hormones: The thymus gland consists of two soft pinkish-gray lobes lying just above the heart in the chest cavity of all vertebrates. It's the master gland of the immune system, as discovered quite independently by Dr. Jacques Miller of Australia and Dr. Robert Good of the United States, and it manufactures a family of hormones which regulate the growth and maturation of a sizable part of the immune system. The first of these hormones, called thymosin, was discovered by Dr. Allan Goldstein, now at George Washington University School of Medicine. Thymosin was used clinically in 1974 to treat a five-year-old girl named Heather who had been born with a faulty thymus. In critical condition from a series of crippling infections because her immune system had not matured, she weighed less than a normal two-year-old child. Injections of thymosin led to a dramatic improvement. Heather grew and is today leading a normal life, although she still needs thymosin.

The various thymic hormones seem to have partially distinct but also overlapping functions. They are being particularly studied in relation to cancer because they may beef up the body's natural defense network. Dr. Marc Weksler of Cornell University Medical College has shown that they may also slow or reverse some of the immune deficiencies of aging.[10] The thymus gland shrinks very early on, becoming noticeably smaller by puberty. As the thymus shrinks, its hormone output declines. The decline accelerates between 25 and 45 years of age. Nobelist Sir Macfarlane Burnet has speculated that the thymus gland may be a primary pacemaker for aging, its shrinkage being responsible for the falloff in immune capacity and the increase in anti-self reactions which characterize aging.

(7) Cellular transplantation: Drs. T. Makinodan of Los Angeles and K. Hirokawa of Japan obliterated the immune and blood cell systems of old mice with heavy doses of X ray, then gave them transplants of thymus glands and bone marrow cells from young mice. The immune responses of the old recipients became youthful. Whether this drastic procedure will prolong maximum life span is not known at present.

Most of the above list of drugs and procedures fall into the category of "immunoengineering," and show that we are learning to manipulate age-associated changes and declines of the immune system, not only to slow them down but in some cases partially reverse them. This augurs well for near-future successes in life-span extension because the immune apparatus is one of the principal life-maintenance support machineries in the body.

Another such machinery, as outlined in the fourth chapter, is the neuroendocrine complex, represented by the hypothalamus in the brain and the various endocrine glands, particularly the pituitary, adrenal, thymus, and thyroid glands. Many brain-reactive drugs are now being introduced to treat neurological and psychiatric disorders in the elderly. An increase in magnesium in the tissue fluids tends to increase neurotransmitter stores in the brain, and to increase the ability of the brain to respond to repetitive stimuli, a clear-cut anti-aging effect. Dr. P.W. Landfield of the Bowman Gray School of Medicine demonstrated that certain drugs which are neural stimulants (PTZ and an analog of ACTH) may actually retard brain aging in rats as measured both by brain structure and the ability to navigate through a maze.[11] The drugs are designed to correct neurotransmitter imbalance, which may also underlie many basic aging processes. The drug L-dopa, used in the treatment of Parkinson's disease, has been successfully employed to extend the average life span of mice.[12] Neurotransmitter depletion may be responsible for both normal and disease-related locomotion problems in the elderly. Drs. J. Marshall and N. Berrios of the University of California compared the swimming abilities of old and young rats.[13] Young rats swam vigorously, keeping their bodies nearly horizontal and their heads above water; old rats tended to swim vertically, struggled to keep their heads up, and repeatedly sank, persistently going "down for the third time." When the old rats were given a neurotransmitter stimulant, they swam like young rats. Similar, albeit less dramatic, results were obtained with L-dopa. According to the investigators, these results indicate that "the central programs for these movements are still intact in aged rats." This is a highly encouraging conclusion.

Drs. A.V. Everitt, of Australia, and Donner Denckla, formerly at Harvard University, have concentrated on the pituitary gland.[14] Hanging down from the base of the brain like a small thumb, the pituitary may be the pacemaker for an aging clock located in an adjacent region of the brain, the hypothalamus. The master endocrine gland, the pituitary secretes hormones which influence all the others. Both Everitt and Denckla have found that if it is surgically removed, but the operated-upon animal kept healthy by injecting it with three of the known pituitary hormones (which it can now no longer manufacture itself), remarkable age-retarding or even rejuvenatory changes occur. The rate of spontaneous cross-linking slows down, age-related kidney damage decreases, the heart does not enlarge and cardiovascular fitness is restored to juvenile levels, DNA function improves, and the immune system behaves like that of a younger animal. Recently Dr.

David Harrison of the Jackson Laboratories in Maine has confirmed some, albeit not all, of these rejuvenatory claims.[15] Denckla believes that with age a program clock in the hypothalamus instructs the pituitary to elaborate a "death hormone," which blocks the responsiveness of the tissues to thyroid hormone. So the trick is to remove the pituitary. No pituitary, no death hormone! You must simply replace the other, desirable hormones which the pituitary also secretes. Neither Everitt nor Denckla have yet succeeded in extending maximum life span in their pituitary-deprived animals, possibly because replacement of the ten or more important non-death hormones which the gland also secretes is at best a ticklish, difficult-to-judge task. Denckla is presently trying to isolate his theoretical "death hormone" and, if successful, to make an antidote or antiserum to it, thereby avoiding the complications arising from removing the pituitary gland itself.

Another possible approach, if the primary clock lies in the hypothalamus, might be to transplant fetal hypothalamic tissues into the aging brain. Formerly it was thought that the central nervous system was incapable of regeneration or of growing if transplanted to a new site. The extent of the adult brain's "plasticity" was not appreciated. But recent experiments with adult rats have shown that when hypothalamic nerves from rat fetuses are transplanted into adults, the nerves grow and restore damaged functions.[16] In addition, an inherited diabetic defect in the brains of adult rats has been improved by fetal nerve cell transplants. Such procedures in old animals might well reset the hypothalamic clock.

There may be two clocks, one in the brain and a separate one in each cell, evolution having devised a fail-safe death trip for our chagrin and its own purposes. Dr. Vincent Cristofalo of the Wistar Institute of Anatomy and Biology in Philadelphia has manipulated the clock in connective tissue cells (the fibroblasts) to achieve about 30 percent more doublings than usual before reaching the Hayflick Limit. Newly discovered tissue-specific growth factors, such as T-cell growth factor and epidermal (skin cell) growth factor, allow longer lives in culture for their respective cells than were obtainable just a few years ago. We see that both clocks are now, to a degree, susceptible to manipulation.

Advances in basic biologic research may have important fallout for life-span extension technology. One area to watch is the control of gene expression and regulation. There are 50,000 to 100,000 genes in a human cell. The genes are the same for each cell, yet the cells themselves are different. A muscle cell is not a brain cell, nor is it an intestinal cell, but all three cells have the same genes. Most of the genes in any one type of cell are not operating. They are "repressed." Those which are operating are "expressed"; they tell the cell what its structure should be and regulate its function. What modulates the level of expression of a gene is a question we cannot answer as yet, nor can we say precisely how the many genes of the cell, once expressed, are coordinated so that they function together in an orderly way. As cells mature from the embryonic state, their genes turn off and on, guiding the maturation, development, and diversification of the cells and organs. The changes observed in the tissues of animals such as insects, which undergo metamorphosis (for example: caterpillar into butterfly), illustrate the programmed extinction of whole tissue systems. All human cells possess a gene which can produce insulin, but only in pancreas cells is this gene expressed. Cells from unborn mice repair damage to their DNA very quickly, but just before birth the repair rate declines. The genes for DNA-repair are there but they are turned down or off. Can we learn how to turn them back on? A major mystery and one of the hottest areas in modern biology is the nature of gene expression and repression; what controls it; what regulates it. (The now famous technique of recombinant DNA was discovered as a side issue in the attempt by Nobelist Paul Berg to understand gene regulation.) If there is a program clock within the cell, it must involve gene expression and repression, particularly of regulatory genes. If we can control gene regulation, and aging is due to a clock, we can control the clock. And according to Dr. John Baxter, official chairman of the First Annual Congress for Recombinant DNA Research held recently in San Francisco, "Understanding the way genes are regulated is the biggest challenge since the discovery of the double helix, and . . . we are making great progress."

The technique of cell fusion has led to results fascinating for gerontology. Under the right conditions, which means adding certain viruses or a solution of polyethylene glycol (antifreeze) to a cell culture, two different cells will dissolve their membranes where they touch and flow together. Their nuclei fuse and the cell wounds heal, producing a single cell with the DNA from both cells. Even cells of different species can be made to fuse, and the fused cells, now called "hybrids," will divide and reproduce. Drs. Tom Norwood and George Martin of the University of Washington and Dr. Gretchen Stein of the University of Colorado have explored this promising area of research.[17] When young and old cells are fused in the test tube, neither nucleus will synthesize DNA. However, when a normal old cell is fused with a transformed or malignant cell, the nucleus of the old cell is induced to manufacture new DNA. DNA synthesis is rekindled in the senescent cell. Thus, the DNA of the old cell is not necessarily irretrievably damaged by aging. The situation is like that of old rats who can be made to swim like young rats by giving them extra neurotransmitter chemicals. The program is not lost or erased, it is just repressed, turned off. That's good, because repression we can learn to deal with, erasure maybe not. Dr. Stein believes that senescence may be caused by a substance produced within an old cell that interferes with the manufacture of the new DNA the cell needs to divide. In that case, by controlling gene regulation, the cells could be "born again." The Hayflick Limit is not inexorably ordained. Intervention is possible.

We know from Chapter 4 that cancer cells and "transformed cells" have escaped the Hayflick Limit. They have cast-off the restraint of growing old. It is possible to take a certain kind of cancer cell, a teratocarcinoma, place it in a young, developing embryo, and have the cancer cell revert to normal and proceed to become part of the embryo. Dr. Beatrice Mintz of the Institute for Cancer Research in Philadelphia has injected teratocarcinoma cells into early mouse embryos. The mice which develop are derived from both the normal embryo cells and the teratocarcinoma cells. They are just as healthy as ordinary mice. In the embryonic environment the teratocarcinoma cells have lost their malignant properties and have developed normally. Such astonishing experimental results and rapidly accumulating knowledge about gene expression will have a major impact on gerontology.

These brief synopses of promising research which is in progress and pertinent to longevity goals show that the chances for a breakthrough in the near future are not merely fanciful or wishful thinking. Part of the fundamental knowledge may already be at hand, and high-level funding of research could see its application rather soon. The scenario I envisage is a piecemeal but fairly large extension of mean and maximum life span secondary to the retardation of aging by nutritional and pharmacologic means, beginning within five years and continuing through the century. Then, by the end of the present century, in short within eighteen years, additional advances in fundamental biology will allow a substantial slowing down or even halting of the aging process. Our individual lives will expand into a new and exciting time-dimension. This expansion will enlarge the possibilities of personal and group activities, and, as I shall presently discuss, introduce a major new era into the future prospects for humankind. Time is indeed a "fourth dimension" in the psychological and sociological as well as in the physical science sense. Along with author-historian H.G. Wells, we can well imagine that given entrance into this new realm of time, "Man will stand upon earth as upon a footstool, and stretch forth his realm among the stars."

9

Transition to the Long-living Society

Lamenting that just about the time in life when we possess the wisdom and experience to give our best to the world and to ourselves, our energies fail and our bodies and brains begin to deteriorate, character Vitek in Karel Capek's play, *The Makropoulos Secret,* exclaims: "Let's give everyone a 300 year life . . . to be a child and pupil 50 years; 50 years to understand the world and its ways . . . and a hundred years to work in; and then a hundred, when we have understood everything, to live in wisdom, to teach and to give example. How valuable life would be if it lasted for 300 years!"

But is that really so? What actually will be the effects on society and the individual of the coming advances in geriatrics and gerontology? Will further extension first of average life span and then maximum life span—not necessarily (at least right off) to 300 years but say to 120 to 150 years—be a boon or a calamity? After learning that life-span extension is at least possible in the near future, people almost always ask me, "How will it affect society and the world? What will it mean for me as a person?" Then there is the moral imperative. Scientists engaged in research which may have a large impact on society are often blamed for not thinking in advance about the possible effects of their work.

Transition to the Long-living Society

An understanding of the situation of the elderly and pre-elderly of today, and how that is changing, may allow us to make some educated guesses about the nature of tomorrow in a long-living society. Even today, the survival of large numbers of relatively healthy elderly persons is a new experience for mankind. In 1850 only 33 percent of U.S. newborn children lived to be 60 years or older, today the figure is 83 percent. Ours is the first century in history in which significant numbers of people can expect to live out all phases of the life cycle. The current elderly and pre-elderly enjoy a new and important frontier to explore in laying out, as we shall see, the social roles of retirement, leisure, reeduction and multiple careers. True, the situation also features some negative aspects. Although maximum life span has not yet been extended, the 50 percent survival is increasing all the time. There are more functionally old people, and there will be even more. In 1900 the United States contained 3.1 million persons over 65 years of age; in 1940, 6.6 million; in the year 2000 the number will reach 30.6 million. In the combined industrialized nations by the year 2020, if present trends continue, there may be as many as 270 million "economically inactive" older persons—about 280 inactive for every 1,000 still active in the labor force, double the current inactive/active ratio.

Society has historically imprinted its members with negative concepts about the old. Even before becoming a major segment of the population, old people often received a bad press from the makers (or reflectors) of opinion, with a few notable exceptions like Plato, Chaucer, Proust, Brecht, and Andersen. Chaucer's Wife of Bath adores life and gets more skillful at exploiting it as she grows older. In her more mature years she becomes enamored of and weds a young lad named Jenkin, the sight of whose legs at her fifth husband's funeral had excited her. Brecht's old woman in "The Unworthy Old Woman" refuses to fit into her prescribed social role but continues to insist on change, experimentation, and free choice. Hans Christian Andersen gives probably the most favorable accounts of old age in fiction. The old and young often act together, or the old act as guardians of youth, or as magicians.

In this context, age is a time of ripeness and wisdom.

Nevertheless, writers who have been mostly negative about age stand clearly in the majority: Aristophanes, Hesiod, Sophocles, Dante, Shakespeare, Swift, Dickens, Molière, Coleridge, Thomas Hardy, Yeats, Beckett, and the Grimm brothers, just to cite a few among the baleful. Western drama often reflects the romantic ideal of virtuous youth pitted against malevolent, unbending old age.[1] *Romeo and Juliet* provides a close parallel with earlier plays by the Roman dramatists Plautus and Terence, where youthful romance is thwarted by blinded, prejudiced parents. Molière's comedy plots frequently reflect a similar situation, but in them the young people survive and win, their lighthearted activities providing the comedy. When old people win, it's usually portrayed as tragedy (Sophocles), or irony (Beckett). In both Goethe's and Marlowe's versions, Faust yields up his hope of heaven in return for a mere twenty-four years of restored youth—hardly a favorable reflection on the allurements of old age. Shakespeare's Polonius is one of the most pedantic bores in literature. King Lear presents a sorry picture of bungling age. Interestingly enough, just as Hans Christian Andersen presents the most favorable views of age, so the fairy tale Grimm Brothers give the grimmest. Remember the witches in *Hansel and Gretel* and *Snow White!* Youth wins handsomely in the Grimms' stories, stamping the evil old into the ground with hardly a second thought. As a source of societal data, literature can be used to find out past attitudes toward age. As we see, they were generally negative, even though before about 1900 the population contained too few old persons to constitute a significant social problem.

Today the attitudes are if anything worse, not so much in literature as in fact, as detailed by the former director of the National Institute on Aging, Dr. Robert Butler, in his book, *Why Survive? Being Old in America,*[2] for which he won a Pulitzer Prize. Both old and new myths about the aged continue to flourish and are compounded now by immense practical problems: medical care, housing, pensions, access to meaningful pursuits, personal security . . . the list is long. Myths that the aged are unproductive, disengaged, inflexible, and senile, nevertheless serenely sitting glued to the television tube in old peoples' collectives, or idling on park benches feeding pigeons and watching the passing parade, yet they keep multiplying in number, a vast swarm of the slowly dying, the undead, wrinkled, and wheedling, a sorry lot and nobody's idea of anything to be desired. Myths that they are useless, uninteresting, and can be safely disregarded, condemned to a foreclosed existence.

> There is . . . a greater debasement, a debasement based on loss of self esteem, of significant social roles, and of a sense of importance. It is the debasement of "agism,"[3] which has been defined by Alex Comfort as "the notion that people cease to be people, to be the same people or become people of a distinct and inferior kind, by virtue of having lived a specified number of years.[4]

An acceptance of these myths and stereotypes has allowed the young and middle-aged to feel guiltless while avoiding the problems of the old. Worst of all, the old people too have accepted the myths. Just as blacks and women once meekly acquiesced in the myths of their inferiority and so abetted their own enslavement, the old tend to respond to stereotypes about the aged by complying with them. "Products of a consumer society, the elders come to believe that they are obsolete products and suffer the fate reserved to old cars and broken plastic toys. They are discarded."[5]

Even seemingly good things may enforce bad myths. When you reach 62 or 65, you no longer have to pay overdue fines at most public libraries; at the National Parks you receive a Golden Age Passport entitling you to free entry; you get a 50 percent discount on recreational area use fees; you are encouraged to apply for Medicare benefits under Social Security; you receive discounts in many stores, buses, restaurants and theaters, an additional exemption on state and federal income taxes, and some young scamp surely says, "You're looking good, Pops." Soon you have accepted the myth, in part because of these benevolent put-downs. And although Falstaff can still keep up with youthful activities, he is told,

> Do you set down your name in the scroll of youth, that are written down old with all the characters of age? Have you not a moist eye, a dry hand, a yellow cheek, a white beard, a decreasing leg, and increasing belly? Is not your voice broken, your wind short, your chin double, your wit single, and every part about you blasted with antiquity. And will you yet call yourself young? Fie, fie, fie, Sir John!

The reality need not be like the above at all. Chronologic age is at best only a rough indication of functional age. Because age norms imposed by society work to constrain behavior, behavior at a particular age cannot be assumed to be a reliable indication of the possibilities of that age. The present old as a class are clearly capable of much more than society allows them to express or experience, or than they allow themselves. Social roles in late life are ambiguously defined, so old age seems pointless, valueless. But it is known that deprived of specific roles, young people will respond the same as the old.[6] In unemployment crises, for example, the young, rendered roleless, disengage, and become apathetic and indolent. Similar circumstances lead to similar responses irrespective of age. Many problems seemingly characteristic of the elderly are evoked by social conditions rather than innate processes.

Modern formal sociological theories agree with the above theses.[7] The major theory today to explain the observed differences between the old, middle-aged, and young is that of "age stratification." Sequential generations manifest different aging patterns because history assigns to each a different position in time. As each new cohort (cohort: a group of individuals born at about the same period) moves from childhood to old age, its members are assigned specific roles according to their age. They learn through complex processes of socialization what behavior is expected of them, what behavior patterns they must conform to.[8] The main idea is one of cohort flow through time. At any point in time the cohorts fit together to form the age strata in the population (Figure 9.1).

Age stratification also involves the process of becoming socialized to new roles as your cohort ages. The stratum to which you belong affects how you are supposed to behave. But as different groups come along, they never enter the same world. The world keeps changing. The old people of tomorrow will not be like those of today whether life span is extended or not.

The "social breakdown theory" seeks to explain part of the problem of today's elderly by asserting that a person already susceptible to psychological problems (secondary to retirement, financial straits, ill health, etc.) is apt to generate negative feedback from society. People tend not to respond positively to a depressed or dissatisfied person. But the ultimate breakdown is caused by continuing adherence to middle-aged values of visible productivity, the Industrial Revolution's chief moral by-product, namely, the work ethic. Thus the problems of today's older persons (besides health problems) stem largely from the use of dominant middle-class, middle-aged life-styles to judge their behavior. Society throws up guidelines permitting an individual to know if he is at the right spot at the right time in his life in terms of educational and career development. Prevailing guidelines for appropriate behavior in late life are often negative and restricting. It is the task of today's elderly and pre-elderly, both for themselves and the future young/old, to break free from dominance by these constricting social values. They have plenty to do.

I find the ideas about the interaction between status and roles[9] among the most intriguing relevant to the present elderly and the pre-elderly, i.e., those who may not themselves greatly benefit from coming gerontologic research but are already beginning to shape the future values of the long-living society. "Status" refers to the position or occupation which locates a person within the social structure, and "role" to the behavior considered appropriate thereto. Status and roles may coexist in three ways, and success and happiness at any age is much influenced by their relationship. The status(+) role(+) connection is commonest. Catholics, doctors, delivery boys,

Age strata.

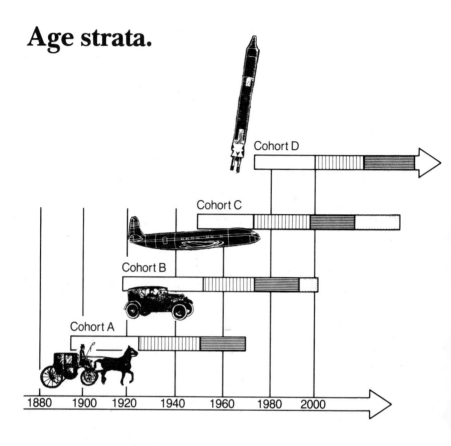

Stages in life course

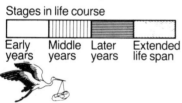

From point to point, the living memories and historical backgrounds of the total population change, as the cohorts flow through time. Digging deep into the strata, you might find still living a World War I mentality, but not one of the Civil War type. A more recent cohort is influenced by its vivid past experience of the Great Depression.

Figure 9.1

opera singers, school teachers, laboratory technicians, manual laborers all have a certain institutionalized status, and their roles and behavior are linked to and determined by it. If they depart too widely from the role, they risk losing the status. If you are a college professor (status), you are more or less coerced by society to behave within certain limits, and display a certain tweedy demeanor (role). The more you depart from the role prescribed by your status, the tougher you have to be to survive.

Another situation, designated as status($+$) role($-$), is characterized by a definite social position but only a vague role. Examples would be any merely honorary position, a consultant to a firm selected because he or she is famous although there really are no duties, anyone who has been "kicked upstairs" in his job, inactive Nobel laureates, former sex goddesses, retired admirals. All these have status according to what they were, but no longer an automatically active time-filling role.

Because old age involves a systematic status loss for an entire cohort, the third situation, status($-$) role($+$), assumes special interest. Here we discover a role behavior lacking status or position but serving a social function, whether positive or negative. Examples: the family scapegoat, rebels, villains, fools, clowns, playboys, gold-diggers, rabble-rousers, "dirty old men," collectors of odd bits of knowledge or trivia, tinkerers, game-players, jet setters, social lions . . . in a word all roles which cannot be linked to an institutionalized status, involve processes independent of social position, and provide essential or at least interesting functions which the major institutional roles don't cover. Note that status($-$) role($+$) individuals provide much of the variety that makes life dynamic and interesting. Their histories are the stuff of novels and movies. Great artists unrecognized throughout much of their lives often fall into this category: Cezanne, for example, or Van Gogh.

Figure 9.2 illustrates how these three status/role categories change with age. We see that the first declines drastically, beginning about the time of retirement. The second increases (but can be boring if that's all you've got . . . counting your awards, your newspaper clippings, but having nothing much else to do). The third holds steady with age. Those with an eccentric side to their personalities seem to age well, and might survive most happily in a long-living society. As a combination of 2 and 3, famous or honored eccentrics, like Bertrand Russell, probably enjoy the most successful old age.

After sociological theory, with its tinge of ethics, we come to economics. Economic theory indicates that additional increases in 50 percent survival—but without concomitant increases in maximum life span—risk creating serious problems. At our stage in history merely squaring the survival curve may be good for the individual (to live a bit longer, remain healthier) but threatens the collective economy. Analyzing the potential effects of further curve squaring for an article in the June 1978 issue of *Science,* economists G. Gori and B. Richter[10] concluded, "If current social, legislative, and economic rules

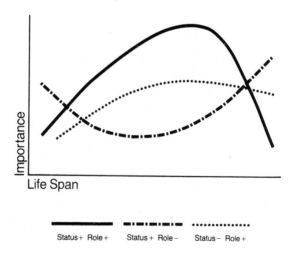

Relative importance of role types in the life span.

Figure 9.2

remain unchanged, a successful policy of disease prevention has a recessive economic potential." Their pessimistic appraisal can be explained by reference to Table 9.1. The table details what the numerical increase in the population at various age-periods would be in the years 1980, 1990 and 2000 if the five major causes of death had all been eliminated as of 1975. The numbers refer to increases in thousands in four age categories beyond current or future census projections. "Increase" means over and above what the population would be if these diseases just went on occurring at their present rates.

Table 9.1

Increase in population (in thousands) over current census projections in U.S. if the five major causes of death had been eliminated starting in 1975 (adapted from Gori and Richter)

Age range	1980	1990	2000
10–29	85	171	219
30–49	154	484	748
50–69	959	1622	2399
over 70	935	2029	4267

The table shows clearly that as the years pass, further conquest of major diseases will cause a progressively larger addition to the over 70-year-old age-group than to younger groups. With curve squaring the "functional" age of people (how active, alive, and vital you are) coincides with the true chronological age. With perfect curve squaring, all seventy year olds would be similar healthwise and free of major diseases, but they would still be 70 and therefore part way down the hill in age-susceptible functional capacities. The end result would be a top-heavy functional as well as chronologic age structure in the society. Gori and Richter calculate that by the year 1995 a medical "success," if limited to curve squaring (increase in 50 percent survival without increase in maximum life span), will cause a 5 percent drop in the expected gross national product, a 32 percent drop in private housing starts, a 126 percent increase in unemployment over the expected figure, and a 157 percent increase in unemployment insurance benefits. Political and business analyst Peter Drucker, considered the founding father of the discipline of management, also presents a negative view: "The more successful a society is in prolonging the individual life span [by which he means curve squaring] the lower inevitably is the rate of genuine capital formation by individuals."[11]

The only positive side of the projected economic picture would be a substantial savings in health care (such as the twelve- and one-half billion annual nursing home expense for senile dementia alone). In any case we are morally obliged to go on learning how to cure the major diseases. Not to do so would be like curing overpopulation by infanticide. So the economy will have to adjust to the negative side effects of a curve squaring technology. From the standpoint of pure, hard-headed economics, however, having increasing numbers even of disease-free elderly persons in the population and outside the workforce is not a rosy prospect. Even today, social security benefits alone account for over one-fifth of the federal budget.

Faced with problems of myth compounded by reality, governments are apt to apply to experts for advice. In 1978 the National Institute on Aging asked the National Academy of Sciences to establish a Committee on Aging, its first charge being to organize several conferences on the subject "the elderly of the future." It was hoped that the conference results would form a basis for institutional and government planning. The government wanted advice about (1) what was coming, and (2) what to do about what was coming.

I happened to be appointed as the only hard-core biologist on this committee. The other members were distinguished sociologists, political scientists, psychologists, economists from such places as Stanford, Harvard, the University of California, the University of Michigan, Duke University, and the like. We were in effect reminiscent of poet Charles Olson's line, "Boy, did you ever see, even in a museum, such a collection of Bodhisattvas!"

Among the Bodhisattvas, I argued hard that at least one of the conferences for which we were choosing subject matter and speakers be devoted to the socioeconomic effects of maximum life-span extension. I insisted that even if the chances of people living to be 120 or 140 years of age were small, even if only 5–10 percent over the next 10 to 20 years, the effects on society would be so profound that we ought to try delineating some of them in order that the government might have at least a rough plan in its side pocket for such a social juggernaut.

I achieved only a little success (a single lecture was to be devoted to this subject), and after impatient debate within the committee it seemed clear to me that a strong emotional resistance hindered most of my colleagues from considering such a topic worthwhile. As though before the atom bomb exploded over Hiroshima, J. Robert Oppenheimer had gone round to his sociopolitical colleagues and forewarned, "There's going to be a hellava big bang that may change a lot of things. What do you think about it? Is it wise or unwise, good, bad? How do you think it will affect mankind?" And without taking their eyes off of their curricula vitae, his colleagues had replied as though part of some Gilbert and Sullivan chorus, "Tell us just before it goes off, please, so we can put our fingers in our ears, put our fingers in our ears, put our fingers in our ears." And then it went off.

In the case of the Committee on Aging, I could not escape the conclusion that the prospect of maximum life-span extension tended to blow the data base and theoretical backgrounds which my expert friends were accustomed to weave together when concocting learned sociological predictions. They resisted the concept because they didn't know how to handle such a theme. So did most of the invited speakers. The speaker selected to address himself to "Political Characteristics of Elderly Cohorts in the 21st Century" marvelously covered subjects such as age-consciousness, educational status, and political organizations, but never once considered that maximum life span might be being substantially lengthened by that rather far-future time. Now most bio-gerontologists do indeed believe that at least sometime within the twenty-first century, if not before, maximum life span will be considerably extended. Present-day social gerontologists, on the other hand, often seem like clerics who don't want to think about resurrection because they'll be out of work. Ideas and data from them on this intriguing subject are shockingly scant. Therefore, we must look at the problems and opportunities with only minimal input from the professional clergy.

Before the seventeenth-century advent of modern thought about the orientation of man toward himself and the universe, the two main theories of history were those of Regression and of Cycles. Regressionists held that in some distant past a golden age existed. The object of human endeavor was to get back to it and rediscover the forgotten secrets of the ancient all-wise sages. The Theory of Cycles, by contrast, pictured society as going through ups and downs without any particular purpose or pattern. With the seventeenth and then eighteenth century philosophers, men like Descartes, Lord Bacon, Benjamin Franklin, William Godwin, and Condorcet, a new theory arose, a new paradigm, the Idea of Progress, which maintained that things could actually be improved by human effort over the passage of time. The Golden Age is not in the past but in the future!

But today we are witnessing the Counterrevolution of Falling Expectations. A growing pessimism manifests itself about man's ultimate abilities to solve his social, political, and economic problems. The failure of nuclear disarmament is a fine example of collectively rushing toward a clearly perceived disaster without being able to stop. On a personal everyday level the middle-class American dream of owning one's own home is becoming no more than that—a dream for most people, for whom dreams end and responsibilities begin. The individual is caught in a complexity which he feels powerless to influence. And if the environment is destroyed or the world fissioned, there won't be much chance anyway of living into the twenty-second century, or even the twenty-first. Charles Darwin himself advised, "... the first thing that must be asked about future man is whether he will be alive, and will know how to keep alive, and not whether it is a good thing that he should be alive." What is needed to keep alive is not another blueprint out of Adam Smith, Karl Marx, or John Maynard Keynes. Simple reworkings and extensions of older economic and political philosophies may not suffice to manage the problems of our current evolutionary stage. What we need is a jump or mutational event in the social structure, a discontinuity, an abrupt historical change in man's whole orientation toward himself and his problems. Significant extension of maximum human life span will in my view comprise such a mutational event, an epigenetic change to be sure, but one as remarkable as the jump from *homo erectus* to *homo sapiens.*

Extending maximum life span means that "functional" or "physiologic" age will no longer equal "chronologic" age. With life span extended to 130 years a person chronologically 75 years old will have the same vigor and appearance as a 50 year old today. The middle years in particular will be spread out, as visualized in Figure 9.3.

Because of this spread, span-extending technologies may yield quite different economic effects than curve squaring ones. The only professional economist who has considered these potential effects is Yale University's Professor Larry Kotlikoff (and even he only initiated his inquiry because of an invitation—my one success—from the National Academy of Sciences' Committee on Aging). On theoretical analysis Professor Kotlikoff finds that population growth anticipated from maximum life-span extension will have a different impact on economic welfare and per capita output than that arising from either curve squaring or altered birth rates.[12] Kotlikoff's measure of economic welfare is "average consumption per year" over an individual's lifetime. Population growth resulting from maximum life-span extension will, he concludes, lead to an increase in the ratio of productive to nonproductive persons, with an increased per capita output regardless of whether the working period increases year for year with life-span extension, or only proportionately. His analysis predicts, for example, that if people were to retire at age 80 instead of 60, and to die at 100 instead of 70, the capital intensity would be raised by 12 percent. This represents a substantial economic increase, as well as a doubling of the number of post-retirement years until death (twenty years instead of ten). A 50 percent survival of 100 years would correspond to a maximum life span of 125 to 130 years, with an even better economic outlook.

Comparison of present and future life spans.

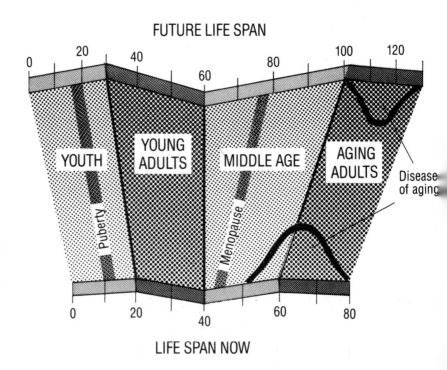

Extending maximum life span will stretch out the young-adult and middle-aged periods, probably with less extension of the period of decline. Longer youth period and later menopause will allow greater leeway in family planning. The diseases of old age will be delayed, and exposure to them will cover proportionally fewer years of the life span than they now do.

Figure 9.3

Table 9.2 shows what the "chronologic" population structure would be in the years ahead if "physiologic" aging had simply been stopped in 1980 and births restricted to replacement levels. It's an extreme-case example because if physiologic aging were absolutely halted, many of those over 65 years of age in 2040 would still be babies. However, the extreme case makes the point: retardation of the rate of aging will cause a striking shift toward an older average chronologic age of the population, but a younger average physiologic age. This change, not really into an "old" society but into what the Abkhazians of the Caucasus mountains in Soviet Georgia rightly call a "long-living" society, will revolutionize humankind and its institutions, not so much by Kotlikoff's economic effects (that too!) but by shifting us toward a more value-oriented society.

Table 9.2

Percent in each population group, assuming aging had been halted in 1980 and births restricted to a steady state level

Age range	1980	2000	2020	2040
under 18	34	26	20	17
18–64	56	47	41	34
65–90	10	21	17	17
over 90	1	6	22	32

Values are notoriously individual. We need therefore to consider the psychology of individuals, their personalities, in a long-living society. There is not much concrete data to fall back on but a fair amount of theory on which to stand. Science fiction has been singularly impotent in realizing the characteristics of people with greatly extended life spans—a sure sign that the characteristics will reflect a psychological paradigm change. The four major immortality themes of science fiction are all too comprehensible for belief. The long-lived or immortal populations are depicted as: wise and all-knowing; wise but evil; jaded and depleted by the ultimate boredom of having seen it all; or just ordinary persons who happen to be immortal because they were not born before the discovery of the immortality pill or serum. These themes are obviously clichés. In any far-future world, Buck, Flash, and Han Solo would all be regarded as irritating psychological throwbacks.

Two potential approaches to realizing the character makeup of citizens of a long-living society stem from existing formal sociopsychological theory: the psychoanalytic interpretation, and the theory of life periods promulgated by Erikson,[13] whose ideas were popularized in Gail Sheehy's book, *Passages.* Searching for lifelong determinants of character that were supposedly formed during early childhood, psychoanalytic theorists assume that the basic tendencies of the personality do not change much thereafter. If this were true, we could understand why some people are against life-span extension, even for themselves. It's enough to struggle with the same inner conflicts and hang-ups for 60–80 years. Who would want to do so for 150? Fortunately, most psychiatrists and psychologists now believe that adult development may involve ongoing personality changes. You are not as stuck with your personality as you are with your collagen fibers.

Erikson described seven stages of the life cycle, each with an identity crisis and a problem to be solved before one could pass to the next. All stages involve interactions between health, career, family circle, psychological attributes, and social responsibilities. We know that in the past several centuries the number of stages has been visibly increasing.[14] Only with the arrival of formal education in the seventeenth and eighteenth centuries did childhood become discernible as having special characteristics. Adolescence assumed its present style and meaning in the latter part of the nineteenth century. "Youth" as a period in life emerged only in the last few decades as a transition between adolescence and adulthood. More recently separated periods include the "young-old," ages 55–75 (healthy and vigorous, economically OK and relatively free from the responsibilities of work and parenthood), and the "old-old."

These life stages, or if you prefer "passages," will doubtless be altered and increased in number by significant extension of maximum life span. If behaviors now popularly regarded as age-inappropriate—such as entering into first marriage or becoming a political activist or provocateur at age 70—engage large numbers of people, they come to be accepted, and often produce major changes in social structure. A persistent tendency to return to college by older or longer-living persons would lead to a restructuring of educational institutions, greater flexibility of movement between education and work, and a general loosening of the age-stratification system.[15]

A primary integrating theme of the last stage of life is recognized by psychologists to be the search for values, for personal meaning, particularly that of one's own life. Near the end of the working career, successes and failures in the major tasks of youth and middle adulthood become clear to most individuals. There is usually (perhaps always) a discrepancy between initial goals and final accomplishments. Nobody gets home free or scores 100 percent. I've heard Linus Pauling admit the main thing he regrets in his long honors-filled life is that he didn't spend enough time with his children.

Age and time stimulate introspection and value judgements which, if successful, allow the enhancement of integrity. A life-review process takes place. To the extent that health and basic survival needs are not overriding problems, late life is far more concerned with identifying values than with running after achievement goals. Reminiscences of the very old, Casanova, Goethe, Ben Franklin, Bertrand Russell, Stravinsky reflect this resolution. In the movie *Raging Bull* it's exposed when ex-champion prizefighter Jake LaMotta, now an unfunny stand-up comedian rehearsing his lines in front of a mirror, suddenly confronts himself as the failure he has been as a human being, and achieves a moment of peace and insight, if not salvation. These moments expand with age, for ordinary as well as great men. The age-related shift toward a kind of super-integrity has been caught by William Butler Yeats in his poem, "The Coming of Wisdom with Time."

> Though the leaves are many, the root is one
> Through all the lying days of my youth
> I swayed my leaves and flowers in the sun
> Now I may wither into the truth.

The period of intense self-preoccupation and review accompanying the initial realization that one is "old" tends to pass with advanced age (90 years or older). Very old individuals are often quite wonderfully tranquil, serene, self-motivated, and, what is most pertinent to our futurist inquiry, pleasingly and stubbornly independent, even radical. "Structural conditions which prodded youth to be open to change and . . . exploration of identity may even today be reappearing among older people."[16] T. S. Eliot wrote, "Old men ought to be explorers." And according to British film director, Nicolas Roeg, *The Man Who Fell to Earth* was best understood by the under–12 and the over–80. They had no problems with it because the very old have gone past cultural conditioning. They don't care anymore. And the young do not yet have preconceptions, which can be so binding."[17]

Some see human development as a struggle to realize one's essence, one's being in purest form, and the successful aged exhibit the adult personality in purest form, with emphasis on self-realization. Extension of maximum life span may mitigate the intensity of the life-review and later processes at ages we now regard as old, but should not abrogate them. And the length of time included within a span-extended life should make experiential self-realization ventures almost guaranteed, a modernization of James Easton's account of one Edward Drinker, who died in 1782 at 103 years of age,

> The life of this man was marked with several circumstances, which have seldom occurred in the life of an individual. He saw the same spot of earth covered with wood, and a recep-

tacle for beasts and birds of prey, afterwards become the seat of a city, not only the first in wealth and arts in the new, but rivalling in both, many of the first cities in the old world. He saw regular streets, where he once pursued a herd, churches rising upon morasses, where he had often heard the croaking of frogs; wharfs and warehouses, where he had seen nothing but Indian canoes; a stately edifice, filled with legislators, astonishing the world with their wisdom and virtue, on the same spot, probably, where he had seen an Indian council-fire. He saw the first treaty ratified between the newly confederated powers of America and the ancient monarchy of France, with all the formalities of parchment and seals, where he had seen William Penn ratify his first and last treaty with the Indians, without the formalities of pen, ink, and paper. He witnessed all the intermediate stages through which a people pass, from the lowest to the highest degree of civilization, the beginning and the end of the empire of Great Britain in Pennsylvania. He had been the subject of crowned heads, and afterwards died a citizen of the newly created republic of America, and triumphed in the last years of his life in the salvation of his country.

In a long-living society the average educational level will increase markedly. Already large numbers of middle-aged women have been returning to school in the United States.[18] Among today's oldsters (those born 1890–1900), 20 percent were immigrants and most came from rural backgrounds and averaged only eight years of education. Of the thirty-nine million Americans 60 years or older today, 58 percent did not complete high school, 35 percent completed high school but not college, and only 7 percent completed college. Even among such cohorts, who obviously were not rendered education-prone by intense early exposure, 5 percent of persons 55–64-years-old and 2 percent of those over 64 are enrolled in university courses. The percentage of those taking such courses in the future will surely increase commensurate with the improved and expanded education of today's youth, because more of those who have been through college tend to seek adult education in later years.

With extended life spans we may expect to find an increasing number of individuals enjoying multiple careers. Even today that is beginning to happen, so it should increase. Ronald Reagan made the switch from B-pictures to professional politics at age 55. When asked why he had left a lucrative private practice in psychiatry to assume the directorship of the National Institute on Aging, Dr. Robert Butler voiced the cool reply, "It's a nice mid-life career change." At age 48, dentist Arild Hammer from Ketchikan, Alaska, left his tooth clinic with its staff of five and its 2,000 registered patients to become a commercial fisherman. He now navigates the waters off Alaska in his forty-seven-foot power trolly, "Infinity." After retiring in 1916, Jane Lillian commenced a new career in working with the aged, wrote *Salvaging Old Age*, traveled to India when 76, studied Mayan inscriptions in Central America at age 86, and died at 92. And to cite an older but stunning example: the Victorian rich man's son, William Morris, translated the Icelandic sagas into English, wrote one of the best of the Utopian novels (*News from Nowhere*), and was a charter member of the Pre-Raphaelite Brotherhood—in short a respectable man of means and letters; but at age 42 he chose a new path, resigned his family directorship in the Devon Great Consols Company, placed his silk top hat, symbol of capital, on a chair, sat on it, and went out to become one of the great eccentric socialist organizers of his day, who, for example, said, "I demand a free and unfettered animal life for man first of all. If we feel the least degradation in being amorous or merry or hungry or sleepy, we are so far bad animals, and therefore miserable men."

Any extension of maximum life span also extends the period of fertility. Example: rats on a caloric restriction regime are still capable of having offspring at the human equivalent of 80 to 100 years. They need to have their food intake temporarily increased to achieve successful impregnation at this late age: a long period of restriction may delay or suppress ovulation. The potential option of pursuing a full unfettered career before raising a family is attractive to many modern women.

Transition to the Long-living Society

I expect the successive career jumps of the long-lived person, and perhaps those especially of the status(−) role(+) category, will sometimes be into professions quite different from his or her earlier ones. Most people who grow bored in middle age or even younger try to just go on living their carefree regular life-style, or what Alan Watts calls "the terrible monotony of everlasting pleasure." They become more and more desperate without actually making the break into a new form, because of anxiety over security and identity. When debonair movie star George Sanders committed painless suicide nine years ago, he left a note saying no one should seek a message or read a scandal into his passing, that he was simply bored. Winston Churchill's last words were: "I am bored with it all." John Wilkes's last words: "It don't signify." Axel (in the play by Villiers de l'Isle-Adam): "As for living, our servants can do that for us." And Francis Bacon in his essay *Of Death:* "A man would die, though he were neither valiant nor miserable, only upon a weariness to do the same thing so often over and over."

Boredom often comes with being stuck in one life-style and within the biases of one nationality—another reason why some people can't abide the idea of very long lives. But perhaps having done what I want to do for my present career, which is, let us say, gerontology or the science of aging, I may elect to become a tour guide to the Museum of Antiquities in Cairo and the sights along the Nile, Abu Simbel, Luxor, the haunts of Anubis, God of the Underworld. My radical turnabout would not only necessitate learning Arabic, Egyptian history, and dressing in a white jelaba, but changing my whole being, becoming an alien to my past while nevertheless preserving that core identity—the "I" which is the sum of remembered experiences; of smells, nightfalls, voices, and the *Los Angeles Times* in the morning, with "coffee and oranges in a sunny chair," as Wallace Stevens phrased it. Or, to choose a status (−) role(+) projection, farming opium poppies in the Turkish highlands, and thinking, as I smoke my long pipe, "Those *L.A. Times*-reading Americans are either devils or fools." Radical personal change takes time, but given time, you gain the freedom and leisure to choose your own vision, outlandish or within the framework of your existing domain.

In social as well as in scientific pursuits, insight and progress often follow the successful melding of dissimilarities. In the past the population was broken into socioeconomic groups: the rich, the middle class, the poor, the aristocracy, the bourgeoisie, the proletariat. Recently we have also become segmented by life-styles. A person may enjoy a good income yet elect to live in a boarded-over storefront in Hollywood, or a loft space in New York. A friend of equal income and the same profession may inhabit a spacious house in Beverly Hills. This segmentation (and other forms of social diversity) are increasing, and according to management consultant Peter Drucker, "Population segmentation is one of the consumer economy's driving forces,"[19] and so bodes a favorable economic forecast. And due in part to the mixing of initial education (the young-young) and reeducation (the young-old) in the same classrooms, we may expect to witness an upswing in intergenerational marriages and love-relationships of which famous examples from literature and science (Goethe and Ulrika van Levetzow, Chateaubriand and Leontine, bacteriologist Robert Koch and his lady, Colette and her twenty-three-years-younger husband) persuade us of their insight-provoking benefits. Polygenerational families would constitute an additional diversifying influence within a long-living society, and, surprisingly enough, a new influence. The popular belief in large households of the past is illusory. Much less than 10 percent of all households in preindustrial England contained more than two generations.[20] With three to five living generations within a single family the average chronologic age can be shown to be 60 years, the average "physiologic" age 35–40 years.

On a personal level the above various changes, as they occur, will lead to important alterations in the individual's social network—a term referring to all contacts he or she may customarily have with other persons.[21] Social networks are important, not only for happiness but for basic survival. In a study of 7,000 adults in California with subsequent nine-year mortality follow-up, the relative risk of death for persons with the smaller compared to larger social networks was 2.3 times for males and 2.8 times for females.[22]

The sometimes bizarre, and greatly extended social networks already visible in today's world should increase within a long-living society. A few months ago I was visited in my office by a wilderness-born Masai warrior whose name is Tepilit Ole Saitoti. He told me that each Masai group sends off its brightest child for a western education. Tepilit Ole Saitoti was educated initially in bushlore by his tribespeople in the east African veldt, and a bit later on Shakespeare by the Dons of Oxford. He now lectures widely and has published an elegant photographic text about his people. But he returns periodically to the barefoot existence of a spearman. A song made famous by the late black singer, Josephine Baker, ran, "Two loves have I, Paris and Savannah." Only a few years later, Tepilit Ole Saitoti has much more diverse loves to keep him warm, thanks to the airplane, the motor car, and the instant safari of TV. Well, why not go from Oxford to the bush? It's merely a change of channel, whereupon at the sight of black warriors dipping their paddles into the steaming river, some one shouts, "Well rowed, Balliol!"

Less bizarre but equally extended future social networks would include multinational, long-term, intermittent, interpersonal relationships and friendships, added to but not replacing the local, constant ones we are more familiar with today. Part of my own experience within the international scientific community is a good example of an extended network. The community of modern biologists dedicated to investigating the major histocompatibility complex (MHC, the cluster of genes which regulate immune function in man) was small when it first gathered in the mid-fifties. Only about eight of us MHC pioneers were around when Professor D.B. Amos staged the first International MHC Workshop in 1965 in South Carolina, but already we constituted an international group hailing from the U.S., Great Britain, Holland, France, Scandinavia, and elsewhere. It transpired without any formal plan that every two to three years one of us sponsored another

Workshop at which the newer aspects of the field were hammered out, nailed together, and flown. The original group became known as the "Councillors" of the Workshops. In them I have by now a dozen twenty-year-long solid friends from many lands. With most of them I am in personal contact only two to three weeks every two to three years, yet I know their lives and personalities quite as well as if they were denizens of Los Angeles—and from a perspective with the dross drained because we have only been together during seasons of activity. Our relationship foreshadows the intermittent friendship possibilities open to the extended life span of the multinational man, leading to a great expansion of what Marshall McLuhan rightly dubbed "global consciousness."

The picture emerging from the above analysis, and much of it based upon existing sociological data and theory—of second and third careers in the same lifetime, intergenerational education, intergenerational marriages, polygenerational families, bizarre and extended social networks—is one of increasing population segmentation and social diversity, in short a more variegated interesting world with a raised, more value-oriented social consciousness. Add Kotlikoff's prediction of improved economy thereto and the picture of what I personally anticipate the long-living society may be like is not unattractive.

I also expect, allowing a bit more fantasy to prevail, that with the extension of time into experience and local into global consciousness, the lopsided achievement-orientation dominating our frantic twentieth century might well change in part into the orientation of games. Presently we have twenty-five years to grow up in and forty years in which to achieve the goals of adulthood, then we slide along horizontally or downhill until death claims us. Men say of us, "He was a great painter, a good scientist, a fine carpenter, a patriotic soldier, an honest and effective politician." Contemporary man is obsessed with earning the highest accolades for his achievements within the time that he has; and since that time is short, he drives his heart and mind forward at a killing pace. But the world of games anticipates another reality, an entirely different organizing strategy which can illustrate for us how different things might conceivably be. To quote from Alan Harrington's fine book, *The Immortalist:*

> . . . men are always trying to get out of real time, to shift their activities into parallel ribbons and blocks of time. Millions take refuge in the divine world of games. The management of games provides us a clue to the satisfying management of immortality. We will see that in the Utopia Beyond Time, our present game structures can serve as models for the structures of the successive lives that each man and woman will someday live out in eternity.[23]

Games orientation has already begun in the modern world —witness publications like *Moves,* the magazine of gaming technics, or *Strategy and Tactics,* or *Dungeons and Dragons* as a simpleminded forerunner of serious business, and on the most refined of levels, Nobel novelist Hermann Hesse's glass bead game. When time expands, time's frameworks are the rules of games. Under these circumstances, and freed of the constant buffeting of compressed events and responsibilities thrust on him or her from outside, each person in the world of games can arrange his existential choices. An antiquarian of the distant future might well write of such a twenty-first-century man:

> The life of this man was marked with several circumstances. He saw the same regions on earth, once covered with fine cities, destroyed by overdevelopment, pollution, and the ravages of deprived multitudes, then rebuilt as gleaming pollution-free metropoles powered by solar voltaic cells. Clean rivers ran through the gardens of the cities, in one of which in his own room he sat at the twentieth-century's almost flaming aftermath, watching prime time news update the impending nuclear war between the superpowers, a war without value, totally negative, an enterprise propelled by cadres of generals and political fools, until . . . he began his own crusade, along with several million of those who were beginning to think of themselves as the first young-old, although they were not so old yet, only en route

along the road to the time of the young-old. Soon people everywhere following their resolute examples began saying "No" to the valueless perpetuation of the war machines. This nay-saying led to the first great reordering, greater than anyone had expected, a paradigm times paradigm change. Afterwards he spent several years in touch with computers and monitors hooked to planetary satellites, becoming reeducated, preparing himself, during the succeeding long course of his life, to assume responsibility for what he would cause to happen, or more often just allow to happen. He embraced the liberties and independence of his generation, a better than average example of the new species of human who had ushered in the early portion of the twenty-first century and triumphed in the last years of his life in the salvation of the world—of course doing so with great good humor, the only way to approach unexplored territory.

Appendix A

The table in this appendix, for which I am indebted to Ms. Susan Ritman, lists nutrient values for ninety-nine common, representative foods, as well as the official Recommended Daily Allowances (RDA) for each of the thirty-two essential nutrient substances (except for sodium, which I personally recommend as being *lower* than 1.5 grams per day, for reasons given in Chapter 7). You will find by playing with the data of the table—and as we have found by extensive computer analyses of over 5,000 possible combinations, done by our computer consultant, Mr. Jochen Haber—that it is difficult to construct a 1,500 calorie per day food combination within the chosen limits for proteins, fats, and varieties of foods (see below) which actually has enough of all thirty-two RDA's, and so can be accurately labeled as entirely fulfilling the criteria of "undernutrition without malnutrition." Some supplementation with vitamins or minerals may be required at these or lower calorie levels (see Appendix B).

Therefore, at least until I or others have done further investigative work on the problem, these appendices (A and B) can only be considered as illustrative guides, and not as failsafe formulations. One must be careful with respect to very long-term low caloric intake. Data do exist (compiled from the medical literature by Dr. Reuben Andres of the Gerontology Research Center of the National Institute on Aging) indicating that, on the average, underweight persons actually have shorter survival than slightly overweight people. These data certainly do not support Nathan Pritikin's anti-obesity campaign, nor do they accord with my own views, nor with the experimental data derived from underfeeding in animals. However, the information given in the table of this appendix, plus our computer experience, may help explain what seems like a paradox. I think the explanation is that people who are underweight because of not eating very much are often malnourished—unless they have been extremely careful and selective in what they have actually eaten. On the typical, slipshod American, and most foreign diets, you are apt to be somewhat malnourished unless you actually overeat—and malnutrition does not promote longevity, regardless of any low calorie benefit.

Nutritive Values of Foods

FOOD Category and Substance	AMOUNT OF FOOD PER DAY		MEASURE		Calories	Total Protein (GM)	ESSENTIAL AMINO			
	Min	Max	Portion	GM			Tryptophan	Threonine	Isoleucine	Leucine
RECOMMENDED DAILY ALLOWANCE						56	180	48	720	960
MEAT & POULTRY										
Hamburger	100	100	3½ oz.	100	174	21	190	700	850	1300
Calves Liver	100	100	3½ oz.	100	137	19	300	900	1000	1750
Chicken (light meat)	100	100	3½ oz.	100	110	23	200	800	1100	1475
Lamb (choice)	100	100	3½ oz.	100	257	17	200	750	800	1200
Pork (thin class)	100	100	3½ oz.	100	275	17	150	600	600	900
Ham (canned)	100	100	3½ oz.	100	184	18	200	700	800	1100
Turkey (flesh only)	100	100	3½ oz.	100	159	24	—	1000	1260	1800
Veal	100	100	3½ oz.	100	184	19	250	850	1030	1400
FISH & SHELLFISH										
Clams	70	70	4 cherrystone	70	74	13	—	450	475	775
Cod	100	100	3½ oz.	100	75	18	—	900	800	1450
Crab (steamed)	50	100	3½ oz.	100	88	17	—	730	745	1400
Halibut	100	100	3½ oz.	100	93	20	—	800	822	1350
Herring, Atlantic	50	100	1 herring	50	167	17	—	1000	1050	1750
Lobster	50	100	1 cup cubed	145	91	19	—	730	745	1400
Mackerel, Atlantic	100	100	3½ oz.	100	184	19	—	1075	1200	1850
Ocean Perch (redfish)	100	100	3½ oz.	100	83	18	—	700	800	1200
Oysters	50	100	med—2 selects	25	63	8.4	—	450	475	775
Salmon										
Atlantic	100	100	3½ oz.	100	209	23	—	800	800	1250
Atlantic, canned	100	100	1 can 6½ oz.	185	196	22	200	875	1025	1500
Sardines, Pacific, raw	50	100	3½ oz.	100	157	19	—	325	330	550
Shrimp, raw	50	100	3½ oz.	100	85	18	—	730	750	1400
Sole	100	100	3½ oz.	100	75	17	—	800	800	1350
Swordfish	100	100	3½ oz.	100	112	19	—	1100	1200	1850
Tuna, canned in water	50	100	½ cup	115	119	28	—	1100	1200	1850
FRUITS										
Apples	150	300	1 med 2¾" diam.	150	67	0.2	3	14	13	23
Apricots	40	80	1 med.	40	58	1	—	16	14	23
Avocado	75	150	1 cup	150	176	2	9	40	47	76
Banana	150	300	1 med.	150	94	1.1	13	38	32	53
Cantaloupe	200	400	½ med.	400	36	0.7	—	—	—	—
Grapefruit	100	200	sections 1 cup	190	47	0.5	—	—	—	—
Grapes	75	150	1 cup	150	78	1.3	3	19	6	14
Orange	90	360	1 med.	180	54	1.0	6	12	23	22
Peaches	100	200	1 med.	100	43	0.6	4	27	13	29
Pears	75	150	1 small	75	66	0.7	—	—	—	—
Pineapple	70	140	1 cup diced	140	59	0.4	—	—	—	—
Raisins	30	60	2 tbsp.	18	320	2.5	—	—	—	—
Strawberries	75	150	1 cup whole	150	39	0.7	9	25	18	42
Watermelon	160	320	1 cup diced	160	28	0.5	—	—	—	—

ACIDS (MG) Lysine	Phenylalanine	Tyrosine	Valine	Methionine or Cysteine	Fat (GM)	Carbohydrate (GM)	Fiber (GM)	VITAMINS A (I.U.)	C (MG.)	D (I.U.)	E (I.U.)	K (MCG)
720	960		840	600	35% of total cals.	50-100GR		5000	60	400	15	70-140
1400	650	555	900	400	10	0	0	20	—	0	0.9	7
450	950	700	1200	450	5	4	0	22,500	36	0-15	2	90
1590	800	650	1000	500	2	0	0	60	—	0	0.6	—
1275	625	500	800	400	21	0	0	—	—	0	0.9	—
1000	500	425	600	325	23	0	0	0	—	0	0.7	11
1250	600	550	790	375	12	0.9	0	0	—	0	1.0	15
2200	960	—	1200	650	7	0	0	—	—	0	—	—
1600	800	700	1000	450	12	0	0	—	—	0	—	—
800	400	400	625	275	1.6	2.0	0	100	10	0	—	—
1700	850	650	900	575	0.3	0	0	0	2	—	0.33	—
1250	650	600	750	450	2	0.5	—	2200	2	0	—	—
1650	650	625	900	400	1.4	0	0	—	—	44	0.9	—
1800	925	775	1200	600	11	0	0	110	—	315	1.6	—
1250	650	600	750	475	1.5	0.3	0	—	—	0	—	—
2300	900	950	1800	650	12	0	0	450	—	1100	—	—
1600	650	625	1100	500	1.2	0	0	—	—	3/med. sized	—	—
800	400	400	625	275	1.8	3.4	0	300	—	0	—	—
1600	675	550	950	500	13	0	0	—	9	154-550	—	—
1800	750	550	1100	600	12	0	0	—	—	220-440	—	—
550	300	250	400	200	9	0	0	—	—	1150-1170	—	—
1250	650	600	750	475	0.8	1.5	—	—	—	150	—	—
1650	650	625	900	400	0.8	0	0	—	—	—	—	—
2300	900	1000	1800	650	4	0	0	1600	—	—	—	—
2300	900	1000	1800	650	0.8	0	0	—	—	—	—	—
22	10	6	15	3	0.6	15	1	90	4	0	0.8	—
23	13	10	19	4	0.2	13	0.6	2700	10	0	—	—
59	48	32	63	29	16	6	1.6	290	14	0	—	—
46	44	29	45	22	0.2	22	0.5	190	10	0	0.45	2
—	—	—	—	—	0.1	8	0.3	3400	33	0	0.18	—
—	—	—	—	—	0.1	11	0.2	80	40	0	—	—
15	14	12	9	23	1.0	16	0.6	100	4	0	—	—
43	30	17	31	12	0.2	12	0.5	200	50	0	—	1
30	18	21	40	31	0.1	10	0.6	1330	7	0	—	8
—	—	—	—	—	0.4	15	1.4	20	4	0	0.8	—
—	—	—	—	—	0.2	14	0.4	70	17	0	—	—
—	—	—	—	—	0.2	77	0.9	20	1	0	—	6
32	23	27	23	1	0.5	8	1.3	60	60	0	0.3	—
—	—	—	—	—	0.2	6	0.3	590	7	0	—	—

FOOD Category and Substance	AMOUNT OF FOOD PER DAY		MEASURE		NUTRITIVE VALUES OF FOODS					
					VITAMINS					
	Min	Max	Portion	GM	Thiamine (MG)	Riboflavin (MG)	Niacin (MG)	B-6 (MG)	Folacin (MCG)	B-12 (MCG)
RECOMMENDED DAILY ALLOWANCE					1.4	1.7	18	2	400	3
MEAT & POULTRY										
Hamburger	100	100	3½ oz.	100	0.09	0.18	5	0.4	7	1.8
Calves Liver	100	100	3½ oz.	100	0.2	2.7	11	0.7	220	60
Chicken (light meat)	100	100	3½ oz.	100	0.05	0.09	11	0.68	6	0.45
Lamb (choice)	100	100	3½ oz.	100	0.15	0.2	5	0.28	4	2
Pork (thin class)	100	100	3½ oz.	100	0.8	0.2	4	0.45	8	0.7
Ham (canned)	100	100	3½ oz.	100	0.5	0.2	4	0.4	8	0.6
Turkey (flesh only)	100	100	3½ oz.	100	0.08	0.14	8	—	10	—
Veal	100	100	3½ oz.	100	0.14	0.25	6	0.34	5	1.6
FISH & SHELLFISH										
Clams	70	70	4 cherrystone	70	0.1	0.18	1.3	0.08	—	98
Cod	100	100	3½ oz.	100	0.06	0.07	2.2	0.23	18	0.8
Crab (steamed)	50	100	3½ oz.	100	0.16	0.08	2.8	0.3	2	10
Halibut	100	100	3½ oz.	100	—	—	—	0.43	12	1
Herring, Atlantic	50	100	1 herring	50	0.02	0.15	3.6	0.37	—	10
Lobster	50	100	1 cup cubed	145	0.1	0.07	—	—	17	0.5
Mackeral, Atlantic	100	100	3½ oz.	100	0.15	0.33	8.2	0.5	—	0.9
Ocean Perch (redfish)	100	100	3½ oz.	100	0.1	0.08	1.9	0.23	9	1
Oysters	50	100	med—2 selects	25	0.14	0.18	2.5	0.05	—	18
Salmon										
Atlantic	100	100	3½ oz.	100	—	0.08	7	0.7	26	4
Atlantic, canned	100	100	1 can 6½ oz.	185	—	—	—	0.3	20	7
Sardines, Pacific, raw	50	100	3½ oz.	100	—	—	—	0.24	16	17
Shrimp, raw	50	100	3½ oz.	100	0.02	0.03	3.2	0.1	11	0.9
Sole	100	100	3½ oz.	100	0.05	0.05	1.7	—	11	—
Swordfish	100	100	3½ oz.	100	0.05	0.05	8	—	—	1
Tuna, canned in water	50	100	½ cup	115	—	0.1	13	0.43	15	2.2
FRUITS										
Apples	150	300	1 med 2¾" diam.	150	0.03	0.02	0.1	0.03	8	0
Apricots	40	80	1 med.	40	0.03	0.04	0.6	0.07	—	0
Avocado	75	150	1 cup	150	0.11	0.2	1.6	0.42	51	0
Banana	150	300	1 med.	150	0.05	0.06	0.7	0.5	28	0
Cantaloupe	200	400	½ med.	400	0.04	0.03	0.6	0.09	30	0
Grapefruit	100	200	sections 1 cup	190	0.04	0.02	0.2	0.034	11	0
Grapes	75	150	1 cup	150	0.05	0.03	0.3	0.08	7	0
Orange	90	360	1 med.	180	0.1	0.04	0.4	0.06	46	0
Peaches	100	200	1 med.	100	0.02	0.05	1	0.024	8	0
Pears	75	150	1 small	75	0.02	0.04	0.1	0.017	14	0
Pineapple	70	140	1 cup diced	140	0.09	0.03	0.2	0.088	11	0
Raisins	30	60	2 tbsp.	18	0.11	0.08	0.5	0.24	4	0
Strawberries	75	150	1 cup whole	150	0.03	0.07	0.6	0.055	16	0
Watermelon	160	320	1 cup diced	160	0.03	0.03	0.2	0.068	8	0

(VALUES PER 100 GM) →

		MINERALS										
Pantothenic Acid (MG)	Biotin (MCG)	Ca (MG)	P (MG)	Mg (MG)	K (MG)	Na (MG)	Fe (MG)	Cu (MG)	Mn (MG)	Zn (MG)	Se (MCG)	Cr (MG)
4-7	100-200	1200	1200	400	1875-5675	1100-3300	18	2-3	2.5-5.0	15	50-200	0.05-0.2
0.6	—	12	200	21	350	65	3	0.06	0.02	3.4	20	0.03
8	100	8	330	16	280	70	9	5	0.17	4	43	0.06
0.8	11	11	218	17	320	50	1.1	0.011	0.02	0.6	12	0.03
0.55	6	10	150	15	90	90	1.2	0.06	0.02	3	18	0.03
0.8	5	10	190	22	120	120	2.5	0.011	0.02	1.4	24	0.03
0.68	5	11	160	19	340	1100	2.7	0.34	0.02	1.7	—	0.03
0.86	—	8	200	28	315	66	1.5	0.037	0.02	2	—	0.03
0.9	2	11	200	15	170	170	3	0.05	0.02	3	—	0.03
0.3	—	70	160	—	180	120	6	—	—	1.5	—	—
0.14	—	10	200	28	400	70	0.4	—	—	—	43	—
0.6	—	43	175	34	—	—	0.8	0.27	0.02	3.6	—	0.03
0.28	8	—	—	—	—	—	—	—	—	—	—	—
1	—	—	260	—	—	—	1.1	—	—	—	—	—
1.5	—	65	200	22	180	210	0.8	—	—	—	63	—
0.24	18	5	230	28	—	—	1	—	—	—	—	—
0.36	—	20	200	—	270	80	1	—	—	—	—	—
0.25	9	90	140	32	120	70	5.5	—	—	—	65	—
1.3	—	80	190	—	—	—	0.9	—	—	—	—	—
0.55	15	270	300	30	400	50	—	0.08	0.02	1.1	—	0.03
1	24	33	215	24	—	—	1.8	—	—	—	—	—
0.28	—	60	170	50	220	140	1.6	—	—	—	60	0.03
0.3	—	12	200	—	340	80	0.8	0.01	0.02	0.3	—	0.03
0.19	—	19	200	—	—	—	0.9	—	—	—	—	—
0.3	3	16	200	—	280	40	1.6	0.01	0.02	0.4	—	0.03
0.11	0.9	7	10	5	110	1	0.3	0.014	0.035	0.012	0.45	0.015
0.24	—	17	23	12	280	1	0.5	0.04	0.01	0.085	—	0.015
1	5.5	10	42	45	600	4	0.6	—	—	—	—	—
0.26	4.4	8	26	33	370	1	0.7	0.11	0.13	0.15	0.95	0.015
0.25	3	14	16	16	250	12	0.4	0.014	0.01	0.14	—	0.015
0.28	3	16	16	12	135	1	0.4	0.04	0.01	0.1	—	0.015
0.08	1.6	16	12	13	160	3	0.4	0.035	0.065	0.035	—	0.015
0.25	1.9	40	20	11	200	1	0.4	0.004	0.008	0.02	1.3	0.012
0.17	1.7	9	20	10	202	1	0.5	0.04	0.01	0.05	0.4	0.015
0.07	—	8	11	7	130	2	0.3	0.04	0.01	0.055	0.6	0.015
0.16	—	17	8	13	150	1	0.5	0.15	1.2	0.08	0.55	0.015
0.045	4.5	60	100	35	760	27	3.5	—	—	—	—	—
0.34	4	20	20	12	160	1	1	—	—	—	—	—
0.3	3.6	7	10	8	100	1	0.5	0.017	0.026	0.085	—	0.015

FOOD Category and Substance	AMOUNT OF FOOD PER DAY		MEASURE		NUTRITIVE VALUES OF FOODS					
	Min	Max	Portion	GM	Calories	Total Protein (GM)	ESSENTIAL AMINO			
							Tryptophan	Threonine	Isoleucine	Leucine
RECOMMENDED DAILY ALLOWANCE						56	180	48	720	960
VEGETABLES										
Asparagus	100	200	4 large spears	100	32	2.5	25	60	55	100
Beans										
Lima	75	150	1 cup	150	126	8.4	200	825	975	1600
Green	75	150	1 cup	100	37	1.9	33	90	90	160
Garbanzos	100	200	1 cup	200	373	21	175	750	900	1500
Soybeans (mature)	100	200	1 cup	200	434	34	525	1600	1900	3200
Soybean Curd (tofu)	60	120	1 piece 2½ × 1 × 2¾	120	79	8	—	2150	2400	3950
Beets										
Greens	75	150	cooked, 1 cup	150	32	2.2	20	60	40	90
Red, raw	70	140	1 cup diced	140	97	1.6	17	60	45	80
Broccoli	100	400	1 lb., 2 large or 4 small	450	41	3.6	45	160	186	240
Brussels Sprouts	100	200	1 lb., 24 × 1" diam.	450	56	5	60	200	230	250
Cabbage	70	200	1 cup finely shredded	90	27	1.3	17	60	50	85
Carrots	80	240	1 carrot 7½ × 1⅛	80	46	1.1	8	33	33	50
Cauliflower	50	100	1 cup whole flowerettes	100	33	2.7	40	120	135	200
Celery	60	120	1 cup chopped	120	21	0.9	14	40	45	75
Corn	100	400	1 cob (refuse 45%)	225	111	3.5	12	80	75	220
Cowpeas	70	140	1 cup	140	354	23	250	850	900	1650
Cucumber	45	130	1 small 6⅜ × 1¾	180	18	0.9	6	21	25	35
Eggplant	100	200	1 cup diced	200	31	1.2	12	45	50	70
Lettuce	90	360	wedge ⅛ of head	90	17	0.9	10	54	50	83
Mushrooms	35	105	1 cup sliced or diced	70	31	2.7	40	100	85	135
Onions	40	160	1 cup chopped	160	43	1.5	20	20	20	35
Parsley	3.5	60	1 cup chopped	60	56	3.6	75	—	—	—
Peas	70	140	1 cup	140	84	6	65	250	275	455
Peppers, Green	25	100	1 cup strips	100	27	1.2	—	—	—	—
Potatoe										
White	100	500	2¾ × 4¼	250	77	2	33	75	75	120
Sweet	90	360	5 × 2	180	118	1.7	22	50	50	70
Spinach	25	100	1 cup chopped	55	32	3.2	35	115	100	200
Squash	65	195	1 cup sliced or cubed	130	21	1.1	—	—	—	—
Tomatoe	50	200	2½" diam.	100	26	1.1	9	25	20	30
Turnip Greens	115	400	1 lb.	450	35	3	—	127	106	210
CHEESE										
American	25	100	1 slice 2¼ × 2¼ × ¼	25	373	22	325	700	1025	200
Cheddar	30	120	1" cube	30	402	25	320	900	1550	240
Cottage (low fat, made from 1% milk fat)	60	240	¼ cup	60	68	12	140	550	700	130
Monterey Jack	30	120	1" cube	30	369	24	300	875	1500	238
Mozzarella (part skim)	30	120	1" cube	30	252	24	—	900	1200	24
Swiss	30	120	1" cube	30	369	28	400	1000	1500	30

Lysine	Phenylalanine	Tyrosine	Valine	Methionine or Cysteine	Fat (GM)	Carbohydrate (GM)	Fiber (GM)	A (I.U.)	C (MG.)	D (I.U.)	E (I.U.)	K (MCG)
720	960		840	600	35% of total cals.	50-100GR		5000	60	400	15	70-140
100	55	45	80	28	0.2	5	0.7	900	33	0	3.7	60
1475	1200	650	1000	250	0.5	22	1.8	290	30	0	—	—
130	100	80	115	30	0.2	7	1	600	20	0	—	14
1375	1150	600	900	200	5	61	5	50	—	0	—	—
2650	2050	1300	2000	525	18	34	5	80	—	0	—	—
3050	2525	1900	2600	700	4.2	2.4	0.1	0	0	0	—	—
60	55	50	45	17	0.3	5	1.3	6100	30	0	—	—
95	65	65	45	35	0.1	10	0.8	20	10	0	—	—
220	175	—	210	60	0.3	6	1.5	2500	110	0	3.0	200
250	170	—	230	45	0.4	8	1.6	550	100	0	1.5	—
50	50	30	70	17	0.2	5	0.8	130	50	0	0.3	125
45	30	25	50	14	0.2	10	1.0	11,000	8	0	0.8	—
160	100	—	155	45	0.2	5	1	60	80	0	0.2	—
27	50	—	55	25	0.1	4	0.6	240	9	0	0.45	—
75	110	70	125	40	1.0	22	0.7	400	12	0	2.5	—
1600	1200	600	1060	270	1.5	62	4.4	30	—	0	—	—
35	20	—	28	8	0.1	3.4	0.6	250	11	0	0.15	—
60	50	45	60	13	0.2	6	0.9	10	5	0	—	—
50	67	102	71	24	0.1	3	0.5	330	6	0	0.8	129
165	75	70	95	17	0.3	4.4	0.8	tr	3	0	0.1	—
60	40	—	30	16	0.1	9	0.6	40	10	0	0.15	—
530	—	—	—	18	0.6	9	1.5	8500	172	0	2.7	—
480	290	200	300	60	0.4	14	2.0	640	27	0	0.15	—
—	—	—	—	—	0.2	5	1.4	420	128	0	—	—
100	80	55	90	25	0.1	17	0.5	tr	20	0	0.07	3
45	50	30	60	22	0.4	27	0.7	8,800	21	0	—	—
160	130	110	130	45	0.3	4	0.6	8,100	51	0	3.7	89
—	—	—	—	—	0.1	4	0.6	400	22	0	—	—
30	20	14	25	7	0.2	5	0.5	900	23	0	0.45	5
157	142	86	136	32	0.3	5	0.8	7,600	139	0	—	650
2100	1100	1200	1300	575	31	1.6	0	1200	0	12-15	—	—
2100	1300	1200	1700	650	33	1.3	0	1100	0	12-15	—	—
1000	670	660	770	375	1.0	2.7	0	37	tr	12-15	—	—
2000	1300	1200	1600	640	30	0.7	0	950	0	12-15	—	—
2500	1300	1400	1500	700	16	3	0	600	0	12-15	—	—
2600	1700	1700	2100	800	27	3.4	0	800	0	12-15	—	—

FOOD Category and Substance	AMOUNT OF FOOD PER DAY		MEASURE		NUTRITIVE VALUES OF FOODS					
					VITAMINS					
	Min	Max	Portion	GM	Thiamine (MG)	Riboflavin (MG)	Niacin (MG)	B-6 (MG)	Folacin (MCG)	B-12 (MCG)
RECOMMENDED DAILY ALLOWANCE					1.4	1.7	18	2	400	3
VEGETABLES										
Asparagus	100	200	4 large spears	100	0.18	0.2	1.5	0.15	64	0
Beans										
Lima	75	150	1 cup	150	0.24	0.12	1.4	0.6	110	0
Green	75	150	1 cup	100	0.08	0.11	0.5	0.08	44	0
Garbanzos	100	200	1 cup	200	0.31	0.15	2.0	0.5	200	0
Soybeans (mature)	100	200	1 cup	200	1.1	0.3	2.2	0.8	170	0
Soybean Curd (tofu)	60	120	1 piece 2½ × 1 × 2¾	120	0.06	0.03	0.1	—	—	—
Beets										
Greens	75	150	cooked, 1 cup	150	0.1	0.22	0.4	0.1	—	0
Red, raw	70	140	1 cup diced	140	0.03	0.05	0.4	0.055	90	0
Broccoli	100	400	1 lb., 2 large or 4 small	450	0.1	0.23	0.9	0.2	70	0
Brussels Sprouts	100	200	1 lb., 24 × 1" diam.	450	0.1	0.16	0.9	0.23	55	0
Cabbage	70	200	1 cup finely shredded	90	0.05	0.05	0.3	0.16	33	0
Carrots	80	240	1 carrot 7½ × 1⅛	80	0.06	0.05	0.6	0.15	14	0
Cauliflower	50	100	1 cup whole flowerettes	100	0.11	0.1	0.7	0.21	30	0
Celery	60	120	1 cup chopped	120	0.03	0.03	0.3	0.06	6	0
Corn	100	400	1 cob (refuse 45%)	225	0.15	0.12	1.7	0.16	33	0
Cowpeas	70	140	1 cup	140	1	0.2	2.2	0.56	70	0
Cucumber	45	130	1 small 6⅜ × 1¾	180	0.03	0.04	0.2	0.04	15	0
Eggplant	100	200	1 cup diced	200	0.05	0.05	0.6	0.08	30	0
Lettuce	90	360	wedge ⅛ of head	90	0.06	0.06	0.3	0.055	37	0
Mushrooms	35	105	1 cup sliced or diced	70	0.10	0.46	4.2	0.13	23	0
Onions	40	160	1 cup chopped	160	0.03	0.04	0.2	0.13	25	0
Parsley	3.5	60	1 cup chopped	60	0:12	0.26	1.2	0.16	120	0
Peas	70	140	1 cup	140	0.35	0.14	3	0.16	50	0
Peppers, Green	25	100	1 cup strips	100	0.08	0.08	0.5	0.26	8	0
Potatoe										
White	100	500	2¾ × 4¼	250	0.1	0.04	1.5	0.25	19	0
Sweet	90	360	5 × 2	180	0.1	0.06	0.6	0.22	50	0
Spinach	25	100	1 cup chopped	55	0.1	0.2	0.6	0.28	193	0
Squash	65	195	1 cup sliced or cubed	130	0.05	0.09	1	0.08	31	0
Tomatoe	50	200	2½" diam.	100	0.06	0.04	0.7	0.1	39	0
Turnip Greens	115	400	1 lb.	450	0.2	0.4	0.8	0.26	95	0
CHEESE										
American	25	100	1 slice 2¼ × 2¼ × ¼	25	0.027	0.35	0.07	0.07	8	0.7
Cheddar	30	120	1" cube	30	0.027	0.38	0.08	0.07	18	0.8
Cottage (low fat, made from 1% milk fat)	60	240	¼ cup	60	0.02	0.17	0.13	0.07	12	0.6
Monterey Jack	30	120	1" cube	30	—	0.4	—	—	—	—
Mozzarella (part skim)	30	120	1" cube	30	0.018	0.3	0.1	0.07	9	0.8
Swiss	30	120	1" cube	30	0.022	0.37	0.09	0.08	6	1.7

Pantothenic Acid (MG)	Biotin (MCG)	MINERALS										
		Ca (MG)	P (MG)	Mg (MG)	K (MG)	Na (MG)	Fe (MG)	Cu (MG)	Mn (MG)	Zn (MG)	Se (MCG)	Cr (MG)
4-7	100-200	1200	1200	400	1875-5675	1100-3300	18	2-3	2.5-5.0	15	50-200	0.05-0.2
0.6	—	22	60	20	280	2	1	0.21	0.18	0.8	—	—
1	—	50	142	180	650	?	? 8	0.18	0.54	0.8	—	0.06
0.2	—	56	44	30	240	7	0.8	0.04	0.27	0.3	0.6	0.06
1.3	10	150	330	—	800	26	7	—	—	—	—	—
1.7	60	230	550	265	1700	5	8	—	—	—	—	—
—	—	130	130	110	40	7	2	—	—	—	—	—
0.25	2.7	120	40	—	570	130	3.3	—	—	—	—	—
0.15	2	16	33	—	335	60	0.7	0.2	0.08	0.3	—	0.03
1.2	—	100	80	24	380	15	1.1	0.011	0.056	0.27	—	0.03
0.7	—	36	80	30	390	14	1.5	0.011	0.11	0.37	—	0.03
0.2	2.4	50	30	13	230	20	0.4	0.06	0.06	0.14	2.3	0.03
0.28	2.5	37	36	23	340	47	0.7	0.011	0.02	0.12	2.2	0.03
1	17	25	56	24	300	13	1.1	0.011	0.16	0.46	0.65	0.03
0.43	—	40	28	22	340	130	0.3	0.01	0.02	0.07	—	0.03
0.54	6	3	110	50	280	tr	0.7	0.011	0.02	0.33	0.4	0.03
1	21	75	430	230	1000	35	5.8	—	—	—	—	—
0.25	—	25	27	11	160	6	1.1	0.01	0.06	0.1	—	0.03
0.22	—	12	26	16	200	2	0.7	—	—	—	—	—
0.2	3	20	22	11	175	9	0.5	0.037	0.07	0.25	0.8	0.03
2,200	16	6	120	13	400	15	0.8	0.26	0.033	1.1	13	0.03
0.13	3.5	27	36	12	160	10	0.5	0.1	0.08	0.11	1.5	0.03
0.3	—	200	60	40	700	45	6.2	—	—	—	—	—
0.75	9	26	120	35	300	2	2	0.13	0.11	1.3	—	0.03
0.23	—	9	22	18	210	13	0.7	—	—	—	0.7	—
0.38	—	7	50	35	400	3	0.6	0.05	0.04	0.2	0.45	0.03
0.82	4.3	30	50	30	240	10	0.7	0.06	0.62	0.16	0.65	0.03
0.3	7	90	50	90	470	70	3	0.08	0.6	0.4	—	0.03
0.36	—	30	30	16	200	1	0.4	0.14	0.1	0.3	—	0.03
0.33	4	13	27	14	240	3	0.5	0.01	0.02	0.046	0.5	0.03
0.38	—	250	60	60	—	—	1.8	—	—	—	—	—
0.5	—	600	750	22	160	1400	0.4	0.11	0.4	3	9	0.17
0.4	3.6	720	500	28	100	620	0.7	—	—	3	—	—
0.2	—	60	130	5	90	400	0.14	—	—	0.4	—	—
—	—	750	440	27	80	500	0.7	—	—	3	—	—
0.08	—	650	460	23	84	470	0.2	—	—	3	—	—
0.4	—	960	600	36	110	260	0.17	—	—	4	11	—

FOOD Category and Substance	AMOUNT OF FOOD PER DAY		MEASURE		Calories	Total Protein (GM)	ESSENTIAL AMINO			
	Min	Max	Portion	GM			Tryptophan	Threonine	Isoleucine	Leucine
RECOMMENDED DAILY ALLOWANCE						56	180	48	720	960
DAIRY										
Whole Milk	120	500	1 cup	244	62	3.3	45	150	200	300
Skim Milk	120	500	1 cup	244	35	3.4	50	150	200	330
Buttermilk	120	500	1 cup	244	41	3.3	35	160	200	330
Yogurt	120	240	1 cup	244	64	5.3	30	210	300	500
EGGS										
Whole	50	50	1 med.	50	164	13	180	600	800	1100
Yolk	29	29	1 med.	29	345	16	240	750	800	1400
White	15	15	1 med.	15	47	11	175	500	600	900
BREAD										
Rye, regular	21	75	1 slice	25	254	9	—	400	400	700
Whole Wheat	25	75	1 slice	25	255	9	150	400	475	475
CEREALS										
Rolled Oats	20	80	1 cup	80	391	14	175	460	500	1000
Rye	20	80	1 cup	80	355	12	—	400	400	700
GRAINS										
Barley	50	200	1 cup	200	357	8	—	400	400	800
Rice, Brown, raw	50	200	short grain, 1 cup	200	356	7.5	—	300	300	650
Wheat Bran	6	18	1 tbsp.	6	353	16	—	500	450	900
Wheat Germ	6	18	1 tbsp.	6	395	27	260	1000	900	1700
Bulgar Wheat	50	200	1 cup	200	361	11	127	340	390	750
FATS & OILS										
Butter, salted	14	28	1 tbsp.	14	733	0.9	12	40	50	80
Corn Oil	14	28	1 tbsp.	13.5	900	0	0	0	0	0
Olive Oil	14	28	1 tbsp.	13.5	900	0	0	0	0	0
Safflower Oil	14	28	1 tbsp.	13.5	900	0	0	0	0	0
Soy Oil	14	28	1 tbsp.	13.5	900	0	0	0	0	0
NUTS & SEEDS										
Almonds	18	36	1 cup whole	144	642	19	175	500	700	1300
Cashew	18	36	1 cup whole	144	598	17	375	650	1100	1700
Peanuts, roasted with skin	18	36	1 cup whole	144	629	26	340	800	1300	1900
Sunflower Seeds	10	36	1 cup whole	80	599	24	200	550	600	950
MISCELLANEOUS										
Yeast, Brewer's, Debittered	7	14	1 oz.	28	317	39	700	2300	2400	3200

(VALUES PER 100 GM)

Lysine	Phenylalanine	Tyrosine	Valine	Methionine or Cysteine	Fat (GM)	Carbohydrate (GM)	Fiber (GM)	A (I.U.)	C (MG.)	D (I.U.)	E (I.U.)	K (MCG)
720	960	840	600	35% of total cals.	50-100GR			5000	60	400	15	70-140
250	160	160	220	85	3.3	4.7	0	13	0.9	3-4 I.U.	0.09	3
270	165	165	230	85	0.18	4.9	0	200	1	—	0.006	—
280	175	140	250	80	0.9	4.8	0	33	1	—	—	—
475	300	275	400	150	1.6	7	0	70	0.8	—	—	—
900	700	500	850	400	12	0.9	0	1,180	0	—	1.6	11
1200	700	700	1000	350	31	0.6	0	3,400	0	100	3.9	—
750	650	400	550	450	tr	0.8	0	—	—	0	—	—
400	500	225	560	170	1.1	52	0.4	0	0	—	—	—
325	550	380	550	200	2.6	49	1.5	tr	tr	—	0.5	—
500	700	450	700	230	7	68	1.2	0	0	0	0.36	20
400	500	225	560	170	1.7	73	2	0	0	0	1.8	—
400	600	365	600	200	1	79	0.5	0	0	0	0.9	—
300	400	275	400	180	2	77	0.9	0	0	0	2	—
600	550	425	680	220	4.6	62	9	0	0	0	2.2	—
1600	1000	800	1200	500	11	47	2.5	0	0	0	90	—
300	480	350	450	200	1.5	76	1.7	0	0	—	—	—
70	40	40	60	21	81	0.06	0	3,000	0	35	2.4	30
0	0	0	0	0	100	0	0	0	0	0	28	10
0	0	0	0	0	100	0	0	0	0	0	20	—
0	0	0	0	0	100	0	0	0	0	0	50	—
0	0	0	0	0	100	0	0	0	0	0	16	—
450	1000	600	1100	500	54	20	2.6	0	tr	0	22	—
950	900	—	1200	300	46	29	1.4	100	—	0	—	—
100	1600	1100	1500	270	49	21	2.7	—	0	0	10	—
30	660	280	750	280	47	20	4	50	—	0	—	—
300	1900	1900	2700	800	1.0	38	1.7	tr	tr	—	—	—

FOOD Category and Substance	AMOUNT OF FOOD PER DAY		MEASURE		NUTRITIVE VALUES OF FOODS					
					VITAMINS					
	Min	Max	Portion	GM	Thiamine (MG)	Riboflavin (MG)	Niacin (MG)	B-6 (MG)	Folacin (MCG)	B-12 (MCG)
RECOMMENDED DAILY ALLOWANCE					1.4	1.7	18	2	400	3
DAIRY										
Whole Milk	120	500	1 cup	244	0.04	0.16	0.08	0.04	5	0.36
Skim Milk	120	500	1 cup	244	0.04	0.14	0.09	0.04	5	0.38
Buttermilk	120	500	1 cup	244	0.03	0.15	0.06	0.034	—	0.22
Yogurt	120	240	1 cup	244	0.04	0.2	0.14	0.05	11	0.6
EGGS										
Whole	50	50	1 med.	50	0.11	0.3	0.1	0.12	65	1.5
Yolk	29	29	1 med.	29	0.22	0.44	0.1	0.3	152	3.8
White	15	15	1 med.	15	tr	0.27	0.1	0.003	16	0.07
BREAD										
Rye, regular	21	75	1 slice	25	0.18	0.07	1.4	0.1	23	0
Whole Wheat	25	75	1 slice	25	0.3	0.1	2.8	0.18	27	0
CEREALS										
Rolled Oats	20	80	1 cup	80	0.6	0.14	1	—	16	—
Rye	20	80	1 cup	80	0.4	0.22	1.6	—	—	—
GRAINS										
Barley	50	200	1 cup	200	0.12	0.05	3	0.22	20	0
Rice, Brown, raw	50	200	short grain, 1 cup	200	0.34	0.05	5	0.55	16	0
Wheat Bran	6	18	1 tbsp.	6	0.7	0.35	20	0.8	260	0
Wheat Germ	6	18	1 tbsp.	6	2	0.7	4	1.2	330	0
Bulgar Wheat	50	200	1 cup	200	0.3	0.15	4	0.2	—	0
FATS & OILS										
Butter, salted	14	28	1 tbsp.	14	0.005	0.034	0.042	0.003	3	tr
Corn Oil	14	28	1 tbsp.	13.5	—	—	—	—	—	—
Olive Oil	14	28	1 tbsp.	13.5	—	—	—	—	—	—
Safflower Oil	14	28	1 tbsp.	13.5	—	—	—	—	—	—
Soy Oil	14	28	1 tbsp.	13.5	—	—	—	—	—	—
NUTS & SEEDS										
Almonds	18	36	1 cup whole	144	0.24	0.9	3.5	0.1	100	0
Cashew	18	36	1 cup whole	144	0.43	0.25	1.8	—	70	0
Peanuts, roasted with skin	18	36	1 cup whole	144	0.32	0.13	17	0.4	100	0
Sunflower Seeds	10	36	1 cup whole	80	2	0.23	5.4	1.3	—	0
MISCELLANEOUS										
Yeast, Brewer's, Debittered	7	14	1 oz.	28	16	4	40	2,500	3900	0

(VALUES PER 100 GM) ⟶

		MINERALS										
Pantothenic Acid (MG)	Biotin (MCG)	Ca (MG)	P (MG)	Mg (MG)	K (MG)	Na (MG)	Fe (MG)	Cu (MG)	Mn (MG)	Zn (MG)	Se (MCG)	Cr (MG)
4-7	100-200	1200	1200	400	1875-5675	1100-3300	18	2-3	2.5-5.0	15	50-200	0.05-0.2
0.31	5	120	90	13	150	50	0.05	0.005	0.01	0.4	1.2	0.015
0.33	—	120	100	11	166	52	0.04	0.005	0.01	0.4	4.8	0.015
0.28	—	116	89	11	150	100	0.05	0.005	0.01	0.4	—	0.015
0.6	—	180	140	17	230	70	0.08	—	—	0.9	—	—
1.7	23	55	200	11	130	120	2.3	0.05	0.02	1.4	—	0.05
4.4	52	140	600	16	100	50	6	0.01	0.02	3.4	18	0.03
0.24	7	9	15	9	140	150	0.1	0.005	0.01	0.02	5	0.015
0.45	—	75	150	40	145	560	1.6	0.017	0.5	1.2	—	0.06
0.8	2	80	250	80	260	530	2.3	0.17	1.2	1.7	70	0.06
—	24	50	400	140	350	2	4.5	—	—	—	—	—
—	—	40	375	115	470	1	3.7	—	—	—	—	—
0.5	31	16	200	37	160	3	2	—	—	—	66	—
1.1	12	30	220	90	210	9	1.6	—	—	—	39	—
3	14	120	1300	490	1100	9	15	—	—	—	—	—
1.2	—	70	1100	340	800	3	9	—	—	—	—	—
0.7	—	30	350	—	230	—	3	—	—	—	—	—
—	—	24	23	2	26	800	0.16	—	—	0.05	—	—
—	—	—	—	—	—	—	—	—	—	—	—	—
—	—	0.18	1.2	0.01	—	0.04	0.4	—	—	—	—	—
—	—	—	—	—	—	—	—	—	—	—	—	—
—	—	—	—	—	—	—	—	—	—	—	—	—
0.5	18	230	500	270	775	4	5	—	—	—	—	—
1.3	—	40	375	270	460	15	4	—	—	—	—	—
2	35	70	400	175	700	5	2.2	0.4	1.5	3	—	0.06
1.4	—	120	800	40	920	30	7	5	0.4	11	71	0.007
12,000	110	200	1750	230	1900	120	17	5.3	0.4	11	71	0.007

Appendix B
Menus and Recipes

In this appendix we give two representative daily menu combinations at 1,500 calories, two all-purpose salads high in nutrition, bulk, and satiety but low in calories, plus listing of food combinations at 1,500 calories. The materials were selected on the basis of the computer analyses of Mr. Haber. Recipes are by Ms. Ritman.

One problem with most popular diets is that the authors often expect you to get very involved with food preparations. The busy modern person is often not willing to do this and wants preparations which taste good but do not require excessive preoccupation with the kitchen. On the other hand, complicated diets are sometimes popular because they give the less busy person something to become involved with. The first is and the last is not our goal in this appendix. The all-purpose salads are examples selected for the busy person. You can eat them alone or with a little oatmeal, fruit, milk, and meat or fish for three days running.

In doing computer work, one must define criteria for the computer to use in making its selections. Ours have been: for the 1,500 calorie combinations, fewer than 15 percent calories derived from fats and fewer than 25 percent from protein. In addition, we have specified, for each day, one or no meat and poultry entrees; one or no fish and shellfish; one to three fruits, two to four vegetables; one or no cheese; one to two dairy goods; one or no eggs; two, one, or no slices of bread; two, one, or no cereal entrees; two, one, or no grains; two or fewer portions of fats and oils; two or fewer of nuts and seeds; one or no yeast portions. For each of these, if selected, the computer was limited to the minimum or maximum quantity or the value halfway between (table of Appendix A). These criteria were chosen because the dieter would want a moderate variety for his daily courses, and so the computer would not suggest, for example, two pounds of lettuce and a spoonful of fish, which might be satisfactory nutritionally for part of the day's diet, but hardly practical.

Our initial computer runs indicated that with these ninety-nine representative foods, there were *no* combinations at 1,500 calories which satisfied the fat, protein, and carbohydrate limits plus the criteria about portions and gave absolutely adequate RDA's for *all* thirty-two nutriments listed. The computer was of course programmed so that if only one of the nutriments was not quite adequate in any particular day's combination, the combination would be rejected. Those RDA's which caused the most frequent rejections were, in order: zinc, vitamin E, copper, sodium (too much), magnesium, iron, niacin, vitamin B_{12}, pantothenic acid, calcium, riboflavin, folacin, vitamin A, B_6, thiamine, vitamin C. After trials, we were able to come up with a reasonable number of food combinations only by neglecting the requirements for one or more random nutriments within any combination, in other words by not insisting on total compliance. But that's chancy for long-term restriction! On the other hand, it's easy to supplement for the B-vitamins by taking an appropriate B-complex tablet or capsule daily, and similarly for vitamins A and C, and for the mineral zinc. By agreeing to supplementation and thereby omitting these items from the actual food requirements, we found a large number of combinations that would supply the RDA's for what was left, and within the 1,500 calorie maximum. For practice, you should use the table of Appendix A to calculate the actual full nutritive values of some of the low calorie Scarsdale and Pritikin diets.

Some of the combinations and food lists given below may seem rather bizarre. That is in part because for "undernutrition without malnutrition" in the human we are still in the investigative stage, although I think solutions are not far distant. And if you find you are still eating such bizarre combinations 120 years hence, you can hardly be displeased with them if they have allowed you to live so long. However, I believe more enticing combinations will reward further study. Some key substances can be helpful in achieving a pleasant low-calorie diet. Because many salads and raw vegetables are apt to be on the diet, you should become acquainted with gourmet vinegars. Compared to other vinegars, these are apt to be expensive, but they are well worth the expense. Look in the gourmet stores for them! The dark Chinkiany rice vinegar available in Oriental groceries, or Aceto Balsamico (Williams-Sonoma; Box 3792, San Francisco, Ca. 94119) are both excellent. If you get to Fauchon's (26 Place de la Madeleine, Paris) you can choose, among seventeen different vinegars, from the expected ones such as sage and tarragon, to the unusual. The same holds for mustards. A low calorie, low meat, low fat diet is itself inexpensive, so you still come out ahead dressing it up with expensive treats like fine vinegars. The supplemental vitamins (see above) are easy to find in drugstores or health food stores. Additional additives, such as antioxidants and some of the other materials I've listed in Chapters 7 and 8, can be obtained from Gerontix Biological Research Products, 2802 Pacific Coast Highway, Torrance, Calif. 90505; (tel.: 213-534-3530); Life Extension Products, 2835 Hollywood Blvd., Hollywood, Florida 33020 (tel.: 305-925-2500); Health Maintenance Programs, Inc., 503 Grasslands Rd., P.O. Box 252, Valhalla, N. Y. 10595 (tel.: 914-592-3155). *However, I do not recommend these materials for indiscriminate use by the general public.*

1,500-Calorie-Day Optimal Nutrition
MENU I

Breakfast

 Brewer's Yeast (1 tbsp.) in low-sodium tomato juice
 Rye Cereal (⅔ cup)
 Wheat Germ (3 tbsp.)
 Wheat Bran (1 tbsp.)
 Strawberries (½ cup)
 Skim Milk (1¼ cup)

Lunch

 Sweet Potatoes (2) and Pears (2) (see recipe)
 Spinach (2 cups)
 Buttermilk (½ cup)

Dinner

 Computer Chicken (see recipe)
 Lima Bean Salad (see recipe)
 Any remaining sweet potatoes and pears
 Green Beans (1 cup)
 Grapefruit (1 cup)

Sweet Potatoes and Pears

2 sweet potatoes
2 pears
juice of 1 lemon
1 tsp. cinnamon
generous sprinkling of nutmeg

Boil the sweet potatoes until partially done. Peel and cut into ¼" slices. Peel, seed, and slice the pears into ¼" slices. Layer the sweet potatoes and pears in a baking dish. Sprinkle with cinnamon, nutmeg, and add the lemon juice. Bake at 350° for 1 hour basting with the lemon juice occasionally. Recipe serves one.

Computer Chicken *(After B'Stilla)*

3 small chicken breasts, skinned
1½ cup water
½ cup chopped parsley
1½" stick of cinnamon
½ tsp. pepper
½ large onion (or 1 small), grated
½ tsp. ground ginger
⅛ tsp. turmeric
⅛ cup lemon juice (fresh)
3 egg whites, beaten
⅜ cup sunflower seeds
2 tsp. apple juice
1 tsp. cinnamon
cheddar cheese (three 1" cubes), grated

Combine the first eight ingredients in a large covered pot. Bring to a boil. Reduce heat and simmer slowly for 30 minutes, stirring occasionally.

Roast the sunflower seeds (if raw) in a 350° oven until they begin to turn brown. Grind them in a coffee grinder, food processor, or with mortar and pestle. In a small bowl thoroughly mix the ground sunflower seeds with the apple juice and cinnamon to make a dry paste. Set this mixture aside.

At the end of the 30-minute cooking time, remove the chicken from the pot. Discard the cinnamon stick. Skim off any fat. Reduce the remaining liquid to about ¾ cup by boiling rapidly. Reduce heat to simmer and add lemon juice. Pour beaten egg whites into the simmering liquid and stir constantly until cooked and slightly congealed. Let the egg whites become curdy but not too dry. Use a slotted spoon to transfer them to a cake pan or other shallow pan. Refrigerate until cool.

Preheat an oven to 425°.

Shred the chicken into pieces 1½" long and put the chicken pieces evenly into a baking dish. Discard the bones. (Three separate little baking dishes may be used if individual servings are desired.) Cover the chicken pieces with the well-drained egg mixture. Sprinkle on the sunflower seed mixture. Top this with the grated cheddar cheese. Cover the dish and bake for 20 minutes. Recipe serves three.

Lima Bean Salad

Soak ½ cup of lima beans in 1½ cups water overnight. Simmer in the same water for 1–1½ hour, stirring occasionally, until the beans are tender but not mushy. (This makes 1 cup of cooked beans.) Allow them to cool. Add:

    1 tbsp. wine or tarragon vinegar
    1 clove garlic put through a press
    ¼–½ tsp. oregano leaves

Mix and refrigerate overnight. Stir well once or twice before eating to be sure they all get marinated. Serves one.

1,500-Calorie-Day Optimal Nutrition
Menu II

Breakfast

Brewer's Yeast (1 tbsp.) in low-sodium tomato juice
Egg White (1) with ¼ cup chopped onion fried in ½
tbsp. butter
Lowfat Yogurt (1 cup) with raisins (2½ tbsp.)

Lunch

Moroccan Skewered Liver (3½ oz.) (see recipe)
Corn (1½ ears) plain or with lime juice and chili powder
Lowfat Yogurt (1 cup) with raisins (2½ tbsp.) and apricots
(2 med.)
Skim Milk (½ cup)

Dinner

Eggplant Salad (1 cup) (see recipe)
Ocean Perch in Vegetable Wine Sauce (3½ oz.) (see
recipe)
Corn (1½ ears) plain or with lime juice and chili powder
Grapefruit (½ cup)

Moroccan Skewered Liver

Preheat broiler.

Heat a non-stick pan and quickly brown 3½ ounces of calves' liver (about ¾ to 1 minute per side). Remove to a plate and cut into small squares. Thread these onto small skewers. Sprinkle with ground cumin and red pepper. Broil, turning once, until desired doneness (1 minute per side for medium rare when squares are about 1"). Serves one.

Ocean Perch in Vegetable Wine Sauce

1 clove garlic, crushed
1 large onion, chopped
2 stalks of celery, chopped
1 carrot, grated
1 large tomato, chopped
¼ cup water
dash of ground pepper
½ cup dry white wine
1 tbsp. chopped parsley

Heat a small amount of water in a non-stick pan and in it "sauté" the garlic, onion, celery, and carrot 10–15 minutes until tender. Add the tomato, water, and dash of ground pepper. Cover and simmer slowly for 10 minutes. Purée the sauce in an electric blender and add wine and parsley. (Sauce is enough for four portions.)

Wash, dry, and broil 3½ ounces of ocean perch fillet about 4" from the flame in a preheated broiler. If fillet is ½" thick, broil 2½–3 minutes on a side.

Return the amount of sauce for this preparation to the skillet. Place the fish in the sauce. Cover and simmer for five minutes.

Eggplant Salad

Cut off the top of an eggplant and bake it in a preheated 450° oven for one hour or until the skin starts looking a little burnt. Scoop out the insides, put into a bowl, and discard the skin. Chop or mash the pulp and mix with:

    6 tsp. lemon juice (fresh)
    2 cloves garlic, put through a press
    2 tbsp. chopped green onion
    2 tsp. capers

Refrigerate overnight and serve at room temperature or slightly cool. Serves two.

Two All-Purpose Salads

Salad 1

1 cup soybeans
¾ cup barley
1 cup beets
½ cup green pepper
¾ cup parsley
1½ cups red cabbage
1 cup yellow squash
2 tomatoes
¼ to ½ lb. Romaine lettuce
1 carrot, shredded
ginger root, 2 tbsp., shredded
1–2 red onions
2 lemons
½ cup gourmet vinegar
1½ cups lowfat yogurt

Heat soybeans and barley together in 3 cups water for 45 minutes in a double boiler. Steam beets for 30 minutes. While these are under way, cut up enough raw green pepper, onion, parsley, red cabbage, and yellow squash to make the above amounts. Also cut up the lettuce, tomatoes and shred carrot and ginger root.

Place all raw ingredients in a large bowl. In a small bowl prepare dressing, mixing the yogurt, juice of the lemons, and ½ or more cups of vinegar. The tastiness of the salad will be greatly improved by using a gourmet vinegar.

Run cold water over the cooked beet(s) while squeezing the skin off, and dice.

Place cooked soybeans and barley in a large sieve and cool with running water.

Add diced beets and soybeans and barley to rest of salad. Add dressing. If desired, season further with one teaspoon of pepper and a low or non-salt seasoning such as Vegit.

Mix everything together.

The above makes about 2,000 grams or slightly more than 4 pounds (10 servings), and with a total calorie count of 1,540 for the entire 4 pounds. It would, however, be difficult to eat this much bulk in one day, illustrating that one need not feel hunger on a very low calorie intake. You can stuff yourself and still lose weight.

Salad 2: Biryani

2 cups brown rice
2 tbsp. butter, unsalted
1 large onion, chopped
1 clove garlic, chopped
1 green chili pepper, finely cut
4-6 whole cloves
4-6 green cardamons
1 stick cinnamon 2"-2½"
1-1½ tsp. cumin seeds
12-18 peppercorns
¼ tsp. cayenne pepper
2 cups potatoes, cubed
2 cups eggplant, cubed
2 cups broccoli flowerettes
2 cups cauliflower flowerettes
1 cup peas
1½ cup carrots, sliced
juice of 2 lemons
¼ cup water
2 cups yogurt
⅓ cup raisins

Boil 3 cups water in a saucepan and add the brown rice. Simmer covered until water is absorbed and rice is not quite completely cooked (around 20 minutes).

In a large fry pan (preferably one with a cover that can also go into the oven) melt the butter and fry the onion, garlic, and green chili for about 3 min.

Add the spices except for the cayenne. Stir 1 min. Add the cayenne and the vegetables and stir until the vegetables are coated. Stir in the brown rice, the juice of 2 lemons and ¼ cup water. Mix the yogurt and raisins and layer that mixture over the rice and vegetables. Cover and put in a 350° oven for 30 min.

Before serving, remove the cloves, cinnamon stick and peppercorns. Depending on your taste, remove or leave the green chili pepper.

Makes 5 servings.

1,500 Calorie Nutritionally Optimal Food
Combinations for 6 DAYS*

I.

Grapes, 75 gm (½ cup); soybean curd, 120 gm; turnip greens,
400 gm; lowfat yogurt, 120 gm (½ cup); buttermilk, 1¼ cup;
sunflower seeds, 23 gm (⅓ cup); barley grain, 125 gm (2/3
cup); orange, 90 gm (½ orange); asparagus, 200 gm (8 large
spears); lima beans, 110 gm (¾ cup); raisins, 45 gm (⅓ cup).

II.

Pineapple, 140 gm (1 cup); black-eyed peas, 105 gm (¾ cup);
lima beans, 150 gm (1 cup); whole milk, ½ cup; skim milk, 2
cups; raisins, 60 gm (½ cup); cantaloupe, 300 gm (¾ cantaloupe); eggs, 50 gm (1 egg); tuna, 50 gm (¼ cup); brewer's
yeast, 14 gm (1 tbsp.); sunflower seeds, 10 gm (1 tbsp.).

III.

Apricots, 40 gm (1 apricot); turnip greens, 400 gm; brussel
sprouts, 150 gm (8 sprouts); skim milk, 2 cups; rye bread, 75
gm (3 slices); cod, 100 gm; rolled oats cereal, 80 gm (1 cup);
sunflower seeds, 20 gm (2 tbsp.); brown rice, 125 gm (⅔ cup);
brewer's yeast, 14 gm (1 tbsp.).

IV.

Grapes, 150 gm (1 cup); sweet potatoes, 225 gm (1¼
potatoes); asparagus, 200 gm (8 large spears); buttermilk, ½
cup; butter, 7 gm (½ tbsp.); celery, 120 gm (1 cup): brown rice,
50 gm (¼ cup); strawberries, 110 gm (¾ cup); barley grain,

*Exact weights are given according to the computer formulation. Figures in
parentheses are closest, easy approximations. 100 gm = 3½ oz.

50 gm (¼ cup); turnip greens, 400 gm; tuna, 100 gm (½ cup); skim milk, ½ cup; sunflower seeds, 20 gm (2 tbsp.); brewer's yeast, 14 gm (1 tbsp.).

V.

Bananas, 300 gm (2 bananas); cucumbers, 180 gm (1 cucumber); lima beans, 150 gm (1 cup); whole milk, ½ cup; lowfat yogurt, 310 gm (1¼ cup); pears, 75 gm (1 pear); rye cereal, 20 gm (¼ cup); brussel sprouts, 150 gm (8 sprouts); calves' liver, 100 gm; sweet potatoes, 360 gm (2 potatoes).

VI.

Apples, 300 gm (2 apples); black-eyed peas, 70 gm (½ cup); turnip greens, 115 gm; buttermilk, 2 cups; skim milk, ½ cup; calves' liver, 100 gm; brewer's yeast, 14 gm (1 tbsp.); egg yolk, 29 gm (1 egg yolk); parsley, 3.5 gm (1 tbsp.); squash, 65 gm (½ cup); whole wheat bread, 25 gm (1 slice); pineapple, 105 gm (¾ cup); brown rice, 50 gm (¼ cup); raisins, 30 gm (¼ cup); lobster, 50 gm (⅓ cup)

Notes

CHAPTER I

1 H. Mason, *Gilgamesh, A Verse Narrative* (New American Library, Mentor Books, 1972).

2 A.R. Omran, "Epidemiologic Transition in the United States, the Health Factor in Population Change," vol. 32, no. 2 Washington, D.C.: (Population Reference Bureau Inc., May 1977).

3 A. Artaud, *The Theatre and Its Double*, trans. Victor Corte (London: Calder & Boyars, 1970).

4 M.L. Jones, "Lifespan in Mammals," Data from a poster for the Gordon Conference on Aging, Santa Barbara, Ca. 22–26 January 1979; A. Comfort, *The Biology of Senescence*, 3rd ed. (N.Y.: Elsevier, 1979).

5 A. Comfort, *Studies in the Longevity and Mortality of English Thoroughbred Horses*, Ciba Found. Colloquia on Aging, 5:35 (1959); A. Comfort, "The Longevity and Mortality of Thoroughbred Stallions," *J. Gerontology* 14:9 (1959).

6 W.J. Thoms, *The Longevity of Man, Its Facts and Its Fictions* (London: J. Murray, 1873).

7 J. Easton, *Human Longevity: Recording the Name, Age, Place of Residence and Year of the Decease of 1712 Persons Who Attained a Century and Upwards From AD 66 to 1799, Comprising a Period of 1733 Years with Anecdotes of the Most Remarkable* (London, 1799).

8 Z.A. Medvedev, "Caucasus & Altay Longevity: A Biological or Social Problem," *The Gerontologist* 14:381 (1974).

9 From *New York Times*, 7 October, 1979.

10 From "Aging Americans," *Wall Street Journal*, 25 October, 1979.

11 *Special Report on Aging, 1979*, NIH Pub. No. 79–1907, September 1979.

12 U.S. Dept of Commerce Bureau of the Census, *Special Studies Series* p-23, no. 59, issued May 1976.

13 Table 1.3 is adapted from the *Wall Street Journal*, 29 October 1979.

14 O. Segerberg, Jr., *The Immortality Factor* (New York: E.P. Dutton & Co, Inc., 1974).

15 A. Abrams, S.S. Tobin, P. Gordon, C. Pechtal, and A. Hilkevitch, "The Effects of a European Procaine Preparation in an Aged Population." *J. Gerontology* 20:139 (1965).

NOTES (pages 20-63)

16 "Procaine and Related Geropharmacologie Agents—the Current State of the Art," in *Proc. First Workshop of Vet. Admin. Geriatric Research, Education and Clinical Centers,* ed. A. Cherkin and A.P. Sviland (California: Sepulveda V.A. Hospital, privately printed, 1975).

17 A. Aslan, A. Urabiescu, C. Domilescu, L. Campeanu, M. Costiniu, and S. Stanescu, "Long-Term Treatment with Procaine (Gerovital H₃) in Albino Rats, *J. Gerontology* 20:1 (1965).

18 A. Comfort, *The Biology of Senescence.*

19 G.A. Sacher, "Maturation and Longevity in Relation to Cranial Capacity in Hominid Evolution," in *Primate Functional Morphology and Evolution,* ed. R. Tuttle (The Hague: Mouton Pub., 1975), p. 417; R.G. Cutler, "Evolutionary Biology of Senescence, in *The Biology of Aging,* eds. J.A. Behuke, C.E. Finch, and G.B. Moment (N.Y.: Plenum Press, 1978), p. 311.

20 S.L. Washburn, and R.S.O., Harding, "Evolution and Human Nature," in *Am. Handbook of Psychiatry,* 2nd edition, ed. S. Arieti (N.Y.: Basic Books Inc., 1975), p.3.

CHAPTER 2

1 A. Harrington, *The Immortalist* (N.Y.: Random House, 1969).

2 E. Kübler-Ross, "Interview," *Playboy Magazine* 28:69 (May 1981).

3 G.J. Gruman, trans. *A History of Ideas about the Prolongation of Life,* Am. Philosophical Society no. 56, part 9 (Philadelphia, 1966).

4 Ku K'uam Yu, *Taoist Yoga* (New York: Weisner, 1970).

CHAPTER 3

1 K.D. Munkres, C. Furtek, and E. Goldstein, "Genetics of Cellular Longevity in Neurospora Crassa," *Age* 3:108 (1980).

2 S.R.S. Gottesman, K.Y. Hall, and R.L. Walford, "A Thesis of Genetic Linkage of Immune Regulation and Aging: The Major Histocompatibility Complex as a Supergene System," in *Developmental Immunology: Clinical Problems and Aging,* ed. E.L. Cooper (Academic Press, 1982 [in press]).

3 F.A. Willius, and H.L. Smith, "Further Observations on the Heart in Old Age. A Post Mortem Study of 381 Patients Aged 70 Years or More," *Am. Heart Jour.* 8:170 (1932).

4 W. Teague, "Senile," *TriQuarterly* 40:164 (1977).

5 A. Comfort, "Measuring the Human Aging Rate," *Mechanisms of Ageing and Development* 1:101-10 (1972). G.A. Borkan, and A.H.

Norris, "Assessment of Biological Age Using a Profile of Physical Parameters," *J. Gerontology* 35:177–84 (1980).

6 Borkan, "Assessment of Biological Age."

7 D. Harrison, "Experience with Developing Assays of Physiological Age," in *Biological Markers of Aging Conference, June 19–20, 1981,* ed. M. E. Reff and E. L. Schneider (National Institutes of Health, 1981), p. 2.

CHAPTER 4

1 R.L. Walford, *The Immunological Theory of Aging* (Copenhagen: Munksgaard, 1969).

2 J. Baines, "The Peace Paradigm," *The Whole Earth Papers* (Fall 1977).

3 L. Hayflick, "The Cellular Basis for Biological Aging," in *Handbook of the Biology of Aging,* ed. C.E. Finch and L. Hayflick (N.Y.: Van Nostrand Reinhold, 1977) p. 159.

4 J. Rener, and R.M. Nardone, "Nucleolar RNA Synthesis in Heterokaryons from Senescent and Presenescent Human Fibroblasts," *Exp. Cell Research* 129:287 (1980).

5 R. Holliday, L.I. Huschtscha, G.M. Tarrant, and T.B.L. Kirkwood, "Testing the Commitment Theory of Cellular Aging," *Science* 198:366 (1977). R. Holliday, L.I. Huschtscha, and T.B.L. Kirkwood, "Cellular Aging: Further Evidence for the Commitment Theory," *Science* 213:1505 (1981).

6 J.R. Smith, and C.K. Lumpkin, "Loss of Gene Repression Activity: A Theory of Cellular Senescence," *Mechanisms of Ageing and Development* 13:387 (1980).

7 P.A. Sharp, *Summary: Molecular Biology of Viral Oncogenes,* Cold Spring Harbor Symposia on Quantitative Biology, XLIV, part 2 (1980), p. 1305.

8 Baines, "Peace Paradigm."

9 G.M. Martin, "Mechanisms of Aging and the Human Condition," in *Biological Mechanisms in Aging,* ed. R. Schimke Bethesda, Md.: N.I.H. Publication No. 81-2194, 1981), p. 1.

10 R.C. Adelman, and G.W. Britton, "Impaired Capability for Biochemical Adaptation during Aging," *Bioscience* 25:639 (1975). M. Rothstein, "Posttranslational Alterations of Proteins," in *Handbook of Biochemistry in Aging,* ed. J. R. Florini, R.C. Adelman, and G.S. Roth (Inc. Boca Raton, Fla.: CRC Press, 1981), p. 103.

11 R. Hart, and R. Setlow, "Correlation between Deoxyribonucleic Acid Excision Repair and Lifespan in a Number of Mammalian Species," *Proc. Nat. Acad. Sci., U.S.A.* 71:2169 (1974).

NOTES (pages 82–22)

12 E.L. Schneider, D. Kram, R.R. Tice, Y. Nakanishi, R.E. Monticone, C.K. Bickings, and B.A. Gilman, "Sister Chromated Exchange in Mice and Man," in *Conference in Structural Pathology in DNA and the Biology of Ageing* (Bonn: Deutsche Forschungs Gemeinshaft, 1980), p. 96.

13 J. Sonneborn, "DNA Repair and Longevity Assurance in Paramedium Tetrautelia," *Science* 203:1115 (1979).

14 W.M. Generoso, K.T. Cam, N. Krishna, and S.W. Huff, "Genetic Lesions Induced by Chemicals in Spermatozoa and Spermatids of Mice Are Repaired in the Egg," *Proc. Nat. Acad. Sci. USA* 75:435 (1979).

15 D. Harman, "Free Radical Theory of Aging: Nutritional Implications," *Age* 1:145 (1978). D. Harman, "The Aging Process," *Proc. Nat. Acad. Sci. USA* 78:7124 (1981).

16 L.H. Korn, and J.B. Gurdon, "The Reactivation of Developmentally Inert 5 S Genes in Somatic Nuclei Injected into Xenopus Oocytes," *Nature* 289:461 (1981).

17 S. Tas, C.F. Tam, and R.L. Walford, "Disulfide bonds and the structure of the chromatin complex in relation to aging," *Mechanisms of Ageing and Development* 12:65 (1980). S. Tas and R.L. Walford. "Increased Disulfide Mediated Condensation of the Nuclear DNA-protein Complex in Lymphocytes during Postnatal Development and Aging," *Mechanisms of Ageing and Development* 19:-73–84 (1982).

18 G.C. Cotzias, S.T. Niller, A.R. Nicholson, Jr. et al. "Prolongation of the Life-span in Mice Adapted to Large Amounts of L-Dopa," *Proc. Nat. Acad. Sci. U.S.A.* 71:2466 (1974).

19 G.S. Roth, "Receptor Changes and the Control of Hormone Action during Aging," *in Aging, Cancer and Cell Membranes,* ed. C. Borek, C.M. Fenoglio and D.W. King (N.Y.: Thieme-Stratton, Inc, 1980) p. 228.

20 R.L. Walford, "The Immunological Theory of Aging, Current Status," *Federation Proceedings* 33:2020–27, 1974; R.L. Walford, R.H. Weindruch, S.R.S. Gottesman, and C.F. Tam, "The Immunopathology of Aging," in *Annual Review of Gerontology and Geriatrics,* ed. C. Eisdorber, B. Starr, and V.J. Cristofalo (N.Y.: Springer Publ. Co., 1981), vol. 2, pp. 1–48.

21 G.S. Smith and R.L. Walford, "Influence of the Main Histocompatibility Complex on Ageing in Mice," *Nature* 270:727 (1977).

22 R.M. Williams, L.J. Kraus, P.T. Lavin, L.L. Steele, and E.J. Yunis, "Genetics of Survival in Mice: Localization of Dominant Effects to Sub-regions of the Major Histocompatibility Complex," in *Immunological Aspects of Aging,* eds. D. Segre and L. Smith (N.Y.: Dekker Pub. Co., 1981), pp. 247–66.

23 I. Emerit and A.M. Michelson, "Mechanism of Photosensitivity in Systemic Lupus Erythematosus Patients," *Proc. Nat. Acad. Sci. U.S.A.* 78:2537 (1981).

24 K.D. Munkres, and R.S. Rana, "A Cellular Longevity Assurance Gene Controls Superoxide Dismutase and Catalase in Neurospora crassa," *Age* 3:108 (1980).

25 R.L. Walford, F.Naeim, K.Y. Hall, C.F. Tam, M. Medici, and R. Gatti, "Accelerated Aging in Down's Syndrome: the Concept of Hierarchical Homeostasis in Relation to Local and Global Failure," in *International Workshop on Immunoregulation,* ed. N. Fabris (in press).

CHAPTER 5

1 R.H. Weindruch, J.A. Kristie, K. Cheney, and R.L. Walford, "The Influence of Controlled Dietary Restriction on Immunologic Function and Aging," *Federation Proceedings* 38:2007 (1979); R. Weindruch and R.L. Walford, "Life Span and Spontaneous Cancer Incidence in Mice Dietarily Restricted Beginning at One Year of Age," *Science* 215:1415–18 (1982).

2 R.H. Weindruch, S.R.S. Gottesman, and R.L. Walford, "Modification of Age-Related Immune Decline in Mice Dietarily Restricted from or after Mid-Adulthood," *Proc. Nat. Acad. Sci. U.S.A.* 79:898 (1982).

3 C.M. McKay, "Chemical Aspects of Ageing and the Effect of Diet upon Ageing, in *Cowdry's Problems of Ageing,* 3rd ed., ed. A.I. Lansing (William & William Co., 1952), p. 139.

4 M. Ross, "Length of Life and Nutrition in the Rat," *J. Nutrition* 75:197 (1961).

5 A.H. Carlson, and F. Hoelzel, "Apparent Prolongation of the Life Span of Rats by Intermittent Fasting," *J. Nutrition* 31:363 (1946).

6 C.L. Goodrick in *Science News,* 1 Dec. 1979, p. 375.

7 M.A. Rudzinska, "Overfeeding and Life Span in Tokophyra infusorium," *J. Gerontology* 7:544, 1952.

8 E.A. Lew and L. Garfinkel, "Variations in Mortality by Weight among 750,000 Men and Women," *J. Chron. Dis.* 32:563 (1979).

9 McKay, "Chemical aspects of ageing."

10 R.L., Walford, *The Immunologic Theory of Aging.*

11 K.E. Cheney, R.U. Lie, G.S. Smith, R.E. Leung, N.R. Mickey, and R.L. Walford, "Survival and Disease Patterns in C57BL/6J Mice Subjected to Undernutrition," *Exp. Gerontol.* 15:237 (1980).

[12] C.H. Barrows, Jr. and G.C. Kokkman, "Diet and Life Extension in Animal Model Systems," *Age* 1:131 (1978).

[13] A.V. Everitt, N.J. Seedsman, and F. Jones, "The Effects of Hypophysectomy and Continuous Food Restriction, Begun at Ages 70 and 400 Days, on Collagen Aging, Proteinuria, Incidence of Pathology and Longevity in the Male Rat," *Mechanisms of Ageing and Development* 12:161 (1980).

[14] M.H. Ross, and G. Bras, "Lasting Influence of Early Calorie Restriction on Prevalence of Neoplasms in the Rat," *Journal of National Cancer Institute* 47:1095 (1971).

[15] M.T.R. Subbiah, and R.G. Siekert, Jr., "Dietary Restriction and the Development of Atherosclerosis," *J. Nutrition* 41:1 (1979).

[16] E.J. Masoro, H. Bertrand, G. Liepa, and B.P. Yu, "Analysis and Exploration of Age-Related Changes in Mammalian Structure and Function," *Federation Proceedings* 38:1956 (1979).

[17] Masoro, "Analysis and exploration."

[18] Weindruch, "Influence"; Cheney, "Survival and disease patterns."

[19] K. Nandy, "Effects of controlled Dietary restriction on Brain-Reactive Antibodies in Sera of Aging Mice," *Mechanisms of Ageing and Development*, 18:97, 1982.

[20] "Malnutrition and Mental Development," *World Health Organization Chronicle* 28:95–102 (1974).

[21] P. Levin, J. K. Janda, J.A. Joseph, D.K. Ingram, and G.S. Roth, "Dietary Restriction Retards the Age-Associated Loss of Rat Striatal Dopaminergic receptors," *Science* 214:561–63 (1981).

[22] N. Pritikin, and P.M. McGrady, Jr., *The Pritikin Program for Diet and Exercise* (Grosset & Dunlap, 1979).

[23] H. Tarnower, and S.S. Baker, *The Complete Scarsdale Medical Diet* (N.Y.: Rawson, Wade, 1978).

[24] R.C. Atkins, *Dr. Atkins Diet Revolution* (N.Y.: Bantam Books, 1973).

[25] Masoro, "Analysis and exploration."

[26] A. Gueniot, *Pour vivre cent ans, ou l'art de prolonges ses jours* (Paris, 1931).

CHAPTER 6

[1] L.K. Kothari, A. Bordia, and O.P. Gupta, "Studies on a Yogi during an Eight-Day Confinement in a Sealed Underground Pit," *Indian J. of Medical Research* 61:1645 (1973).

[2] H.C. Heller, L.I. Crawshae, and H.T. Hammel, "The Thermostat of Vertebrate Animals," *Scientific American* 235:102 (April 1978).

[3] R.K. Liu, and R.L. Walford, "The Effect of Lowered Body Tem-

perature on Lifespan and Immune and Non-Immune Processes," *Gerontologia* 18:363 (1972).

4 B. Rosenberg, G. Kemeny, L.G. Smith, I.D. Skurnick, and M.J. Bandurski, "The Kinetics and Thermodynamics of Death in Multicellular Organisms," *Mechanisms of Ageing and Development* 2:275 (1973).

CHAPTER 7

1 G.A. Lindegoom, "The Story of a Blood Transfusion to a Pope," *J. Hist. Med.* 9:455 (1954).
2 Committee on Dietary Allowances and the Food and Nutrition Board, *Recommended Dietary Allowances,* 9th rev. ed. (Washington, D.C.: Academy of Science, 1980).
3 H.N. Monro, and V.R. Young, "Protein Metabolism in the Elderly," *Postgraduate Medecine* 63:143–49 (1978).
4 R.J. Wurtman, "Nutrients That Modify Brain Function," *Scientific American* (April 1982): 50.
5 R.J. Williams, "On Your Startling Biochemical Individuality," *Executive Health* vol. 12, no. 8 (May 1976).
6 D.M. Kramsch, A.J. Aspen, and L.J. Rozler, "Atherosclerosis: Prevention by Agents Not Affecting Abnormal Levels of Blood Lipids," *Science* 213:1511 (1981); T.H. Jukes, "Sursum corda," *Nature* 270:380 (1977).
7 J. Bjorksten, "The Place of Vitamin E in the Quest for Longevity," *Rejuvenation* 3:38 (1975).
8 *Food Chemical News,* 3 April 1978.
9 R.D. Lippmann, A. Agren, and M. Uhlen, "A New Method Which Investigates Lysosomal Sensitivity to Superoxide with Endocytotic, Site-Specific Chemiluminescent Probes," *Mechanisms Of Ageing and Development* 17:275 (1881); R. D. Lippman, "The Prolongation of Life: A Comparison of Antioxidants and Geroprotectors Versus Superoxide in Human Mitochondria," *J. Gerontology* 36: 550 (1981).
10 W.O. Hoekstra, "Biochemical Function of Selenium and Its Relation to Vitamin E," *Federation Proceedings* 34:2083 (1975).
11 N.W. Revis, C.Y. Horton, and S. Curtis, "Metabolism of Selenium in Skeletal Muscle and Liver of Mice with Genetic Muscular Dystrophy," *Proc. Soc. Exper. Biol. Med.* 160:139 (1979).
12 R.A. Sunde, and W.G. Hoekstra, "Structure, Synthesis and Function of Glutathione Peroxidase," *Nutriton Rev.* 38:265 (1980).
13 Nat. Acad. Sci. *News Report,* March 1979, p. 4.
14 "Selenium in the Heart of China," *Lancet,* 27 Oct. 1979, p. 899.

[15] D. Harman, "Free Radical Theory of Aging; Origin of Life, Evolution, and Aging," *Age* 3:100 (1980).

[16] D. Harman, "Free Radical Theory of Aging: Effect of Free Radical Reaction Inhibitors in the Mortality Rate of Male LAF$_1$ Mice," *J. Gerontology* 23:476 (1968).

[17] H.S. Hlack, and J.T. Chan, "Supression of Ultraviolet Light Induced Dimer Formation by Dietary Antioxidants," *J. Inv. Derm.* 65:412 (1975).

[18] D. Harman, and D.E. Eddy, "Free Radical Theory of Aging: Effect of Adding Antioxidants to Maternal Mouse Diets on the Lifespan of the Offspring," *Age* 1:162 (1978).

[19] S. Oeriu, and E. Vachitsu, "The Effect of the Administration of Compounds Which Contain Sulfhydryl Groups on the Survival Rates of Mice, Rats, and Guinea Pigs," *J. Gerontology* 20:417–25 (1965).

[20] D. Harman, "Roles des radicaux libres dans le vieillissement," *Revue francaise gerontologie* 9:125 (1963).

[21] E. Edes, S.K. Clinton, D.R. Truex, and W.J. Visek, "Intestinal and Hepatic Mixed Function Oxidase Activity in Rats Fed Methionine and Cysteine-Free Diets," *Proc. Soc. Exper. Biol. Med.* 162:71 (1979).

[22] S. Tas, C.F. Tam, and R.L. Walford, "Disulfide Bonds and the Structure of the Chromatin Complex in Relation to Aging," *Mechanisms of Ageing and Development* 12:65 (1980).

[23] S.A. Weitzman and T.A. Stossel, "Effects of Oxygen Radical Scavengers and Antioxidants on Phagocyte-Induced Mutagenesis," *J. Immunology* 128:2770 (1982).

[24] Sunde, "Structure, Synthesis and Function."

[25] J.E.W. Davies, P.M. Ellery, and R.E. Hughes, "Dietary Ascorbic Acid and the Lifespan of Guinea Pigs," *Exp. Gerontol.* 12:215 (1977).

[26] D.F. Horrobin et al., "The Nutritional Regulation of T-lymphocyte Function," *Medical Hypotheses* 5:969 (1979); L.H. Chen, "An Increase in Vitamin E Requirement Induced by High Supplementation of Vitamin C in Rats," *Am. J. Clinical Nutrition* 34:-1036 (1981); B.K. Nandi, A.K. Majumdar, N. Subramanian, and I.B. Chatterjes, "Effects of Large Doses of Vitamin C in Guinea Pigs and Rats," *J. Nutrition* 103:1688 (1973).

[27] R. Anderson, R. Oosthuizen, R. Maritz, A. Theron, and A.J. Van Rensburg, "The Effects of Increasing Weekly Doses of Ascorbate on Certain Cellular and Humoral Immune Functions in Normal Volunteers," *Am. J. Clinical Nutrition* 33:71 (1980).

[28] B. Sokoloff, N. Sqelhof Hori, C.C., T. Wrzolek, and T. Imai, "Aging, Atherosclerosis and Ascorbic Acid Metabolism," *J. Am. Geriatrics Soc.* 14:1239 (1966).

29 E. Cameron, and L. Pauling, *Cancer and Vitamin C* (Menlo Park, Calif.: Linus Pauling Inst. of Science and Med., 1979).

30 "Ascorbic Acid: Immunological Effects and Hazards," *Lancet*, 10 Feb. 1979, p. 308.

31 Davies, "Dietary Ascorbic Acid."

32 J.A. Tillotson and E.L. McGown, "Steady State Ascorbic Acid Metabolism in the Monkey," *Am. J. Clinical Nutrition* 34:2397 (1981).

33 Lippmann, "A New Method." Weitzman, "Effects of Oxygen."

34 D.B. Milne, S.T. Omaye, and W. H. Amos, Jr., "Effect of Ascorbic Acid on Copper and Cholesterol in Adult Cynomologus Monkeys Fed a Diet Marginal in Copper," *Am. J. Clinical Nutrition* 34:2389 (1981).

35 Lippmann, "A New Method."

36 P. Sinet, J. Lejeune, and H. Jerome, "Trisomy 21 (Down's Syndrome) Glutathione Peroxidase, Hexose Monophosphate Shunt and I.Q.," *Life Sciences* 24:29 (1979).

37 Hochschild, "Effects of Various Drugs."

38 R.J. Williams, *Nutrition Against Disease* (Pitman, N.Y., 1971).

39 E.P. Ralli, and M.E. Dumm, "Relation of Pantothenic Acid to Adrenal Cortical Function," *Vit. and Hormones* 11:133 (1953).

40 R. Hochschild, "Effect of Dimethylaminoethanol on the Lifespan of Senile Male A/J Mice," *Exp. Gerontol.* 8:185 (1973); R. Hochschild, "Effects of Various Drugs on Longevity in Female C57/BL/6J Mice," *Gerontologia* 19:271 (1973).

41 Hochschild, "Effects of Various Drugs."

42 A. Cherkin, "Dimethylaminoethanol Did Not Extend Survival of Aged Japanese Quail," *The Gerontologist* 15:25 (1975).

43 K. Nandy, D. Baste, and F.H. Schneider, "Further Studies on the Effects of Centrophenoxine on Lipofuscin Pigment in Neuroblastoma Cells in Culture: An Electron Microscopic Study. *Exp. Gerontol.* 13:311 (1978).

44 K.R. Brizzee, and J.M. Ordy, "Age Pigments, Cell Loss and Hippocampal Function," *Mechanisms of Ageing and Development* 9:143 (1979).

45 A. Tappel, B. Fletcher, and D. Deamer, "Effect of Antioxidants and Nutrients on Lipid Peroxidation Fluorescent Products and Aging Parameters in the Mouse," *J. Gerontology* 28:415 (1973).

46 J. Gardner, "The Effect of Yeast Nucleic Acid on the Survival Time of 600 Day Old Albino Mice," *J. Gerontology* 1:445 (1946).

47 T.B. Robertson, "On the Influence of Nucleic Acids of Various Origins upon the Growth and Longevity of the White Mouse," *Austr. J. Exptl. Biol. Med. Sci.* 5:47 (1928).

48 A.M. Connell, "Dietary Fiber and Diverticular Disease," *Hospital Practice*, March 1976, p. 119.

49 K. Watanabe, B.S. Reddy, and D. Knitcheusky, "Effect of Various Dietary Fibers and Food Additives on Azoxymethane or Methyl Nitrosourea-Induced Colon Carcinomas in Rats," *Federation Proceedings* 37:267 (1978).

50 W.L. Chen, and J.W. Anderson, "Effects of Plant Fiber in Decreasing Plasma Total Cholesterol and Increasing High-Density Lipoprotein Cholesterol," *Proc. Soc. Exp. Biol. Med.* 162:310 (1979).

51 R.M. Kay, "Pectin and Serum-Cholesterol," *Lancet*, 9 Oct. 1976, p. 799.

52 J. Robertson, W.G. Brydon, K. Tadesse, P. Wenham, and M.A. Eastwood, "The Effect of Raw Carrot on Serum Lipids and Colon Function," *Am. J. Clinical Nutrition* 32:1889 (1979).

53 *Coronary Heart Disease in Seven Countries*, Am. Heart Association Monograph, no. 29, 1970.

54 J. Currens, and P.D. White, "Half a Century of Running: Clinical Physiologic and Autopsy Findings in the Case of Clarence DeMar ('Mr. Marathon')," *New Eng. J. Med.* 265:988 (1961).

55 W.W. Spirduso, "Physical Fitness, Aging, and Psychomotor Speed: A Review," *J. Gerontology* 35:850 1980.

56 "Energy Requirements: How Much Is Enough?" *Nutrition Reviews* 38:337 (1980).

57 F.G. Benedict, W.R. Miles, P. Roth, and H.M. Smith, *Human Vitality and Efficiency under Prolonged Restricted Diet* (Washington, D.C.: Carnegie Inst., 1919).

58 *Nutrition Action*, August 1981, p. 11.

59 G.R. Meneely, and H.D. Battarbee, "High Sodium-Low Potassium Environment and Hypertension," *Am. J. Cardiology* 38:768 (1976).

60 R.H. Hall, *Food for Naught, the Decline in Nutrition* (N.Y.: Harper & Row, 1974).

61 M.J.A. Farthing, E.B. Janetl, B. Williams, and N.A. Brawford, "Essential Fatty Acid Deficiency after Prolonged Treatment with Elemental Diet," *Lancet*, 15 Nov. 1980, p. 1088.

62 M.H. Ross, and E. Lustbader, "Dietary Practices and Growth Responses as Predictors of Longevity," *Nature* 262:548 (1976).

63 R. Mann, "Swanson: A Life at the Top Table," *Los Angeles Times*, 20 Nov. 1980, Part VI, p. 3.

CHAPTER 8

1 P. Dickson, *The Future File* (N.Y.: Avon Books, 1977).

2 J. Sonneborn, "DNA Repair and Longevity Assurance in *Paramecium tetraurelia*," *Science* 203:1115 (1979).

3 A.G. Schwartz, "Correlation between Species Lifespan and Capacity to Activate 7, 12-dimehylbenz (a) Anthracene to a Form Mutagenic to a Mammalian Cell," *Exp. Cell Research* 94:445–47 (1975).

4 A.G. Schwartz, and A. Perantoni, "Protective Effect of Dehydroepiandrosterone against Aflatoxin B,-and 7, 12-dimethylbenz (a) Anthracene-Induced Cytotoxicity and Transformation in Cultured Cells," *Cancer* 35:2481 (1975).

5 A.A. Driedger, A.P. James, and N.J. Grayston, "Cell Survival and X-ray Induced DNA Degradation in *Micrococcus radiodurans,*" *Radiation Research* 44:835 (1970).

6 E.G. Bliznakov, "Immunological Senescence in Mice and Its Reversal by Coenzyme Q10," *Mechanisms of Ageing and Development* 7:189 (1978).

7 N.L. Heidrick, J.W. Albright, and T. Makinodan, "Restoration of Impaired Immune Function in Aging Animals. IV. Action of 2-mercaptoethanol in Enhancing Age-Reduced Immune Responsiveness," *Mechanisms of Ageing and Development* 13:367 (1980).

8 D.F. Horrobin et al. "The Nutritional Regulation of T Lymphocyte Function," *Medical Hypotheses* 5:969 (1979). D.F. Horrobin, "The Reversibility of Cancer: the Relevance of Cyclic AMP, Calcium, Essential Fatty Acids and Prostaglandin E_1," *Medical Hypotheses* 6:469 (1980).

9 R.B. Zurier, D.M. Sanadoff, S.B. Torrey, and N.F. Rothfield, "Prostagladin E, Treatment of NZB/W Mice 1. Prolonged Survival of Female Mice," *Arthritis Rheum.* 20:723 (1977).

10 M.E. Weksler, "The Immune System and the Aging Process in Man," *Proc. Soc. Exp. Biol. Med.* 165:200 (1980).

11 P.W. Landfield, R.K. Baskin, and T.A. Pitler, "Brain Aging Correlates: Retardation by Hormonal-Pharmacological Treatment," *Science* 214:581 (1981).

12 G.C. Cotzias, S.T. Miller et al. "Prolongation of the Life-Span in Mice Adapted to Large Amounts of L-Dopa," *Proc. Nat. Acad. Sci. U.S.A.* 1:2466 (1974). Interview with W.D. Denckla in *Omni*, November 1981, p. 91.

13 J.F. Marshall, and N. Berrios, "Movement Disorders of Aged Rats: Reversal by Dopamine Receptor Stimulation," *Science* 206:477 (1979).

14 A.V. Everitt, and J.A. Burgess, eds., *Hypothalamus, Pituitary and Aging* (Springfield: Chas. C. Thomas, 1976).

15 D.E. Harrison, J.R. Archer, and C.M. Astte, "The Effect of Hypophysectomy on Thymic Aging in Mice," *J. Immunology* (in press).

16 "Brain Transplants: A Growing Success," *Science News*, 20 and 27 December 1980, p. 389.

[17] T.H. Norwood, H. Hoehn, A.O. Martinez, and G.M. Martin, "Synkaryon and Heterokaryon Analyses of Clonal Senescence," in *Senescence-Dominant or Recessive in Somatic Cell Crosses?*, vol. 2, *Cellular Senescence and Somatic Cell Genetics*, ed. W.W. Nichols and D.G. Murphy (N.Y.: Plenum, 1977), p. 23.

CHAPTER 9

[1] G. Banziger, "Intergenerational Communication in Prominent Western Drama," *The Gerontologist* 19:471–80 (1979).

[2] R.N. Butler, *Why Survive? Being Old in America* (N.Y.: Harper & Row, 1975).

[3] J. Baines, *Aging and World Order*, The Whole Earth Papers, no. 13. (East Orange, N.J.: Global Education Associates, 1979).

[4] A. Comfort, *A Good Age.* (N.Y.: Simon & Schuster, 1976).

[5] A. Fontana, *The Last Frontier: The Social Meaning of Growing Old* (Beverly Hills, Ca.: Sage Publications, 1977).

[6] M.W. Riley, "Age Strata in Social Systems," in *Handbook of Aging and the Social Sciences*, ed. R.H. Binstock and E. Shanas (N.Y.: Van Nostrand Reinhold Co., 1976), p. 189.

[7] J. Rendricks, and C.D. Hendricks, *Aging in Mass Society: Myth and Realities*, 2nd ed. (N.Y.: Winthrop Pub. Co., Inc., 1981).

[8] B.L. Neugarten, and G.O. Hagestad, "Age and the Life Course," in *Handbook of Aging and the Social Sciences*, ed. R.H. Binstock and E. Shanas (N.Y.: Van Nostrand Reinhold Co., 1976), p. 35.

[9] I. Rosow, "Status and Role Change through the Life Span," in *Handbook of Aging and the Social Sciences*, ed. R.H. Binstock and E. Shanas (N.Y.: Van Nostrand Reinhold Co., 1976), p. 457.

[10] G.B. Gori, and B.I. Richter, "Macroeconomics of Disease Prevention in the United States," *Science* 200:1124 (1978).

[11] P.F. Drucker, *Managing in Turbulent Times* (N.Y.: Harper & Row, 1980).

[12] L.J. Kotlikoff, "Some Economic Implication of Life Span Extension," in *Aging: Biology and Behavior* ed. J. March, J.L. McGaugh and S.B. Kiesler (N.Y.: Academic Press, 1982), p. 97.

[13] E.H. Erikson, "Identity and the Life Cycle," *Psychological Issues* 1:18 (1959).

[14] Neugarten, "Age and Life Course."

[15] Riley, "Age Strata."

[16] R.S. Laufer, and V.L. Bengtson, "Generations, Aging, and Social Stratification: On the Development of Generational Units," *J. Soc. Issues* 30:181 (1974).

[17] A. Insdorf, "Roeg: Visual Puzzles are his Métier", *Los Angeles Times*, Calendar Section, 16 Nov. 1980, p. 33.

[18] Riley, "Age Strata."

[19] Drucker, *Managing*.

[20] P. Laslett, "Societal development and aging," in *Handbook of Aging and the Social Sciences*, ed. R.H. Binstock and E. Shanas (N.Y.: Van Nostrand Reinhold Co., 1976), p. 87.

[21] Rendricks, *Aging*.

[22] L.F. Berkman, and S.L. Syme, "Social Networks, Host Resistance and Mortality: A Nine-Year Follow-Up Study of Alameda County Residents," *Am. J. Epidem.* 109:186 (1979).

[23] A. Harrington, *The Immortalist* (N.Y.: Random House, 1969).

Index

Index

Index

Index

Index

Index

Index

Index

Index

Index